The Imagination of Evil

Continuum Literary Studies Series

Related Titles Available in the Series:

Contemporary Fiction and Christianity, Andrew Tate
Modernism and the Post-colonial, Peter Childs
Novels of the Contemporary Extreme, edited by Alain-Phillipe Durand and
    Naomi Mandel
Women's Fiction 1945–2000, Deborah Philips

The Imagination of Evil

Detective Fiction and the Modern World

Mary Evans

continuum

Continuum International Publishing Group

The Tower Building   80 Maiden Lane
11 York Road   Suite 704, New York
London SE1 7NX   NY 10038

www.continuumbooks.com

British Library Cataloguing-in-Publication Data
A catalogue record for this book is available from the British Library.

ISBN: 978-1-4411-7968-5 (paperback)

Library of Congress Cataloging-in-Publication Data
A catalog record for this book is available from the Library of Congress.

Typeset by Newgen Imaging Systems Pvt Ltd, Chennai, India
Printed and bound in Great Britain by the MPG Books Group

Contents

Acknowledgements

I was very much helped in the reading for this project by Kathy Davis and Hazel Johnstone. They were indefatigable in their suggestions about who to read and in the provision of those texts. Shared enthusiasms about various authors became the basis for hours of happy reading.

Writing about detection took place after I became a Visiting Fellow at the Gender Institute at the London School of Economics. The study of detective fiction was beyond the remit of the curriculum, but the intellectual vitality and sense of academic community at the Institute was a source of endless, and considerable, encouragement. To everybody who contributed to that context, my very warm thanks.

As always, I have been helped by many people with whom I have talked about both the general theme of detection and more specific instances where the skills of detection can be directed towards various kinds of social and political events. I am very grateful to all those with whom I have talked about these questions, an essential part to that initial work of the detection (and hopefully, the understanding) of the workings of the social world. It has been a great privilege to share in these richly diverse and sympathetic conversations. I should, however, remark that while always being enthusiastic about inter-disciplinary work (and conversation) I have written this book with an emphasis on the social. This inevitably means that many interventions from literary critics about detection are not explored here. Nor was it possible to write about all authors of detective fiction. All readers will no doubt have their favourites to add to the list of those considered here. Part of the fascination of detective fiction is that there are always additional authors of detection to be read.

My sons Tom and Jamie have been enormously supportive and helpful. They have taken the time to read some of the fiction mentioned here and – even better – have told me about detection in genres other than print. It has been a great pleasure to work in this domestic context and I am extremely grateful to Tom for his help at a crucial stage in the editing of this book. It is, of course, the case that all the faults in the following pages are mine; I have to admit that *I did it*.

Introduction

Crime Writing

I think it is a mistake to assume from the content that this is purely a genre piece.
I mean I guess it is a genre piece but what we were really looking at are major themes
in modern American life . . . But it is my belief that The Wire *story in American*
fiction and in American literature has become an essential genre since Chandler
and Hammett and it is as elemental to our understanding of ourselves as the west-
ern was in earlier years of the twentieth century.
            (David Simon, The Wire, *Session One, Episode One, audio commentary)*

'Sir Iain lived and worked by the same ground rules as a lot of villains swore by.
He was selfish without appearing to be, full of arguments and self-justifications.
He espoused the public good, but lined his pockets with the public's money.'
            (Ian Rankin, Let it Bleed*)*

Crime is one of the central concerns of western societies, sometimes through
a dramatic and sensational presence in the media, sometimes as a mundane
part of twenty-first century life, but always a topic that excites attention and
engages the attention of readers or viewers. The kinds of crimes that attract
the most attention are generally those crimes committed by one individual
against another (most obviously, murder) but other kinds of crimes – the
swindle, the theft of large amounts of money – will also receive attention.
Crime is, at least in its appearance in print rather than reality, hugely popular; as a recent fiction reviewer remarked: 'The murder rate just goes up
and up'.[1] This book explores some of the many themes in western crime-
writing of the past two centuries. But these themes are seen in terms of an
argument about crime-writing: the argument being that crime fiction
demands and deserves more public and critical attention than it is often
given. Too often, crime and detective fiction is written as another sub-genre
of fiction, similar, for example, to romantic fiction, a sub-genre that is perhaps interesting but not truly significant in the same sense as conventional
fiction. It is this view that is rejected here on two grounds.

The first argument for elevating crime and detective fiction to a place of greater significance in our critical pantheon is that in doing so we might avoid the worst excesses of those tediously hierarchical views in western culture which distinguish between the 'high' and the 'low' in culture. Although the advent of more culturally democratic times has limited some of the more flagrant absurdities of this view (absurdities often based on the class position of readers rather than any intrinsic value of the fiction), there still remains a sense in which some forms of fiction, and crime and detective fiction is one, are afforded less cultural esteem. In this context, there is a real loss to the cultural and social world because as citizens we refuse the possibilities of the imaginative about those fractures in society that involve us all. Writers of detective and crime fiction inform their novels with debates about the collective world: about those subjects of social order, social morality and the various tensions between rich and poor that may form the context rather than the foreground of more conventional fiction. Above everything, detective and crime fiction is, by its very subject matter, about morality: its limits, its meaning and its value. We can trace, over the past 200 years of crime-writing, shifting relationships about the relationship of morality to the law. We can, for example, observe in the second half of the twentieth century the emergence of a perception, articulated very often by those most involved in the detection of crime, that there is a growing and considerable moral space between the legal views of 'crime' and crime itself and that those crimes against both the person and the social world, which are truly important, are often outside the formal remit of the law. The moral separation – the estrangement – of law and morality becomes a key theme in crime literature in the latter part of the twentieth century, just as writers in the early part of the twentieth century had argued through their various accounts of the causes of crime, that motives for crime were often social rather than particular. Thus, a significant tradition in crime-writing today suggests that our western construct of the law, and boundaries between legal and illegal, leaves untouched those crimes that have the most destructive impact on human lives.

It is this second argument that can make crime and detective fiction so relevant and so prescient; it is allowed (and it allows itself) the fictional space to explore not just the biography of one person but the biographies of whole groups of people, the people who, for example, run organizations such as the police force or political parties and the people, who may be viewed and interpreted as individuals but who are nevertheless part of a social world. Throughout its history, detective and crime fiction has also recognized the ongoing tension within bourgeois society: the tension between, on the one hand, a moral code, which presents itself as omnipresent and relevant to all, and on the other, the very considerable differences in social power (and social influence), which are consequences of societies divided by class, race and gender. Of all forms of fiction, it is perhaps detective and crime fiction that is the most democratic of all fiction since the eighteenth century: it explores the world (and aspects of the world) that is largely ignored by much of conventional fiction. For example, in the western, Protestant societies of that time, which have long histories of assuming a coincidence of the homologous relationship of hard work and positive morality, detective and crime fiction gives us pictures of people at work and of their various relationships to that central part of most people's lives. It also provides two powerful correctives to conservative views of the social order: first, crime fiction allows the rich and powerful its due quota of human evil, and second, crime fiction has an honourable history of maintaining a social presence for radical views about crime and punishment. Thus, for example, crime fiction (certainly in Europe) was an early convert to the abolition of capital punishment; in the past 30 years, we have seen a number of detective writers (for instance, Ian Rankin and Henning Mankell) reawaken that theme of social, rather than individual, corruption, which Dashiell Hammett had developed in the 1930s. No longer do writers maintain the comforting view that the guilty party is merely the one rotten apple in the social barrel; now, there emerges a highly sceptical view about the health of the whole barrel. We are asked, by writers of crime fiction, to think of social questions that many people would rather ignore: questions about the origins of human actions and the social responses to both the merely unconventional and the more dangerous and damaging.

Crimes against others (be it murder, theft or fraud) are as ancient as human societies; writing fiction about them is rather more recent. The religions of the book (Judaism, Christianity and Islam) all contain numerous comments about how human beings should live and the kinds of punishments that they would suffer should their behaviour become transgressive. Each of the great books of these religions contains stories about various transgressors and the judgements meted out to them by diverse embodiments of righteousness. The Ten Commandments of Mosaic law are taken as the bedrock of moral laws of western society and the various sanctions in chapters 20 to 23 of the *Book of Exodus* (especially perhaps 'Eye for eye, tooth for tooth, hand for hand, foot for foot, Burning for burning, wound for wound, stripe for stripe') have echoed down the ages both as prescriptions for penal policy and legitimations for human revenge.[2]

Modern western societies have (with certain exceptions such as the United States) abandoned many of the more vengeful aspects of biblical law. However, no western society has abandoned either the practice of crime or the pursuit of the criminal. Punishment has, at least in theory, shifted to an emphasis on the rehabilitation of the offender and a commitment to attempting to understand the causes of crime. Both these shifts can be discerned from the beginning of the nineteenth century, and although the shift did not occur overnight (and students of the popular press might argue that this transformation is still far from complete), there is a sense in which many of those professionally concerned with the arrest and identification of 'the criminal' have become markedly less retributive in their practises.

It would, however, be wrong to attribute this greater western attempt at understanding the origins of crime and the genesis of the criminal to a greater social toleration or enlightenment about the meaning of crime. Many people before the beginning of the nineteenth century understood very well that poverty and brutality as well as greed and envy were the 'causes' of crime; public executions were stopped in Britain less because of the greater humanitarian feeling of the public than the threat to public order, which these massively popular events created. State policy in Britain towards the criminal changed because it became apparent to many that various forms of the more physically violent punishments did not work. Pragmatism, in this context as in others, became the underlying dynamic of reform and change.

Parallel to this greater state interest in crime and its causes ran the emergence of a fictional exploration of the criminal. Again, the presence in fiction (be it prose or drama) of the 'bad' person was no novel development; the temptations of the world, and especially envy for the possessions of others in the world (whether they be persons, power or worldly goods), have always been considerable and the temptations that were never universally resisted. But the fiction about crime that emerged in the nineteenth century featured a new fictional person: the detective. Rather than evil-doing being unmasked and discovered through social events (the 'unravelling' of human actions), it has now become the case of a detective setting out to identify and arrest the criminal, whether they be murderer or thief or, quite often, both. What this new form of fiction did, quite as much as other new forms of fiction did for other possibilities of the human condition in other contexts, was to elicit in the reading public a tremendous enthusiasm for this novel form of social agency – that of detection. 'Clues' and 'evidence' became part of public and popular discussions of the world, various attempts were made to identify (before they could commit crimes) the criminal and, perhaps of the most long-term significance, certain social spaces and social relationships became associated with the criminal. As the public imagination about crime grew, developed and acquired traditions and habits of its own, so this imagination would imprint upon the social world (and especially the urban world) those categories of 'dangerous' and 'threatening'.

In the early crime-writing (writing, for example, in Britain and the United States in the 1840s), the physical world of the city acquired, as the country-side had done through the pens of Romantic poets, a moral meaning of its own. This 'moralisation' of the social space has played a central part in the building and re-building of cities for the past 200 years. Thus, although it is often remarked that Paris was rebuilt by Haussmann in the late nineteenth century in such a way as to eliminate the risks of popular uprisings (and the making of barricades across narrow streets), it was equally the case that Paris and other cities were often remodelled in ways dictated by fears about 'breeding grounds' for criminals. Social hygiene demanded that cities become open to the gaze of the police and at the same time offer little in the way of places in which criminals might hide.

Reading fiction might have helped city planners to question their association of the criminal with the squalid and the poverty-stricken areas of the city. A degree of petty theft and vandalism may well have been part of the urban landscape of poverty but as any professional and sane thief would have remarked there was little or no point in pursuing one's profession among the poor; they had nothing either to steal or to kill for gain. The rich, on the other hand, had rather more to offer. This point was grasped by the writers of detective fiction from the first; although Edgar Allen Poe (often described as the first major writer of crime fiction) constructed various images of dark deeds in dark areas of the city, later writers, and certainly from Sherlock Holmes onwards, grasped the essential point that major crimes such as murder for material gain are more likely to occur among those who have been blessed with wealth. It is all the more surprising, therefore, that much writing about detective fiction expresses surprise that (and particularly in England) a great deal of serious crime (and especially murder) seems to take place in the drawing rooms of the wealthy. Where else, we might ask rhetorically, is it supposed that murder for gain might take place? The poor might murder out of rage at each other (or even at their condition) but given the long-term ghettoization of the European poor, it is unlikely that circumstances will effect a mingling of the social classes other than in those most rigidly defined contexts of domestic service or factory employment, where structures of command keep the most privi-leged from the most powerless. Indeed, given some of the demands made

upon domestic servants throughout Europe in the nineteenth and twentieth centuries, what is remarkable is that so few servants killed or robbed
their employers.

The reality of relations between the social classes in much of Europe for
much of the nineteenth and twentieth centuries was often, in fact rather
than in fiction, of a remarkable tranquillity. Notwithstanding events such
as the Paris Commune of 1870 and strikes and civil disturbances, many
European cities, particularly outside the capital city or the locus of state
power, were, at least in terms of public events, relatively peaceful places. Yet
evil, wrong-doing and danger were increasingly portrayed, in fiction, as the
everyday reality of these places. It is this perception of *fantasy* evil, rather
than its reality, which is the major concern of this book. The argument here
is not about dismissing the various crimes, both social and individual, of the
past 200 years. Such an argument in the face of the death and destruction
of the twentieth century would be impossible to make. But what is argued
here is that the imagination of 'evil' played a considerable part in the construction of fears and fantasies about possible threats to both the individual
person and the collective way of life of western societies, as a result of which
communities have turned to the endorsement of a built environment of
separation and constraint. The desire to construct walls, barriers and various forms of safety against wicked outsiders is, again, no new thing in human
history.[3] But what is perhaps different, from the early years of modernity in
the nineteenth century, is the enthusiasm with which considerable general
social energy has continued to be devoted to the identification and pursuit
of the disruptive, 'evil' person or persons in our midst. We have, as Keith
Thomas has pointed out, abandoned the pursuit of witches, but instead of
witches, we have 'witch-hunts', instances where often terrifying amounts of
hatred are directed against either non-existent or largely harmless individuals or collectivities.[4]

It would appear, therefore, that the Europe of the period after the
Enlightenment, although in many ways 'enlightened' and often moving
towards the apparently more humane and thoughtful treatment of social
outsiders and deviants, could not abandon its more ancient enthusiasm for
'imagining evil'. That imagination of evil gave rise, at its most vicious form,
to the persecution (among others) of non-white people, Jews and homo-
sexuals. At its most trivial form, it created various forms of social exclusion,
from dress codes to bans on the entry of divorced people to elite social
occasions. Keeping ourselves safe from others remains, even as we mock
at these past forms of difference, a major social concern and, in the early
years of the twenty-first century, a form of considerable commercial and

industrial enterprise in the provision of various forms (from global arms expenditure to household security systems) of defence against others.

Fiction about crime thus has two meanings: the first is the straightforward sense of writing, which takes the occasion and detection of a crime (usually, a murder) as the central theme of the plot. The second meaning, of considerable importance in the political and social worlds, is the public imagination about crime: our fears and our terrors about the dreadful acts that might be committed, both against us as individuals and against the social world in which we live. The great psychoanalyst Hannah Segal has spoken of the way in which the contemporary world is threatened less by actual wickedness than by 'a delusional inner world of omnipotence, and absolute evil, and sainthood'. These 'delusional' worlds both create and enlarge terrors: they perceive, for example, political terrorism when none exists and magnify (and radically misunderstand) real dangers. At the same time, the same world, and the same forces, encourages us to see both enemies and saints where neither is actually present.

So this study of detective and crime-writing in the past 200 years is both about some of the novels themselves but also about the contribution, which they made to our social understanding of 'evil'. It is, therefore, an attempt to offer through fiction, an ethnography of the way in which people in the west have imagined crime and 'evil'. What will become apparent in these pages is that it has not been the case that all detective and crime fiction is on the side of the rich and the powerful; in certain cases, the sympathies of the author are manifestly with the deprived and the powerless. Nevertheless, it is a characteristic of much western detective fiction that the people, who feature in its pages both as villain and pursuer, are generally white and middle class. Non-white people seldom appear in mainstream western detective fiction (although there is now, as Ruth Morse has pointed out, a sub-genre of 'post-colonial' detective fiction) nor that consistently criminal group: young, working-class men.[5] To many critics, crime and detective fiction is a homogeneous genre, which is not altogether 'serious' literature. This view is not part of this book; on the contrary, an opposing suggestion is made: that of all fiction in the past 200 years, it is detective and crime fiction that has most vividly and often persuasively engaged with social reality. This is not to say that the great works of canonical literature have not explored the social world; they clearly have done this. But that exploration has often emerged from the class politics of western societies in such a way that only certain aspects of the social world have received full consideration and discussion. Moral questions, the questions about how to act in relationship to others and the wider community have widely informed all imaginative literature, but crime and detective fiction has perhaps made a further unique contribution in its assumption that 'good' and 'evil' are part of the same moral continuum, with the same connections to the social world.

Many of the themes which are at the centre of detective and crime fiction are as old as human society and in this sense detective and crime fiction has a certain timelessness, which much of the other fiction does not have. Yet, while the themes might be timeless, the portrayals of the murderers and criminals are not, nor are the various explanations, which authors provide for the genesis of the crimes. Indeed, what much of crime fiction illustrates very well is Marx's dictum that '[t]he more powerful the alien, objective world becomes which he brings into being over and against himself, the poorer he and his inner world become and the less they belong to him'.[6] Whether it relates to detective or villain, these remarks (written in 1844) have a considerable resonance to detective fiction. Most noticeably, many detectives in the fiction, written in the second half of the twentieth century, exhibit both a powerful sense of moral ambiguity about crime and a growing sense that the moral categories that they have been asked to police have any lasting value or significance. As we shall also see, the 'inner world' of many late twentieth century detectives becomes one in which the avoidance of emotional poverty is a constant battle.

Despite the increasing blurring of the lines between the world of the detective and the world of the criminal that becomes so noticeable in more recent detective fiction, many of the institutions of the 'real' world express opinions of increasing moral certainty and absolutism. Those Enlightenment values, which underpinned the more humane treatment of criminals are, for example, challenged by those media campaigns for the return to capital punishment and the public identification of those who have committed offences against children. The public's hunger for punishment sometimes seems to have weakened only slightly (if at all) from the days of public hanging; in Britain, for example, in recent years, sections of the press have been able to create considerable public fervour for more punitive regimes of imprisonment.

Detective fiction, however, does not have a single moral stance nor does it, in the main, actively encourage revenge and punishment outside the processes of law and order. In that sense, much of detective fiction exists 'within' the law. But, where it does not is, as we shall see, very often in the United States where the 'licence to kill' is taken literally by fictional detectives. The real nightmare of some of the worlds of contemporary detective fiction in the United States is not, therefore, that terrible crimes are committed but that only physical, armed force can prevent the continuation of these crimes. This theme, however, is only one possibility which emerges from that important constituent of detective fiction: the fear of crime and the criminal. Of this, one researcher on the 'fear of crime' has written that '[p]ublic anxieties about crime thus have a long history; the "fear" of "crime" is not new'.[7] The period, which that particular researcher considers, is limited to the late twentieth century but the argument here is that 'fear of crime' has a much longer history than is commonly supposed and has been vividly developed by various forms of literary invention. The pages that follow discuss the imagination of crime and at the same time how that imagination of crime offers highly pertinent but often largely ignored insights into social life.

Chapter 1

Making Crime

In the twenty-first century crime, fear of crime, prosecution of the criminal all make frequent headlines in the media; these subjects can dominate political debates and make or break governments. Anyone who watches television or film can detect the same preoccupation: set against the self-improvement sagas about house and person are the programmes about detection, about finding out 'who done it' and bringing that individual to justice. Corporate crime (or the kind of deception perpetrated by governments) invades the small or the large screen much less; it is typically an individual, who commits crime and who has to be tracked down by the detective. It is possible to predict that every day, on every television screen throughout the world, there is some version of the crime or detective story.

This phenomenon of the energetic engagement with the process of detection has changed little since the beginning of the nineteenth century, and this book is an attempt to engage with fictional accounts of crime and detection, and play detective with this form of fiction in the same way as the fictional detective plays detective with their audience. This is the literature in which we find those household names of Miss Marple and Hercule Poirot, or more recently Morse and Frost, men known, like God, only by their surnames. We watch and we read great quantities about detectives and their work, bookshops and libraries carry considerable stocks of both, and there is, as there is with general fiction, a world of awards and prizes, which rewards works of distinction.[1]

In the bibliographies about detective and crime fiction, there are three studies that are generally mentioned, and a set of distinctions, which are equally frequently made. The texts are *Bloody Murder* by Julian Symons (first published in 1972 and revised in 1985), T. J. Binyon's *Murder Will Out* (first published in 1990) and Ernest Mandel's *Delightful Murder* (first published in 1984).[2] All these texts – although they are far from alone, and the critical literature on crime and detective fiction is now considerable – place the origins of the genre at the beginning of the nineteenth century, and all of them cite distinctions between crime, detective and mystery fiction. These distinctions are challenged by Symons, and this author, as largely super-fluous and of little interest or assistance in the discussion of the genre; the first chapter of Symons's text is an elegant challenge to those various authorities who assumed that strict distinctions are possible between crime, mystery and detection. The one subject that all writers in the genre seem to be concerned with is that something bad has happened in the social world and 'we', various collective interests in the social world, need to find out 'who did it'. At the same time, in social worlds, which seem to many people to be increasingly opaque and demand ever more complex skills of their citizens, 'detection' is perhaps becoming a social skill, which is demanded as much of every person as of the professional detective.

But, of course, the social world is not opaque to all of us. As Ernest Mandel reminds us, quoting Marx, western culture has a great deal to be thankful for in the person of the criminal:

The criminal produces an impression, partly moral and partly tragic, as the case may be, and in this way renders a 'service' by arousing the oral and aesthetic feelings of the public. He produces not only compendia on Criminal Law, not only penal codes and along with them legislators in this field, but also art, belles-lettres, novels, and even tragedies. The crimi-nal breaks the monotony and everyday security of bourgeois life.[3]

The remarks may not seem relevant or appropriate to many victims of crime (and, for example, to victims of rape, they may seem even deeply offensive) but then Marx was writing (although less so Mandel) at a time when it was possible to write of 'bourgeois life' and assume a certain clarity of political understanding about its meaning. The theoretical certainties of the nineteenth and twentieth century had not yet given way to the uncer-tainties of the post-modern and the re-drawing of global politics after the 'fall' of the Berlin Wall and the attack on the World Trade Centre. The 'modern' criminal (and those writing about them) thus operated in what might appear to contemporary readers to be much more secure moral and political boundaries than those of their later counterparts. Whether or not this was actually the case, or whether this account of the past is yet another example of our nostalgia for vanished 'Edens', is a matter of some contention.

This study of crime fiction is thus an exploration of crime fiction in the West for the past two 200 years. It is also an exploration which sees crime

fiction as a far more important guide to our changing moral and social attitudes than is sometimes supposed, not in the sense that crime fiction
'reflects' our attitudes but in the way in which crime fiction often rejects or
develops our views about crime. There is, throughout the history of crime
fiction, both fictional writing about crime which does little more than exaggerate public concerns about the danger to individuals of 'evil' people,
while on the other hand, there is writing about crime, which refuses the
given boundaries between the criminal and the non-criminal worlds. In
much of crime fiction, there is an ambiguity about our moral codes, which
is not found in normative public discourses; crime fiction, therefore, can
satisfy public demand for fiction which provides the reassurance of capture
and disclosure, but it can also provide something of an imaginative bulwark
about facile judgements of guilt and innocence familiar to many discussions of crime in the real world. In a contemporary political climate, which
often suggests an obsession with the pursuit of 'evil', we need to ask if this
is simply a continuation of what various critics see as a near pathological
interest in that criminal world (a world which the majority of us never
encounter), or some combination of this with the fictional representation
of a world in which 'crime' is defeated and social order always restored. But
together with these possible explanations, there is another possibility that
reading fiction about crime is the most vivid account that we have of western societies' various fears and preoccupations. For this reason, this account
does not follow the usual chronological account of authors but instead
looks at the themes which have been central to crime and detective fiction
and the way in which they articulate social concerns. For example, the
detective and crime fiction of the nineteenth century is discussed in terms
of northern Europe's terror and vicarious delight in the city, a dual morbid-
ity which informs the work of Edgar Allan Poe, Wilkie Collins and others.
In the same vein, we can read recent writing by female authors about crime
as indicative of the long-standing dialogue between women about both the
possibilities of emancipation and fears about it. For example, Mary Astell,
the English essayist of the late seventeenth century, wrote eloquently in
favour of more independent lives for women. At the same time, her politics
remained, in the context of the world in which she lived, deeply conservative. We find this fault line throughout the subsequent centuries and no
more vividly present than when women write about crime.

The questions are not therefore about how much detective or crime
fiction we read and watch, but why this genre of literature has such a hold
on the public imagination and why we are so concerned with the detection
of events (most often murder) outside general experience. One of the most

salutary contributions of the academic study of crime in the past 30 years
has been to demonstrate that most people living in the west will have little
or no direct involvement in serious crime. Murders are seldom random;
the idea and the fear of being attacked by a strange person are happily
seldom realized.[4] As ever, and as everywhere, the place where violent death
(in peacetime) is most likely to occur is in the home or the immediate
neighbourhood. Motives and emotions that are as old as human civilization
(greed and jealousy most conspicuously) dominate the 'causes' of murder.
We live, on the whole, lives uninterrupted by crime or premature death,
assault or kidnap. For the great majority of western citizens, these events are
only ever experienced at a distance, through fiction or media reports. Many
western Europeans have lived, since 1945, in a relatively peaceful part of
the world, in which violence between individuals themselves, and the state
and individuals (at least in the domestic context) is limited. But we should
also note that although we may think of the state in the past as hideously
ruthless in its treatment of convicted murderers, there were, in fact, relatively few executions. In the year 1831, for example, 1,601 people were condemned to death in England and Wales, but of that number 'only' 52 were
executed including 12 convicted murderers. What this statistic also demonstrates is that numerous offences carried the death penalty at that time,
although the number of capital offences had fallen from over 200 in 1800
to merely 8 in 1831. We might congratulate ourselves that the western
European state has become less punitive in its attitude to criminals than in
the past (and clearly the abolition of the death penalty supports this view),
but at the same time we need to recall that the numbers of people, who
are incarcerated (particularly in the United Kingdom), shows little sign of
decreasing and is often a matter of rabid public enthusiasm.

It is appropriate at this point to note that while the relative domestic and
civic peacefulness and prosperity of our lives has been a feature of much of
the west since 1945, we are nevertheless assured by various voices that we
live in an age of 'anxiety' and a 'culture of fear'.[5] Books on these subjects
(which have extended the discussion to areas such as concerns by parents
about their children and to individual fears about health) have filled the
shelves of libraries, and something of a consensus has begun to develop
that contemporary lives are ruled by fears and anxieties of various kinds.
Much of this literature is simply ahistorical in the most extreme and simplistic sense: it grants no credence to the experiences of people in the past
or indeed the condition in which they lived their lives. For example, the
case of childbearing shows us how different are our expectations from those
of our grandmothers or great-grandmothers, for whom this event was

surrounded by entirely justifiable fears about the actual survival of both mother and baby. Modern anxieties may focus on the effect of childbearing on, for example, personal relations or appearance, but very few people would include anxiety about actual survival in their list of worries and concerns. In the same way, the past, and the struggles of people within it to make better lives for themselves, is betrayed when it is assumed that contemporary concerns about debt and employment are some kind of historical novelty. Illness and unemployment are devastating today, but 100 years ago they brought with them the *certainty* of poverty and degradation in which no state safety net provided any kind of support.

The romantic view of the past (consistently intact families, happy children, home-cooked food and whatever other myths can be invoked) is today usually seized upon by various pundits (be they politicians or academics) when they wish to suggest a contrast with the dissolute or variously negative habits of the present day world. Avner Offer's *The Challenge of Affluence* is one such example of this argument.[6] The book (in common with a consistent tradition within social history and sociology) describes a state of crisis (in Offer's book, a crisis of 'family breakdown, addiction, mental instability, crime, obesity, inequality, economic insecurity and declining trust') and then offers various reasons for this state of affairs. This tradition (of what might be described as 'crisis creation') has a heady appeal in modern western societies, since it largely entirely ignores material explanations for the nature of the world in which we live and suggests ideological reasons for our various crises and reasons that apparently allow us the freedom of changing the nature of our lives and those of others. Offer's work , and that of, for example, George Puttnam in *Bowling Alone*, is richly researched and entirely committed to the betterment of human existence; yet, it is also arguably part of that same rich vein of contemporary western culture, which offers us endless information about self-improvement and self-management.[7] The 'psychic law and order' to which Elizabeth Wilson once referred when speaking about bowdlerized versions of psychoanalysis is as much part of this vein as more clearly scholarly works: all share a wish to work towards the creation of a culture that makes order and coherence out of the disorder, the inequality and the potential for social and individual aggression of global capitalism.[8] Thus, those pundits who write of 'the age of anxiety' or the 'breakdown' of the social world do so with generally little to say about the context of these apparently traumatic states or the possibility that, perhaps, worry and concern are not inventions of the twentieth century. Although we can trace numerous examples, across historical time, of fear of social change, it is a remarkable feature of modernity that it is accompanied by often furious resistance to the changes that it brings. Among those many examples are the terror which seems to have been produced in sections of various societies by changes in the gender order: the emancipation of women, even when manifested by relatively trivial examples such as the use of cosmetics, has produced intensely hostile comments.

So, why, we might ask, since most of us live generally safe, relatively prosperous and 'crime free' lives, are we so fascinated by the pathology of crime, by the process of identification of the murderer or the unmasking of the criminal? Is this interest, along with our interest in the health (or otherwise) of our bodies part of the social pathology of contemporary western societies, in which daily life has become generally predictable and in which we are drawn to the deviant by the very pressures and repetitions of our conformity? We may have, as some sociologists have argued, more personal freedom than at any time in our history (most notably in the relatively free choices of our 'personal' lives), yet at the same time what is expected of us in the workplace and indeed the home has become, arguably, more demanding. The state of society at the beginning of the twenty-first century is, like other 'state of the world' examinations, a divisive topic; as always, decline and decay has its protagonists; those holding this view are as passionate in their arguments as those who suggest positive change and greater human emancipation. The 'decline' of the west has been so long predicted that the reiteration of this view is never surprising, the only event, which truly has been surprising in recent years, has been the collapse of the old Soviet empire. Capitalism, as the historian E. J. Hobsbawm has suggested, has been left wondering what happened and how to construct a new defence of itself.[9] The once straightforward defence, that we could partially justify capitalism in terms of 'defending the bad against the worse' (as C. Day Lewis famously suggested in the 1930s) no longer has the same enemy of wicked communist empires.[10] It may be the case that 'terror' has taken the place of communism as the enemy of the west, but its boundaries remain diffuse and in the context of detective and crime fiction, this recent 'fear of terror' replicates much of the long lasting fears of terror, which have been part and parcel of the possibilities of urban life since the early nineteenth century. For many people, the city and the urban have always been saturated with 'terror' and 'evil'.

These 'big' questions, about the state of the world and our place in it, are usually overtaken in our everyday lives by the more local problems of our work, our health and our families, the long-standing questions of concern. Certainly, since the sixteenth century, and notwithstanding the greater control which we have acquired over the natural world, we have become more concerned with our social 'performance'. Indeed, for many people living in the west, we have been required to become more concerned about how we 'perform' in certain social ways: the need for qualifications and credentials has massively increased and more educational provision (and a longer time spent in education) has much lengthened those years in which we have to worry about the quality of our scholastic achievements. Thus, just as we might, arguably, have reached a point at which the social world becomes both relatively safe and relatively reliable, we have also imposed upon ourselves a myriad of new anxieties, in particular, the question of how to live up to the expectations of an (apparently) highly qualified world, in which we are led to believe that the material rewards of the world are there for all to possess. Previous generations rightly fought to throw off the assumption that the rich man should be in his castle and the poor man at his gate, but that world view, with its hideous refusal of human capacity and equality, did not encourage democratic ideas about equal access to (and certain achievement of) general prosperity and status. Accustomed as we are to a society, which persuades us to assume that the world is everyone's oyster, the obvious state that this brings with it is anxiety about achievement and, of course, depression and a sense of failure if we cannot meet our professional and material aspirations. 'Affluenza' Oliver James argues, has made us all materially, and unhappily, ambitious.[11] The ancient endorsement of the idea that wealth does not 'buy happiness' has now been recognized, for western societies, by such pundits as Richard Layard.[12]

For many persons who are writing about the contemporary world, it is little surprise that the picture that they see is one of unrelieved gloom and social tension. This account of the western world is backed up by sophisticated forms of measurement of the social world: armies of social scientists are able to tell us how we live, how we feel and what we want. What they cannot do is to tell us how this differs from the past; the present is a well-measured country, and the past, for many people, is a hazy mixture of nostalgia and obscurity. There are numerous studies conducted in Great Britain in the first decade of the twenty-first century which demonstrate a profound ignorance about our own history, let alone anyone else's. Were it not for the fact that the Second World War appears (in the form, most predictably of the British fighting the Germans) on the British television screen on every week of the year, there would be almost no sense of the real past in the popular media, other than as a place to be (literally) dug up or to provide a context for emotional drama in period costume.

Except, of course, that the past is the backdrop to those hugely popular dramatizations of the crime novels of Agatha Christie and Dorothy Sayers, the sanitized version of the interwar years is the one in which the china is always impeccable and the clothes beautifully ironed. The real old steam train of the Kent town of Tenterden appears over and over again as endless heroes and villains arrive and depart. The steam from this train never appears to dirty the clothes of the characters, just as the physical build of the characters (the long and lean twenty-first century version of the ideal body) bears little resemblance to the rather more rounded (and certainly shorter) people of those years. We look back at this world, and see a place with clear boundaries of right and wrong, with vivid contrasts between innocence and depravity and with the promise (always fulfilled) of punishment for the evil-doer. As a refuge from much of the world of the twenty-first century, this world is a paradise as uncomplicated as the original Eden; unfortunately, as in the first Eden, there is a snake ('more subtil than any beast of the field') who attempts to destroy it. But Poirot or Miss Marple, and many others, are on hand to restore Eden to its harmonious state. Indeed, many detective novels suggest that the resolution of a murder brings with it a new state of liberation: at last, a certain truth has been discovered, and people can make their lives in a new sense of freedom. Yet, as in chapter 3 of the book of Genesis, 'what has been unmade is not the same when it is recovered:' Adam and Eve acquire knowledge and in the same way we, as readers, acquire both knowledge of the identity of the sinner and a reiteration of that biblical message about the punishment of the guilty.

One of the many questions which the book of Genesis leaves unanswered is the question of why the serpent had any interest in ensuring that Adam and Eve acquired knowledge. With knowledge – and this is made transparently clear in Genesis – comes binary categories (the first one we hear about is naked and clothed). The serpent, like many later perpetrators of evil, was somewhat overconfident in assuming that 'knowledge' would not turn somewhat critically in its own direction. Thus, the serpent becomes associated with evil, fear and characteristics that are hostile to human beings. Cultures might demonstrate that they can 'charm' snakes, but this reversal of the Bible story (the man, tempted by the woman who is tempted by the serpent, becomes the man who acquires a control over the seductive beast) does not disturb the essentially negative qualities of the snake. Nor, until the late twentieth century, has anyone bothered to ask how, in the original Eden, it was possible for two characters, Adam and Eve, who were supposed to live in a world untroubled by knowledge and presumably the knowledge of sexual difference, to have different vulnerabilities to seduction. It was, like much else about gender difference, just taken for granted that women were susceptible to temptation in ways which men were not. The great paradox of the story, of course, is that it is Eve who is tempted by the idea of possessing knowledge, a capacity, which men later attempt to own for themselves.

The metaphors about Eden, and the seductive quality of knowledge, infuse detective and crime fiction from its earliest days, the days which are usually dated from the novels of Edgar Allan Poe, the author of classics such as *The Fall of the House of Usher* and *The Murders in the Rue Morgue*. Poe, himself, never an inhabitant of any form of Eden, died at the age of 40 after a life whose end, his biographer Peter Ackroyd suggests, was as mysterious as the plots of many of his novels. Yet by that time he had achieved considerable fame and was recognized in both his native United States and in Europe.[13] Among the first people to translate Poe was the French poet Charles Baudelaire and in that connection, we can trace links between Poe's work, on the haunting of the new urban space by the unknown and the monstrous, with the writing on the city and its people of both Baudelaire and that later reader of his work, the twentieth-century German critic Walter Benjamin.[14] Within this same context, we can observe the depiction of the sense of menace in city spaces where human beings are unknown to each other, and where social life can only work if unfamiliarity is taken for granted.

In this sense, the city presents the context for all those fears about 'origins', which Marx and Nietzsche observed were characteristic of the bourgeoisie. For Marx, the unspoken 'fear' of the bourgeoisie was about the origin of their wealth; those energetic attempts of maintaining the façade of the civilizing process would come to nothing if awkward questions were asked about the ways in which money was accumulated. In much the same way, Nietzsche suggested that the bourgeoisie – as much as it did not like having questions asked about its wealth – did not like to dwell too closely on the origins of 'modern' values. The awful possibility, in this latter case, would be that modern values would be exposed as mere rationalizations of social convenience. To Marx and Nietzsche, we might add a third person, Sigmund Freud, who was also to make public connections that were thought to be best left unsaid, in this case that all of us owe our origins to a sexual act and that our sexual identity is made rather than given. This trio – Nietzsche, Marx and Freud – all took on the role of social detective; for each and every one, the purpose of their work was to uncover and to reveal the hidden structures and dynamics of the social world. The first question, which we have to ask about detective fiction, therefore, is whether or not it is the domestication of this general 'fear of origin', which we can observe in nineteenth century culture.

While we might ask this question, however, we have to recall that the dynamic of 'unmasking' is as old as the history of carnival and urban celebrations. Disguising our identity has long been one of the forms of play in diverse cultures and historical periods; in the same way as children 'dress up' so adults have for centuries made elaborate efforts to conceal their real identities in various forms of disguise. In doing this, rank and status (and occasionally gender) can be transformed and what cannot be said or acted out in other contexts acquires a degree of social freedom. While carnival or other forms of celebration allow us these possibilities, the narrative of masks and disguise is one in which there is always a final degree of revelation. Detective fiction takes on this narrative form: the murderer remains unknown throughout the novel, and it is only in the concluding chapters that his or her real identity becomes known.

At the same time as the murderer is finally revealed, what is also restored is social order, and it is possible to see this restitution of social order as the definitive contribution of the detective story to social unease about 'origins'. There is little detective fiction, which is not, in some sense or another, restorative; the 'bad apple' in the barrel is removed, and the calm of the social world is once more in place. Detection is, in this sense, a hugely healing and redemptive form of fiction and as such is immensely calming to what might be a general, if unspoken, unease about the potential chaos of the social world. When we can watch or read about the discovery of the mad, the bad and the dangerous in print, film and television, we can rest safe in the knowledge that restoration is possible and that the fault lay not in our created world but in an individual psyche. Nowhere is this more transparent than in public reactions to the murder or the abduction of children. Seldom is it suggested that the sexualization of our culture might play a part in these events; the problem is always the deranged or 'evil' murderer. For all its abandonment of sexual taboos and inhibitions, twenty-first century western society is singularly unwilling to consider what Freud asked us to consider: that children are sexual beings and that all of us, as both children and adults, can exercise and recognize that sexuality.

The attempt to 'un-mask' the social world, to discover the reasons for social change and social continuity, is generally assumed to be a product of the nineteenth century. Indeed, in terms of the development of the social sciences and the systematic study of social life, there is obvious evidence for this view. All the disciplines of the social sciences such as sociology, psychology, criminology and economics emerge as distinct and codified areas of study in the late nineteenth century. But, if we think about the investigation of the social world outside non-fiction, there are others, notably the writers of fiction, who have claims that are at least as strong to be considered as the first real investigators of the social world. The discussion (and consequences) of human motivation is as old as written culture but arguably the narrative fiction of England in the eighteenth century is the cultural location of the most apparent shift towards the study of why people act in the way they do. In the fiction of Henry Fielding and more particularly Jane Austen, we find expressed, as an interwoven theme of their narratives, the view that the social world is full of puzzles and mysteries. In *Bloody Murder*, Julian Symons makes the point that puzzles are everywhere in western literature, but this does not constitute a detective story; Symons, unlike many other writers, accords the title of the novel which first strikes 'the note of crime literature' to *Caleb Williams* by William Godwin, which was first published in 1794.[15] This choice of a novel by the partner of Mary Wollstonecraft and the father of Mary Shelley fulfils all possible expectations: both author and period exactly coincide with the beginning of what we think of as the 'modern' and in particular of the emergence of modern genre fiction.

But, I shall argue in the following chapter, what defines the beginning of writing about crime and murder is not to be found in one particular author but in the emergence, in the eighteenth century, of the idea of sensation and the sensational. This century saw the growth of a print culture, the development of an urban world, which was defined in part – and continues to be so – in terms of its cultural difference from the rural world. The city 'needed' ideas and the city, through the various associations which it nurtured, created ideas. One of the ideas, articulated through newspapers and pamphlets, the original 'popular' press, was that of the extraordinary event. This is not to say that there had been no such thing as an extraordinary event in previous history (the seventeenth century alone in Britain had seen civil war and regicide) but the novel 'extraordinary events' of the eighteenth century were increasingly about ordinary people, finding themselves in strange situations. In the twenty-first century, we speak of 'sensationalisation' and often decry it as a vulgar and vulgarizing form, but what the form established for us in the eighteenth century was the idea that the daily round, the ordinary event, the domestic and local social relations, could be transformed – by a single event or action – into something extraordinary. This, in itself, was arguably greatly enriching for our culture since it gave us a chance to see the way in which the 'quotidien' has richer (even if often darker) possibilities than we had previously imagined. Writing about crime and detection became the way in which the social world, as the normative and interventionist order of the state became increasingly omnipresent, could maintain an association with disruptive ideas and behaviour.

The Christian moral order of the west had been founded on the idea of original sin and the possibility of evil; as those beliefs became increasingly marginalized, it was, perhaps, increasingly necessary for there to be some social space for the exploration of both. This book is therefore concerned with the idea of the creation of the figure of the detective as a replacement for the figure of God and the 'text' of the detective novel as the place in which moral values are contested, debated and – at least in some senses and some ways – upheld.

As many other critics have pointed out, Christian ideas about morality and judgement have never fully disappeared from western culture. England is not alone in the west in continuing to fall back on explanations of 'evil' when faced with particularly problematic social events. However much we may assume that we know about the ways in which human beings can learn and acquire brutal behaviour, we do not easily accept that we are socially 'made'. Indeed, the resistance to this idea can be endlessly illustrated by the way in which 'nature' rather than nurture still holds a powerful explanatory hand in questions about 'innate' differences between women and men or differences in intelligence between children. Detective and crime fiction has continued to explore this idea throughout its history and perhaps the sharpest division within this literary genre is between those writers who view a capacity to murder or harm as 'naturally' given and those who view it as socially created. In the following pages, we will see how this dialogue continues in the pages of crime fiction and how different writers assign responsibility for savage and, literally, murderous behaviour. Yet, between these two accounts of human motivation, there remains a common thread: that the perpetrator of crime must be named and responsibility for crime made socially apparent. The ancient Christian dynamic of the naming of sin, followed by judgement and redemption, underpins all crime fiction. In this dynamics, the detective plays either the part of God or that of God's assistant: the evil-doer is brought to divine retribution through human agency and the detective is the person who reveals to the world the identity of the sinner and the way in which the 'rules' have been broken. The following chapters explore the various ways in which, through detective fiction, we have for some time clung to that ancient pattern of motive, crime, discovery and redemption and are only now coming to consider the possibility that the formal punishment of offenders is neither morally necessary nor of any great social value. More particularly, I want to suggest that once many of us had renounced the idea of the Devil, we had to replace him (or her). Thus, part of the hidden dynamic of contemporary western society is that of the endless re-creation of the Devil; in detective fiction, a largely harmless exercise, allowing us a comfortable, and unthreatening, brief association with what we uncritically call 'evil'. But outside fiction, the dynamic is far more dangerous: our enemies, those who disagree with us, those who are violent towards us, become 'evil', 'little devils' and other titles beloved to sections of the media. This book, therefore, has as its main subject crime fiction, but it is also concerned with the social function of that fiction and of what appears to be a social dependence on the existence of the evil 'other'. In making 'evil' part of the threat which we are led to believe we confront in everyday life we construct for ourselves a moral world in which we (unless we are among the few who commit serious crime) are always innocent and can match our actions against those who are truly 'evil'.

This argument itself rests on the familiar idea that all societies have to organize themselves through some form of moral order. Whether or not we care for the moral order so created is a matter of politics and individual taste; what is universally the case is the way in which the social world cannot tolerate the absence of a socially agreed morality. As many writers have pointed out, from the beginning of the European Enlightenment to the present day, the loss of the authority of religion gives rise to the need for other forms of morality and ethics and to locations other than those of religions for the discussion and the validation of moral codes. It is not perhaps entirely coincidence that the emergence of the novel coincided in Europe with the coming of a more secular society. Although there are numerous material reasons for the development of prose fiction (for example, the emergence of reading publics through the growth of increasing leisure and literacy and urban life), the intellectual dynamic for the birth of the novel lay in the recognition that it remained necessary to discuss moral dilemmas. If Adam and Eve became yesterday's characters in the moral sagas of the west, so there was a cultural and social space for new characters, for characters who could embody the ordinary and demonstrate the moral quandaries which continued to beset human beings.

The detective (and the crime) novel did not immediately appear as a definitive sub-genre of fiction. But, there was from the early days of the novel an element of 'detection' in all fiction. This did not necessarily involve the detection of the identity of the murderer, but it did often involve other elements of detection (for example, of parentage in Henry Fielding's *Tom Jones*) or, more generally, in Jane Austen, the question of who actually loves whom. In all these instances, and other cases, the narrative depends upon revelation, on finding out the truth about the characters and their motivations. Indeed, that uncertainty about the self, which is assumed to be a characteristic of secular societies, is widely explored in eighteenth and nineteenth century fiction.

While the characters of Austen, the Bronte sisters, George Eliot and Elizabeth Gaskell search for a sense of themselves (or the partner with whom they can realize their sense of self) a parallel tradition in fiction explored the identity of the disruptive self, the self who does not bring about reconciliation but subverts and disturbs social order. Detection thus became – whether in its explicit form of the detective novel or in more general fiction – a central characteristic of post-Enlightenment literature. With it came, or continued, a continuing sense of the possibilities of 'evil', evil in the form of the wicked and the corrupt or evil in actions that arose out of 'ordinary' and commonplace human emotions. Evil took various embodiments, with the continuing appearance of outsiders of various kinds as the more likely perpetrators of evil. Moral panics, throughout the past 200 years, have always given rise to the creation and identification of characters who fit the characteristics of those most feared or demonized. One of the many useful lessons of reading detective fiction is to recognize that the 'terrorist' is not just a figure of the early twenty-first century: the evil outsider is an ancient figure in literature, as are the motives of greed, jealousy and obsession, which drive them. It is therefore the case that what follows is as much an investigation into 'why they done it' as into 'who did it' and why we appear to need them to continue to do so. But it is also helpful to recall the comment of Stieg Larrson in *The Girl who Played with Fire* (the second volume of his Millennium Trilogy) that 'There are no innocents. There are, however, different degrees of responsibility'.[16]

Chapter 2

The Making of the Detective

As with all literary genres, there is considerable discussion about who was the 'first' detective and the point of origin of detective fiction. But the guilty party, as certain detective fiction has always supposed, is not necessarily a single person. Thus, this investigation begins with the creation of 'sensation' together with social concern and interest in the exceptional disruptive event, the event that causes social puzzlement and dislocation.

This investigation, therefore, begins in Europe in the eighteenth century, a period in history associated with the Enlightenment and various social and cultural changes that were to make up much of what we know and understand by the 'modern'. Crucial to these changes was the gradual emergence of a public secular space. Whatever doubts individuals might have had about the existence of a (Christian) God were seldom publicly expressed in previous centuries but in the eighteenth century Voltaire and Rousseau were among those who suggested that belief in God, and support for the Roman Catholic Church as the source of moral authority, were not absolutely necessary conditions of existence. However much churches condemned these men, a world view was being established that made God optional, and publicly so. This, as many people have pointed out, then left something of a vacuum in the moral order of the social world. The Ten Commandments and various interpretations of the Bible had allowed Judeo-Christianity to occupy a relatively straightforward moral space for hundreds of years, but once these teachings – and their central character – became less significant and less credible, then the question arose of how people should act.

Initially, in the period between the late eighteenth century and the mid-nineteenth century, forms of Christianity other than those of the established churches began to campaign for more vigorous forms of Christianity, a different governance of the church and a Church which was more engaged with the world of the majority of the population. These attempts to restore the intellectual and social authority of religion did not succeed in reclaiming the overall social place of religion although 'God' was frequently invoked at times of national emergency or personal transition (birth, marriage and death). What had disappeared was the sense of God as the origin of moral unity of the social world. By the end of the nineteenth century, the French sociologist Emile Durkheim was arguing that morality was essentially about regulation and discipline and the ability to live a life in which it is possible to establish clearly defined (as Durkheim describes them) relationships; 'self-mastery', writes Durkheim, 'is the first condition of all true power, of all liberty worthy of the name'.[1]

In this assertion, we can see the ways in which the Enlightenment moved the focus of the moral order from the individual's obedience to God to the ability of the individual to contain and regulate his or her inclinations and emotions, in order to live the kind of life which makes social order and social cohesion possible. Those other landmarks on the journey to a secular morality (Kant's categorical imperative and the utilitarian's concept of the maximization of human happiness) had, by the beginning of the twentieth century, evolved to a point where the general social good had taken the place of a deity. But, of course, just as ideas about morality had been changing, so had ideas about much else in society, not least that taste for the 'sensational', which had become part of the eighteenth century world. But the two themes are closely related, and as such surely related to the emergence of a new kind of social investigation: that of detection.

We can perhaps begin to 'detect detection' in the fault lines that we can observe in the various currents of the loss of God, the increasing valorization of the social and enthusiasm for the sensational from the eighteenth century onwards. The nineteenth century discovery of 'society' as something other than a public space that has to be ordered and controlled carried with it the need to understand possible disruptions to the social order. What might have, for example, once been defined as 'riot' or 'rebellion' (whether individual or social) now becomes a matter of concern about the workings of the social world: where did this disorder 'come from', who was responsible for the disturbance? In individual terms, this emergent new understanding of the disruptive becomes associated with a new mindset about the 'discovery' of the master criminal or the murder. Despite the fact that in many crimes (and most particularly murder) the villain is more or less immediately identifiable, the tale is one which we increasingly tell backwards: we have to learn about the circumstances of the crime, the other possible culprits and the implications of the crime.

But I want to argue here that it is not to Godwin's choice of *Caleb Williams* where we should look for our first glimpse of detection in fiction but to the fiction of Jane Austen, that hugely vital presence in English culture and literature whose name has fuelled not just an academic and commercial industry but also a certain way, for sections of the English literary classes, of looking at the world. Austen, writing very largely of a pre-industrial world, is sometimes presented as the defender all that a conservative imagination could desire. That view – for example, in the work of Marilyn Butler – is located within conventional meanings of both conservatism and radicalism.[2] Austen certainly had no wish to defend the excesses of the French Revolution, and the limited material which we have about her political views, would suggest that her vote would have gone to the Tories rather than the Whigs. But, and it is a very important 'but', there is considerable evidence in her work that she had no veneration for social hierarchy, unearned wealth, the 'natural' authority of either men or the rich and certainly no toleration for untutored views. Austen, we might consider, does not defend convention so much as demand an understanding and justification for it. One of the many great misapprehensions of the British culture industry is the uncritical acceptance of the view of Austen as the defender of conservative, middle-class, provincial England. Her world was, in many ways, much more demanding and much more dangerous than anything that has since been known in the English Home Counties, even if that danger, and those demands, is seldom emphasized in accounts of her work. A measure of how aspects of the English past are romanticized is the way in which the life of an eighteenth century country village – without a welfare state or clean water – can be seen as a paradise compared to its twenty-first century incarnation.

Danger, threat, disruption and deceit are all part of Austen's world and part of any case for her radicalism must be that she understood the ways in which petty and trivial acts can become the origin of events which do serious harm to human beings. Austen, unlike many later enthusiasts for her work, does not assume that individuals possess unique capacities for evil; we all possess them and we all have the capacity either to refuse them or allow them to flourish. In contrast to some of the women writers of crime fiction in the late twentieth century, Austen did not take the view that the capacity for 'evil' arises out of nowhere or that it is difficult to understand human motivation. Austen does not write of mutilated bodies, fear stalking the city streets or random violence attacking the innocent victim, but she does write of both the seven deadly sins and their implications.

Let us take just a few of the range of characters in Austen and see where the villains lie, and then consider the ways in which the author suggests how these individuals demonstrate their less than admirable qualities. First, we can identify the trail of male seducers who exist throughout Austen: men like Wickham in *Pride and Prejudice*, Willoughby in *Sense and Sensibility* and Henry Crawford in *Mansfield Park* have little or no respect for given conventions of sexual behaviour, and make assumptions of their own 'rights' which transcend time and culture. Of this morally unlovely, if seductive, trio, it is perhaps Henry Crawford who is the most developed character and the most relevant to subsequent ideas about 'evil'. Henry Crawford is no lumpen thug, but an assured, poised and socially extremely adept social actor. Like later villains in the pages of explicit crime fiction, Henry Crawford is not a social outcast but the much more interesting figure of the person who uses social convention for his own purposes. Henry Crawford is practised in the arts of heterosexual seduction: in fact, one of his major social characteristics is that he recognizes the value of words, of conversation, of talking to women. Two centuries later, the central male character of the film *Alfie* explained his success with women by saying, 'Just make them laugh'. Henry Crawford did not necessarily make women laugh but what he could do was to light up the ordinary and the everyday. His prowess as a reader of Shakespeare may not engage twenty-first century tastes, but what it does is to suggest the power of the word in what are, if not battles, then at least contests, between the genders. 'Silver-tongued', the 'talk of the devil', 'smooth talker' are all expressions from both sides of the Atlantic, which suggest a degree of cultural suspicion about highly articulate men, which inform numerous accounts of seduction, murder or other criminal deeds.

In Austen's *Mansfield Park*, Henry Crawford, who has, according to his sister, made most of the women that he has met fall in love with him, sets out to make the heroine of the novel, the shy, the retiring and the morally determined Fanny Price, follow this path. In many ways, we might judge Henry's decision to do this as actually worse than the act itself; he is simply bored in the country and decides that since he has nothing better to do he will 'make Fanny Price fall in love with me'.[3] In this decision, he establishes the beginning of a long trail of cold-hearted villains who embark on paths of crime or seduction in order to amuse themselves or to enlarge their own sense of capability. Equally, we might see Henry Crawford as the first of the great figures in fiction who troubled by *ennui*, turns to the corruption of virtue to offer some interest to the mind that is satiated by the boredom of the everyday and the familiar. Henry Crawford seeks 'sensation', that appeal of the unknown or the different, to the person whose life is little challenge, a way of life which is a defining characteristic for the lives of generations of those living in wealth and without need.

Henry Crawford comes close to securing the affection of Fanny Price. But only close; his own vanity encourages yet another possible seduction, and in that he loses both Fanny and at least a degree of his social standing.

Henry has, of course, committed no 'crime' in the conventional sense; his adulterous relationship with one of Fanny's cousins is not a criminal offence in England in the early nineteenth century, and there are certainly no corpses left behind to testify to his crimes. But the character of Henry has allowed us to see something about the way in which individuals move towards acts which are, if not criminal, then at least deliberate in their attack on the autonomy and the well-being of others. Fanny Price is punished for her refusal of Henry Crawford's proposal of marriage by being sent into a form of social exile with her poverty-stricken family. In this context, we see some other dynamics which fuel the making of crime and the criminal: the innocent is made responsible for the 'crimes' of others. Fanny Price is a very long way from being in any sense 'raped' by Henry Crawford, but in her fictional story we see the way in which social power can distort the meaning of innocence and guilt. Just as the victims of rape have often been made systematically 'responsible' for their 'crime', so Fanny Price is made to feel that it is she, and not Henry Crawford, who is responsible for his disappointment.

A disappointment in love (and vanity) for a member of the early nineteenth gentry may not be one of the greatest crimes of the past 200 years, but there are in Austen's work other cases where the sexual incontinence of men brings real harm to young and vulnerable women. Willoughby in *Sense and Sensibility* seduced and left to a life of shame and poverty a young woman; Wickham in *Pride and Prejudice* would have done the same had it not been for a fortunate intervention. Again, these are ancient tales of seduction, but they are also about the boundaries of the social world, and the ways in which the conventional Anglo-Saxon world has always operated standards of morality which are often double and even triple. As numerous feminist writers in the nineteenth and twentieth centuries have pointed out, it is women who are made to carry the 'guilt' of seduction, and men whose behaviour is allowed. In all her work, Austen protests against these distinctions and asks us, as readers, to think a little more closely about the nature of the boundaries between good and bad, acceptable and unacceptable.

Part of the way in which Austen does this is to offer a highly critical gaze at the assumption that behaviour in a socially conventional way is a guide to morally acceptable behaviour. In this context, her work (notwithstanding the way in which her work has been annexed by those who see in it a heaven-sent legitimation for the existence and the behaviour of sections of the English middle class) stands as an important corrective to the idea that social conformity is a guide to moral integrity. It is in this way that Austen offers her second contribution to both the subversion and the disturbance of the social world: her profound scepticism about the similarity, in codes of manners, between behaviour and meaning. Thus, Austen initiates a narrative curiosity about the 'surface', the appearance of the social world, which is to continue until the present day. Her novels do not, in the same sense as the work of Wilkie Collins or Edgar Allen Poe, actually include 'real' murders, but they certainly include much which can be defined as theft or the infliction of real damage on another human being.

Heterosexual seduction is the major form through which Austen's villainous male characters damage vulnerable women and set in motion those patterns of abandonment, poverty and social exclusion which, until very recently, have been the lot of the single, unmarried mother. The characters thus damaged are seldom part of the more visible narrative of Austen's fiction (let alone the film and television reworkings of her novels), but they nevertheless stand as an integral part of its social relations. It is not only, as genteel readers of Austen might hope, that occasional, individual men are just somewhat irresponsible in their behaviour towards women, but that a system of sexual relations requires of women absolute obedience to that code. We have then, in this structure, an account of the social world which suggests various parallel codes: the rules of behaviour in social places (what we might call manners), the actual behaviour of human beings towards each other (behaviour, which is structured by legal frameworks but also interpreted by various forms of greed and avarice) and the various forms of resistance which particular groups (notably, but not exclusively, women) attempt to construct for their own defence and for the realization of actual, rather than imposed virtue.

Fanny Price, in this universe, is something of a standard bearer for her own view of the moral world. She is materially the poorest of Austen's heroines, the most socially and personally deprived, and yet she emerges at the conclusion of *Mansfield Park* as the definitive embodiment of many of the ideals of the Enlightenment, the French Revolution and various other landmarks in human emancipation. She has done this by thinking about what she does, discussing it and sticking to it in the face of various forms of bullying and pressure. More than anything else, for the purposes of Austen's novel and for this discussion of crime and the criminal, she does not take the social world at its own valuation. At the other end of the moral continuum, we might place Mrs John Dashwood, in *Sense and Sensibility*, who is nothing except determined by the social world and who, in one chapter of the most brilliant and perceptive writing in English literature, is allowed by Austen to condemn generosity, material need and any possibility of the concept of fairness. Here is Mrs John Dashwood arguing against any support for her husband's mother and stepsisters:

> 'Altogether, they will have five hundred a-year amongst them, and what on earth can four women want for more than that? – They will live so cheap! Their housekeeping will be nothing at all. They will have no carriage, no horses, and hardly any servants; they will keep no company, and can have no expenses of any kind!'[4]

This comment, and the chapter from which it was taken, constitute an important point in English fiction, since it is one of the most articulate accounts of the way in which the needs of one group of people can be overridden by another person's greed. The quoted passage denigrates the needs of women in various ways: the implications of Mrs Dashwood's comments are that women living without a man will eat little, never go out or entertain. Life beyond the blessing of the patriarchal other is clearly a very limited life, and even if we allow that Mrs Dashwood is exaggerating her account for her own purposes, what we see at work here is the kind of greed for money, which has always been an essential ingredient of various forms of crime. Mrs Dashwood suggests nothing illegal in her advice to her husband, but she does epitomize that fierce hunger for money, which can be socially acceptable in any form of society but which is, in various manifestations, a central ideological building block of capitalism.

Sense and Sensibility was first published in 1811 and has generally been read as the history of two sisters, Elinor and Marianne, with different temperaments and different capacities for fantasy. In Austen's novel, the fantasies which Marianne entertains, are those of romance and of a future life with her (initially) beloved Willoughby. The life which she constructs for herself is furnished with various kinds of material goods and corresponds in kind, if not in detail, with many later western versions of the ideal life of the comfortably married woman, the much parodied suburban life of the home, the car, the husband and the two children. For Marianne, as for her later sisters, this fantasy is made possible through marriage to the romantically engaging partner. The object of Marianne's affection turns out to be something of a rogue, as self-mystifying in his own way as Marianne and certainly avaricious in his pursuit of a wealthy wife. But the important aspect of the sentimental education of Marianne is that in the conclusion to the novel, she abandons fantasy and turns to a marriage of both social convenience and social convention.

In this restoration of Marianne Dashwood, we see a character brought back to what we might describe as 'reality' by that salutary bout of illness, which is so often a fictional vehicle for self-education. Yet, what has been introduced into fiction in *Sense and Sensibility*, just as *ennui* has become a motive in *Mansfield Park*, is a portrait of the power of fantasy in constructing individual actions and choices. Marianne Dashwood has been dreaming of romantic male heroes long before she sets eyes on Willoughby; if she had not, it is highly unlikely that she would have invested so much in her relationship with him. What Austen does is to show us how the modern world invites us to construct fantasies for our lives: how the degree of consumerism and leisure, which had just begun to be available to the English middle class in the early nineteenth century both depended upon and encouraged fantasies of 'the good life'. Throughout Austen's fictions, we find young women, and young men, dreaming of lives which they very often cannot afford or can only afford through considerable personal compromise. Single men with money become the keys to this good life; however unlovely or unattractive personally, they are able to provide the means to support a desirable world. Single men without money have to seek rich women, and it is entirely consistent with some of the plots of Austen's fiction to rewrite her famous first line to *Pride and Prejudice* as 'A single man in possession of no fortune must be in want of a rich wife'. To this end, the male fortune hunters of Austen's novels (Wickham, Willoughby and Mr Elliot of *Persuasion*) all set out to secure their social position through a financially advantageous marriage.

In this situation, the scene is set for the emergence of that first motive for crime and murder: money. A world of desirable material things, accessible to greater numbers of people, had arrived and was to continue to arrive in an even greater flow of goods and consumer possibilities throughout the nineteenth century – a world which led by the nose those with material aspirations. It is not, of course, the case that the nineteenth century invented greed or avarice; both are an ancient part of human history. But what was brought within the range of an increasing number of human beings was a share in the 'good' things of life, which at this historical point might have included access to travel, elegant homes and dress, an existence underpinned by a servant class. As Fanny Price realizes, when she is sent off to her impoverished family in Portsmouth to encourage her understanding of the meaning of poverty, to be without servants involves acquiring a different set of human capabilities: the woman demanded by the exigencies of poverty, is a person with practical domestic skills and an ability to be not just an 'angel in the house' but a useful and hard-working person within it.

The lines which Austen offers to us between poverty and wealth, between need and affluence, occur far more often and are far more fragile than some accounts of her novels would suggest. Becoming poor, the novels suggest, is an all too common human occurrence, and while Austen clearly loathes financial greed and excessive monetary calculation, she is also highly sceptical of those who do not think rationally about the existence, or otherwise, of money and place themselves in some sense 'above' the recognition of securing an income. In this, we can detect (and the word is used deliberately here) an authorial attitude to money, especially money as income, which demands an understanding of the power of both. In many ways, this view of money is very different from the acquisitive view of money (and the things, which it can buy), which is becoming visibly more characteristic of the west in the nineteenth century – as a culture grows up around a new pageant of consumerism. Austen sees money as the means of securing a way of life, a life in which it is possible to know security of place and position and to have some access to a literate and educated world. On the other hand, those of her characters who are consumed with greed and an intense longing for material delights are much less concerned with ideas about stable incomes than with money as the means to establishing a position in the world of commodities. The fine clothes, houses and carriages that seduce certain of Austen's characters are less about ancient greed than about an individual ability to take part in a world of fashion, and implicitly a world of change and endless aesthetic disruption. The sneers directed against the Bennet sisters in *Pride and Prejudice* by the worldly Miss Bingley are about the way in which the provincial Bennet girls cannot keep up with the changing fashions of the metropolis.

In Austen, we therefore find accounts of the power of fashion to seduce and to become naturalized as an essential part of the social world. Capitalism, as the twentieth century has made very clear, has to be kept alive by innovative demands: in those parts of the world where primary material needs have been generally satisfied, it becomes crucial that other needs are created and maintained. Austen, in writing about dress and personal appearance, does her very best to maintain the value of 'neatness' in her aesthetic, but it is apparent that this particular aesthetic is under constant attack from those who see 'neatness' as dowdy and indicative of a certain kind of separation from the world. For later women writers of detective fiction, this problem of dress is to echo the same questions which Austen saw: Miss Marple is taken 'out' of fashion while other female detectives are either allowed a compete refusal of interest in dress or only occasional excursions into the world of what has become 'designer' fashion. A preoccupation and concern with dress, and more specifically fashion, is to become a consistently negative personal characteristic in a tradition which stretches from Austen to women writers of crime fiction in the late twentieth century.

This comment on dress, and its underlying aesthetic in Austen, is made to emphasize the moral importance which dress, and appearance, have for women writers of all forms of fiction, including that of detective and crime fiction. Austen is transparently clear on the subject: her valued heroines may be beautiful, but they are not extravagant in their choice of clothes. The aesthetic of the person which Austen advocates is one which values the appropriate, the modest and above all that degree of self-concern, which respects the limits of its subject. No lover of elaborate clothes emerges from Austen with any moral standing, in much the same way as all the great English women writers of the nineteenth century are united in their opposition to what we might describe as 'flashy dressing.' Indeed, to read the Bronte sisters or George Eliot on the matter of clothes, one could argue that the serpent was deeply misinformed about the generally seductive power of knowledge; it was the varied possibilities of getting dressed and exploring the world of fashion that truly attracted Eve.

In her six completed novels, Austen suggests a set of moral and social values which have remained subjects for discussion for nearly 200 years. This is not the context to discuss the many interpretations which exist about Austen's work, but it is the place to emphasize again her understanding of the ways in which 'evil' is created and 'virtue' upheld. Writing in a world in which criminals of all descriptions were treated harshly and in which severe moral boundaries were often used to underpin various forms of social exclusion and social stigmatization, Austen sets out a recognizably liberal account of the origins of the behaviour which infringes laws, both written and unwritten. She creates 'villains' out of 'ordinary' bored people living in the country, out of women seduced by the promises of town and fashion and of people of both sexes too idle to do much to maintain the world in which they live. Henry Crawford, and his yawning dissatisfaction at the seemingly endless empty days of the countryside, is just one of the characters who prefigures much that is to occur in the western world in the years after Austen.

While Henry Crawford epitomizes every over-privileged person with little to do, other characters in Austen illustrate other social situations, which have become familiar and which do so much to inform fictional writing about crime. The desire for money and wealth is omnipresent in Austen and is accompanied by the need to maintain a self whose appearance demonstrates the possibilities of fashion and the fashionable. This wish to associate oneself with fashion and change is all the more important as society begins (as it did in Britain at the beginning of the nineteenth century) to change rapidly. Not being 'fashionable' puts one outside the social world; it gives the impression that as a social actor the individual is in various important senses not part of the world that is around her. The desire, the hunger for change, which appears in Austen's uncompleted last novel, *Sanditon*, is predictive of the consumer society which is to become a defining characteristic of the world of the nineteenth and twentieth century society. Equally, that same fragment, with its family of hypochondriacs (Diana Parker, Susan Parker and Arthur Parker) foretells the concern with health (entirely rational in the early nineteenth century), which is to become often close to pathology in the west by the end of the late twentieth century. Reading *Sanditon*, it is possible to see many of the strands which are to inform aspects of social life in the contemporary world: a relentless energy and desire for novelty, accompanied by the complexity and difficulty of explaining this particular social appetite.

What Austen demonstrates is an understanding of the human energy, which propels change and seeks for the new. It would be wrong to read Austen as simply resisting change; there is no evidence in her work that she wishes to deny the possibilities of what might generally be called 'improvement'. Indeed, as critics have pointed out, the idea of the 'improvement of the estate' is a sign of moral worth in Austen; respected people do not waste or ignore the goods, which they possess.[5] But on the other hand, only idiots (of the calibre of Mr Rushworth in *Mansfield Park*) want change for its own sake. At the same time, those characters, who refuse to act usefully in the social world in which they live, are held up for criticism by Austen. As readers we might love and admire Mr Bennet, who views the world (and especially members of his family) with a critical and distant gaze, but Austen does not allow us to forget that it is Mr Bennet's Olympian detachment from the world, which has brought his family to a point of material insecurity and done much, a sympathetic reader might suggest, to feed his wife's anxiety. The Bennet girls have to marry; they have been propelled by the material disengagement of their father into a situation where all depends on their ability to attract a husband to provide for them. In the case of the two elder Bennet sisters, the fairy-tale ending is produced, but not before the sheer naked precariousness of their position in the world has been made clear.

Mr Bennet's distance from the world occurs in the genteel surroundings of his study, where he shelters against the onslaughts of domestic life, his wife and his five daughters. In *Mansfield Park*, two other forms of individual fecklessness are presented to us: the incorrigibly idle Lady Bertram and the poor harassed Mrs Price. Mrs Price (who, despite her surname, all too obviously did not understand either the price or the value of anything) cannot cope with her large family and little money. Equally clearly, the marital relationship of Mr and Mrs Price was as sexually energetic as the relationship of her sister, Mrs Norris, with Mr Norris, was not. For Fanny, the experience of her immediate family demonstrated again the need for the vulnerable to learn to protect themselves. Learning to protect oneself against the world was a lesson which Fanny Price had to learn at an early age, indeed her behaviour echoes the behaviour of those other Austen characters, Elinor Dashwood in *Sense and Sensibility* and Anne Elliot in *Persuasion*, who essentially disguise their feelings and have learned the protective value of self-concealment.

Readers of Austen will know that in the final pages of all her novels she achieves the kind of resolute conclusions that are to become a characteristic of detective fiction. Indeed, in all Austen's novels, there is the kind of clarity to the conclusion which is later echoed in much detective fiction; in both, a potentially disrupted world is restored to peace and harmony; there is a sense of the good rewarded and the rather less good, punished. Even if the 'crimes' committed in Austen never conform to the expectations of crime fiction (there are no mutilated bodies, no literal theft – although Mrs Dashwood comes close – and little real physical danger to any of the characters), there is nevertheless a sense that readers are being encouraged to look beyond the appearance of the world to the sometimes dark and threatening possibilities which lie within it.

Again, we encounter here an aspect of continuity in western culture, namely the presence in any social world of an 'underworld' beyond the visible surface of everyday life. One of the great themes of the European Enlightenment was the discussion of 'reality', of what was (and is) the case rather than what we would like to be the case, or what God says is the case. The emergence of narrative prose fiction in the eighteenth century can be seen as an aspect of this new wish for 'realism' and the 'realistic'. But, at the same time, the paradox of this emergent idea was that the context of a new demand for realism was actually fiction and the fictional. The acknowledgement of 'the real' and the everyday existed long before the eighteenth century (for example the work of the Dutch masters of painting in the seventeenth century demonstrated a determination to portray 'the real', which was far ahead of anything which at that point existed in literature), but the new fiction of the eighteenth century began to examine how a 'real' person, for example, in the shape of Henry Fielding's Tom Jones or Moll Flanders organized their moral universe in a world in which God had become more uncertain and in which the established church had become something of a figure of fun. Those who assume that Austen stood as a resolute supporter of the Church of England might do well to remember that merciless picture of the Reverend Collins in *Pride and Prejudice*, this picture is as caustic and irreverent a picture of the clergy as anything in Fielding.

In the contexts of the fiction of both Fielding and Austen, we can see aspects of the emergence in England in the eighteenth and early nineteenth century of a moral order which is to become formative for sections of British society. It is a moral order which embraces aspects of Protestantism (the moral value of work and respect for property and other resources, together with a disdain for ostentation, whether material or of the person) and unites this with a degree of social responsibility which is to inform various progressive social movements and organizations throughout the nineteenth and twentieth century. The psychic traumas of the French Revolution and the War of Independence in the United States were part of a context, which led, as Auguste Comte and others were to suggest, to an emergent recognition of the power (for both good and evil) of the 'social'. While aspects of this recognition might be seen as generally socially progressive (in that it allows necessary social interventions and judgements about individuals which are not solely derived from naturalistic judgements), it also carries with it, as Michel Foucault and those influenced by his work have pointed out, a degree of regimentation in the understanding and the organization of the social world. The new state infrastructures, which become part of northern Europe in the nineteenth Europe, made possible legislation about matters such as child labour and public labour, but they also depended upon clarity in the definition of the person. The Italian political theorist Georgio Agamben has suggested that:

> But what the state cannot tolerate . . . is that singularities form a community without claiming an identity, that human beings co-belong without a representative condition of belonging.[6]

This comment is highly pertinent if we consider the most serious crime, that of murder, the pattern of which has not changed for centuries (that is, that most murders are committed by persons on intimate terms with the murdered). The new urban spaces of the nineteenth century did not 'invent' or 'encourage' murder and yet, by the end of the first decade of the nine-teenth century, the idea was on the way to being accepted in the minds of many people that murder was a general and everyday threat. In one sense, of course, this perception was entirely accurate, in that it was (and is) the case that the great majority of murders occur within the boundaries of the everyday and the domestic. But in another sense, it was hugely inaccu-rate in that the chances of murder by a stranger were – and again are – extremely rare. Moreover, although few murders are actually committed by people who then stand over the body holding the proverbial smoking gun, the guilty party is usually easy to identify. Why then, we might ask, did we need to invent not just the fictional detectives of our culture (and the cul-ture of detection, which goes with it) but the vast professional apparatus of detection. Not all villains are as helpful as the burglar who leaves behind letters addressed to himself, but little crime is as anonymous as we are some-times led to suppose. (The burglar who leaves behind his address is not a person of fiction; examples of this are numerous, such as the burglar, who left behind a bill addressed to himself when he stole various possessions from the home of Sir Oswald and Diana Mosley. Such was the unpopularity of the couple at the time that this particular burglar came close to becom-ing the 'good' thief of the Robin Hood tradition.[7])

The history of the creation of the infrastructure of policing in England (and elsewhere) has been provided in various studies of the organization of police forces. But, one of the many interesting aspects of fiction about crime, dating from the early days of organized policing, is that an amateur sleuth was immediately in place – a sleuth who was always more effective than the police themselves. From the first, therefore, the police in detective fiction written in Britain were cast as the plodding agents of the state, incapable of intelligent thought and only useful when large scale social intervention was necessary. On the other side of the Channel, however, the police appeared in a more positive note in the semi-fictional form of the ghostwritten memoirs of Inspector Vidocq. Vidocq was a criminal turned police informer (and a one-time head of Napoleon's police department), whom the writer Emile Gaboriau created as a detective. He was a man who, in the words of Ernest Mandel, 'combines deductive powers with the pains-taking investigation of clues'.[8] Vidocq, who has the ability to be both intui-tive and systematic in a way which seemed to have been problematic for the British police from the first, became a hugely popular figure in both French and English popular culture, and what seemed to have been so much an element of his popularity was his appeal to move between different sections of society with allegiances only to himself. Here, Agamben is again relevant, in that although the state might want its citizens to be neatly categorized and organized, the public itself has a huge sympathy for the eccentric outsider and indeed for those somewhat dubious or even clearly criminal figures, who have little or no respect for conventional expectations. Thus, when political theorists such as Agamben (and equally Michel Foucault) write of the extension of the normative and punitive powers of the state in the early nineteenth century, it is possible to place alongside this the continuation of disruptive popular traditions, which both remained and flourished and had scant allegiance to the state's crusade for moral order. The fiction about crime which emerges in the nineteenth century suggests many of the paradoxes in the relationship of citizens to the state which is to continue to this day; on the one hand, a sense of the state's responsibility as a protector of its citizens and on the other, a refusal of the view that protective responsibilities necessarily carry with them an automatic right to all pervasive authority.

Nowhere is this paradox more apparent than in the case of many of the fictional policemen who are part of subsequent British crime writing, in which the relationship between the extent of the intellectual acuity of detectives and their tolerance of conventional society is such that the greater the acuity, the lower the level of social conformity. The most successful professional policemen are almost universally those who are most hostile to conventional judgements about the world and every form of bureaucratically imposed procedure. Those late-twentieth century British policemen who have become most beloved by both readers and television viewers (Frost, Morse and Rebus) are well known for their consistent refusal to take part in the expected orthodoxies of personal and professional life. What fiction appears to be saying here (and saying with remarkable consistency) is that social conformity kills the intellect and that any kind of puzzle-solving necessarily involves the imagination, and the intellectual freedom from a rigid normative order, to consider unorthodox possibilities. This point has been made, and enlarged, in some detail in Kate Summerscale's study of a real-life murder of a child in England in 1860, a case, which, in the various failures of the police investigation, demonstrated all the failures of an institutional imagination shackled by assumptions about class, gender and the location of crime.[9]

It probably remains the case that the ability to think critically (and outside social conventions) remains stronger in fictional detectives than in their colleagues in reality. From the early years of crime fiction, senior fictional policemen in British crime-writing embrace various forms of social deviance – an aberration from the expected – that suggests that various tensions around the question of policing and being policed have consistently existed in British society. Returning to Agamben here, when he remarks that the state dislikes people (the 'singularities' of the quotation) who have no formal identity, he is suggesting a way of conceptualizing the part that fictional detection and detectives might have in the creation of a shared public perception of that 'fear of crime', which becomes so much a part of British (and indeed western) politics in the nineteenth and twentieth century. It is that rather than pursuing the explanation of the potentially criminal which Austen suggests, in which the location of the motive for crimes rests in various human responses to the collective social world; other writers of fiction pursue the possibility that 'criminals' (be they murderers or thieves or both) belong to a different kind of collectivity. We know that murder has scarcely changed across centuries, in its location or its quantity; yet, when we 'collectivise' murderers rather than the origins of murder, we also change our perception of murder. The inevitable question, however, is how – and in whose interests – that perception of crime changed.

The first, and most generally cited, location of the origin of the fear of crime is the city; more specifically, the 'new' industrial city of the nineteenth century. The literature on this new form of collective life is considerable but among those who have written of it, there is a consensus about some of the 'usual suspects', namely the relative anonymity of the city in terms of both its topography and its inhabitants and the various temptations (personal and material), which the city contained. David Frisby points out, in his *Cityscapes of Modernity*, that:

> The mystery of the city presupposes that it can be deciphered or 'solved'. In turn, this presupposes a notion of reading the city as text. . . . As Dana Brand argues in this context, the detective 'comforts city dwellers by suggesting that the city can be read and mastered, despite all appearances to the contrary'.[10]

David Frisby's work on detection in the city provides a richly detailed account of the emergence of the profession of detection (most specifically, private detection) in western cities. Yet, in the quotation from the work of Dana Brand, the word 'mastered' also suggests some of the ways in which it is possible for other interpretations of detection to be offered. Crucial to those other interpretations are ideas about gender and the cultural tensions produced through gendered patterns of knowledge.

In his account of the mystery of the city, and in particular, the 'new' industrial city of the nineteenth century, David Frisby remarks that 'The city always remains to be detected'.[11] This sentence has clearly become something of a mantra for those writing in the twenty-first century about the city (and urban life), as much as it was implicitly endorsed by those who investigated the city in earlier centuries. Yet, although we can see how novelists 'discovered' the city in the nineteenth and the twentieth centuries (and Elizabeth Gaskell and Virginia Woolf are two particular examples of avid explorers of the city), it is also important to recognize something of the way in which gender informs the whole process of discovery. One of the most famous poems of English literature is John Donne's *Elegie XIX* that contains the much quoted line 'O my America! My new-found-land', a sentence that brings together the exploration of a woman's body with images of a more geographical exploration.[12] It is an image, which is continued in *Elegie XX*, where the 'fayr free Citty' becomes another site of metaphorical exploration.[13] Both these images have conjured up for generations of readers a sense of exploration, which is both of a particular person and at the same time similar to that of the exploration of a strange place. In both contexts, we might initially fear, or at least feel anxious, about the unknown, but then we might also come to know those places, which are pleasant and welcoming. Both the metaphorical city and America, however, are being explored by men, and in both cases, women become the place that is explored. The city is not, we might remember, at least in our imagination, either a gender-free or a gender-neutral place, but a place to which we take our gendered imagination.

It is hence that what we 'detect' in the city are not simply places of danger or districts, which might harbour vice and miscreants of various kinds but places and locations which have various kinds of meanings for women and men. One of the most obvious ways in which the city has a deeply gendered topography is the way in which certain parts of all cities have districts to which 'respectable' women do not go but to which all men are allowed to go, not least to meet 'un-respectable' women. The ancient Madonna/whore distinction of western culture is as much part of its built culture as it is of its representational art. It is this gendered sense of the forbidden and the transgressive in the city that frequently provides the backdrop for fiction (both crime and otherwise) in the nineteenth century; the detective, in this world, has to be male because it is only men who have general access to the 'body' of the city. Although women writers of fiction in the nineteenth century allow themselves moments of 'detection' in the city, and the crossing of lines between the 'respectable' and the 'transgressive' city, this generally arises from an exercise of charity rather than that of pursuit.

Two great women writers of the nineteenth century clearly illustrate this relationship of women to the city. Both Elizabeth Gaskell and George Eliot allow their female characters to go where women of their class and gender would not be expected to go. (To clarify further, they follow the example set by Jane Austen's heroine Anne Elliot in *Persuasion* who, in order to assist an old friend living in poverty sets off, to the horror of her snobbish father, to visit her: "'Westgate-buildings!' said he; 'and who is Miss Anne Elliot to be visiting in Westgate-buildings?'".[14]) In the same vein, Elizabeth Gaskell's heroine Margaret Hale in *North and South* encounters her own class-based assumptions about the city when she has to make her own way around a northern industrial town, encountering a way of behaving in the city, which is alien to her:

> The tones of their unrestrained voices, and their carelessness of all common rules of street politeness, frightened Margaret a little at first . . . She did not mind meeting any number of girls, loud spoken and boisterous though they might be. But she alternately dreaded and fired up against the workmen, who commented not on her dress, but on her looks, in the same open fearless manner.[15]

The above mentioned quote is a salutary reminder that long before second wave feminism (and campaigns about 'improving the image of construction'), women were both annoyed and embarrassed by men's behaviour towards them in the streets of cities. The 'fired up' emotion, which Margaret Hale experiences is part of that all too familiar situation for women in which we are not expected to answer back; like many later women, Margaret Hale must have thought longingly of speaking back to those who, in the language of the twenty-first century, 'invaded her space'.

But Margaret Hale, as a carefully brought up member of the Victorian middle class, has now been removed from the genteel surroundings of her youth and as such must move through the urban world on her own if she wishes to carry out any ordinary household errand. For other members of the female middle class, that same financial insecurity was always present. We often see the world of the Victorian middle class as one of absolute security and predictability; yet, for many people who assumed themselves to be middle class, the possibilities of poverty were always there and with it a transition, like that of Margaret Hale, to the unknown places of the city and residence with those who had previously been supposed to be both different and potentially dangerous. Again, we can trace a tradition from Austen onwards of the possibilities of the loss of class security: Mrs Bennet in *Pride and Prejudice* is rendered hysterical by it, Mrs Dashwood and her daughters in *Sense and Sensibility* are shown experiencing it, and Fanny Price in *Mansfield Park* is sent off into class exile when she refuses to marry into the wealth and plenty offered to her. The sense of security, which many people have projected onto the past was certainly not there for many who lived within it; on the contrary, it was a place of fear about poverty and loss, as well as the more day to day fears about the possible dangers of class 'pollution' that might arise from exposure to poor areas of cities; the places of the 'Westgate buildings' so feared by Sir William Elliot.[16]

What we therefore need to remember about the past, which informs our perception of the present within which we live, is that it was insecure, precarious, ridden by disease and pain and without those safety nets of, for example, welfare systems and effective medical care that are a taken-for-granted part of the twenty-first century western world. Recalling these aspects of the past reminds us that the kinds of fears which we have about living in the contemporary city (terrorist attack, for example, or assault by unknown people) were matched by other or similar terrors in the past. Those terrors and fears were, as today, a potent mixture of the very limited real possibility of harm and a much more generalized fear of the unknown other and attack by them. Fantasies about the danger of the city and the urban world today have, in this, a great deal in common with the world of the past and campaigns about 'making the city safe' could have appeared at any time in the past 200 years.

As various writers on the city and the urban world have also pointed out part of our long-standing fear of the city has been the nature of the city itself. It is a place where we cannot know everyone or be familiar with every street. The city is therefore always a place in which we have to discover, detect and hopefully 'un-mask' the people with whom we come into contact. Ordinary, day-to-day life becomes a matter of detection since individuals seldom know or experience every place in the city which they inhabit; for many, the city is actually experienced as a village, a place to be lived in as a constantly 'local' place, which is only left for special and isolated reasons. In a study of young women living in south-east London in the early twenty-first century, for example, Sarah Evans found that many of them had little or no idea of London as a whole, and when faced with the prospect of making a journey to unknown parts of London, they became panic-stricken.[17] The very scale and complexity of the city stifles movement and exploration and may become a place where fear of the unknown is magnified through the actual, physical existence of the unfamiliar.

For all this, the city has always offered to certain people rich resources for pleasure and personal betterment. The journey to the city, in order to make a fortune or find a rich spouse, is a well-known journey of English literature. The expectation that the streets of London will be 'paved with gold' is almost as old as the city itself, and searching for riches and advancement in the city is as familiar a venture today as it was 200 or 300 years ago. For the English (and for other people living in countries with identifiable capital cities), the capital city is the magnet for the ambitious poor. Hence, it is in the city that the hopes and fears of individual enrichment are worked out, and there is little in western experience (except perhaps for the search for gold in various countries) that has matched London (or Paris or New York) as the place where the ambitious take their hopes and aspirations.

But individual ambitions, and especially ambitions organized around the desire to accumulate money, are seldom achieved in the simple terms of hard work and dedication. The various clichés and folk legends around the making of fortunes all attest to a general assumption that no one makes a great deal of money entirely honestly. It may be the case that an entrepreneur 'happens' to sell or invent just the right product at the right time (and that of course is part of the mythical world which surrounds capitalism), but in many of the histories of great fortunes (particularly those related to manufacture or the ownership of property), there are other stories about the unprincipled exploitation of human beings and the evasion of moral and legal codes. The degree of ruthlessness, which certain male characters in Victorian literature demonstrate towards others (whether in a collective or an individual sense), was replicated on countless occasions in the 'real' city. The sympathies for his workers which Mr Thornton finally demonstrated in Elizabeth Gaskell's *North and South* were as rare in fiction as they were in reality. The city, the place where civilization was made evident, remained in many ways uncivilized until philanthropy, bourgeois self-interest and political determination brought to it some measures of regulation and order.

Until that point, which for most large European cities did not occur until the end of the nineteenth century, European cities remained places of paradox. On the one hand, they were places of display, elegance, learning and aspiration, and on the other, they were locations of disease, poverty and endless hardship. In this situation, the city provided an ideal site for the manufacture of detection as we now know it: not merely the detection of the nature of the individual (which is as ancient as the idea of the 'masking' of human beings), but of the detection of the guilty individual and the specifically *bad* person. In worlds where there was no absence of questionable relationships between human beings (both as individuals and as groups of people), the detection of the one very bad person provided a comforting reassurance that lines could be drawn between virtue and vice and between the wicked and the good. In a world where, in everyday terms and in every-day experience, there was very little chance of knowing the general other, the particularly bad other provided a moral framework for others.

In this situation, the early days of the modern city provided a fertile breeding ground for the moral contours within which we know live. The modern city was, as suggested, simply too big and too complex for everyone to become familiar with all of it. In this situation, it was potentially a world of moral chaos and a place to be feared. Gaskell's *North and South* and Charles Dickens's *Bleak House* both portray that sense of the city as a place of fear and human confusion. The opening passages of *Bleak House*, as various writers have pointed out, speak of the terrible fog, which can enfold London – a fog which is to remain part of London's experience until the 1950s. But only a few pages further on, Dickens also writes about other kinds of fog, the less literal kind of fog, which obscures human actions. Writing of the conduct of a legal case Dickens remarks:

> How many people out of the suit, Jarndyce and Jarndyce has stretched forth its unwholesome hand to spoil and corrupt, would be a very wide question. From the master, upon whose impaling files realms of dusty warrants in Jarndyce and Jarndyce have grimly writhed into many shapes; down to the copying-clerk in the Six Clerks Office, who has copied his tens of thousands of Chancery-folio-pages under that eternal heading; no man's nature has been made better by it. In trickery, evasion, procrastination, spoliation, botheration, under false pretences of all sorts, there are influences that can never come to good.[18]

Here is the city as the place where the very institutions for which it is known, and which constitute so central a part of its existence, are those that distort and misrepresent human action. It is not, therefore, only the physical conditions of life in the city which make existence difficult, it is also the social relations, which produce, as Dickens suggests, various forms of 'trickery'.

Bleak House was published (in parts, and between 1852 and 1853) and *North and South* in 1855. In her biography of Elizabeth Gaskell, Jenny Uglow notes that Gaskell had observed how women were often 'excited yet disturbed' by Manchester; we might conjecture that the city was exciting in its raw energy and yet at the same time deeply disturbing given the way in which it seemed to abandon known ways of behaviour and bring into existence entirely novel forms (at least as far as middle-class women were concerned) of human behaviour. Central to these new ways of behaviour is, of course, the social forms through which we 'organise' the body, and Uglow, in common with other critics, suggests ways in which the Victorian novel offers a sense of the body, and its social and interpersonal messages, in a literature bound by conventions about the absence of the explicit body.[19]

What we are told about the body (until the twentieth century) is very little in the explicit terms of later writing and yet, at the same time, the body literally *makes itself felt* in endless ways. Perhaps most important, for the purposes of detective fiction, is the way in which fear, and in particular, the fear of the possibly hostile or dangerous unknown other, works (as Sara Ahmed has suggested) 'to align bodily and social space'.[20] In this way, the city becomes, throughout the nineteenth century, ever more demarcated in terms of the 'dangerous' and 'safe' areas, while these definitions are made and supported by a collective unease about the presence of potentially dangerous bodies. Throughout the twentieth century, people living in cities had to learn ways of moving about and of appropriate behaviour in public places, which would allow other people to identify them, and their social and personal agenda, correctly. Moving about the city was not, therefore, simply about becoming what is now known as 'street wise', which is primarily about minimizing interaction with potentially dangerous others, it was also about being able to convey the correct messages to others about oneself. Verbs such as 'to skulk' or 'to saunter' became part of the literary vocabulary about the city – all words, which carried certain 'clues' about the person concerned.

It is this sense of the ever present threats and dangers in the physical presence of others in the city that is used by writers of crime and detective fiction to such good effect. It may also in part account for the way in which in crime fiction it is the private individual, as Symons, Frisby and others have pointed out, who can be the most active citizen in the pursuit of crime. The private citizen can move unnoticed in the city, with no uniform to identify him (and only much later, her). At the beginning of the nineteenth century, most European countries did not have anything approaching an organized police force, and it is important to recognize that much of the investigatory energy of most states had been employed, since the sixteenth century, in the pursuit of perceived 'enemies' of the realm rather than ordinary citizens with criminal tendencies. The wrong doing that actually mattered to the state, therefore, took the form of allegiances to foreign powers or to religions deemed subversive or dangerous. (We may, of course, take the view that this is still the case even if the public perception of 'policing' has taken the form of a wholehearted concentration on 'ordinary' crime).

Thus, while the British state was energetic in its pursuit, for example, of those thought to be sympathetic to Napoleon, it was much less energetic in its interest in more domestic, everyday crime. The second oldest profession (as Philip Knightley has pointed out) is that of the spy rather than the detective; the latter appears relatively late on the list of professions.[21]

It was thus not surprising that should a fictional murder take place the person who would set off in pursuit of the murderer would be a private citizen. It was also thus that the long tradition (which still continues) of the amateur sleuth began, not through the state's refusal of policing but through the state's definition of policing and what really mattered to its interests. The dates of the establishment of formal policing throughout Europe demonstrate just how late was any effective commitment to civilian policing: it was 1842 before a detective department was established in London, and in other countries it was often private detectives who were the primary form of investigator. In his account of class relations in the nineteenth century, the historian E. J. Hobsbawm points out that 'bourgeois masters' often had to exercise authority by 'private armies of Pinkerton men'.[22] For much of the twentieth century, we have taken for granted that the detection of crime has been central to the responsibilities of the state, and yet, it was the detection of the subversive, the political agitator and the person likely to threaten the political order, which was the primary focus of policing for much of the nineteenth century and indeed the twentieth century. For example, in his autobiography E. J. Hobsbawm writes of the way in which both his membership of the communist party and his deceased mother's Austrian nationality made him unsuitable for an army cipher course. Hobsbawm describes the explanation given to him thus:

> 'Nothing personal, but your mother was not British,' said the captain as he told me to take the next train from Norwich back to Cambridge. 'Of course you're against the system now, but naturally there's always a bit of sympathy for the country your mother belonged to. It's natural. You see that, don't you?' . . . 'I mean I have no national prejudices. It's all the same to me what the nations do, as long as they behave themselves, which the Germans aren't doing now'. I agreed.[23]

The lapse in good manners, which the Germans demonstrated in 1939 was something which the British has long assumed them to be capable of. But what this passage also suggests, besides the various prejudices and assumptions of the British security services, is the strength of the ongoing concern in the 'hidden' regions of the British state about questions of national security, the possibilities of the destabilization of the state and the unspoken sense that the state only holds onto power with some difficulty. It is for this reason, as much a feature of the nineteenth century as the present day, that it is possible to suggest that the ongoing strength of the 'amateur' in the detection of murder and other forms of serious crime was in large part a reaction to the recognition by much of the public that the state's institutional priorities were not about the investigation of these real, committed crimes but about the possibility of sedition, treason and destabilization. Thus, there exists in British fiction a tradition of the detection of spies (by authors such as John Buchan, for example, and Rider Haggard, as well as some of the earlier works of Agatha Christie), which persists throughout the nineteenth and twentieth century. But, what is striking about this fiction is that it shares with fiction about orthodox crime a central character of an amateur sleuth, who is very often more effective in detection than the ranks of the professionals.

What this parallel amateur tradition of the detection of the spy and/ or the traitor also has in common with the tradition of the detection of 'ordinary' crime is that it is largely not until after the Second World War that both the British police force and the secret service (the institutions of detection) become blessed with intelligent individuals, even if many of these individuals (from Harry Palmer in the novels of John Le Carré to Inspector Morse in the novels of Colin Dexter) are themselves somewhat less than wholly conventional in their personal lives. Until the end of the Second World War, British detective and crime fiction is dominated by famous amateur detectives while the truly perceptive and successful 'ordinary' policemen are few and far between. (In this context, British crime fiction has much in common with similar fiction in the United States where intelligence and perception is seen to reside more or less entirely in the human form of 'private eyes'.)

The most famous amateur sleuth of the nineteenth century in Britain was, of course, Arthur Conan Doyle's Sherlock Holmes. Conan Doyle, as his intervention in the case related to George Edalji was to make clear, was no fervent respecter of either the value of the taken-for-granted or the ability of the police to see beyond it. (George Edalji was an Anglo-Indian solicitor accused, wrongfully, of malicious attacks on cattle. When Edalji was found guilty and imprisoned, Conan Doyle took a considerable part in securing his release and the recognition of his innocence.[24]) In his creation of Sherlock Holmes, Conan Doyle presented to the public a man with considerable

intellectual talent but little appetite for the conventional world. The first
Sherlock Holmes story appeared in July 1891 and was immediately successful. Holmes – and his friend Dr Watson – investigated 56 cases, all of them
involving on the one hand the demonstration of Holmes's near psychic powers of deduction and, on the other, the complete bafflement of Dr Watson
about what is going on. Holmes always knows the answer and Watson is
always surprised by it; although the Holmes–Watson relationship has always
attracted attention because of its homosexual overtones, it is this relationship between two people and knowledge which is perhaps the more interesting. Holmes – a man who openly takes cocaine – has no great respect for
organized knowledge per se: it is the plodding Dr Watson who has achieved
professional recognition and the right to public credentials. Holmes is a tal-
ented violin player and has some knowledge of some aspects of the world; yet,
at one point, Watson is able to record that he 'knows nothing' of Holmes's
knowledge of literature, philosophy and astronomy. Holmes is thus very far
from a polymath; in fact given his public credentials, he would be unem-
ployable, and it is only the good fortune of his private income that allows
him to live the life of a gentleman in rooms in Baker Street, London.

In terms of other detectives, in both the nineteenth and the twentieth
century, Holmes comes closest to the model of those private eyes of the
1930s and the professional European policemen of the years after 1945,
who live personally unconventional lives, somewhat removed from bourgeois and petit bourgeois order. What we see emerging in Holmes is the
idea of the detective as the person outside society: this is no genial policeman, who has a kind word for the guilty, or a person fully integrated into
a set of professional and personal conventions. This is a man who can
recognize 'evil' in either the form of possibilities or accomplishments, and
who can look beyond the kind of conventional 'surface', which never fails
to impress (and befuddle) Dr Watson.

The world of Sherlock Holmes, the last decade of the nineteenth century,
is often presented by social and cultural historians as the last decade before
all forms of bourgeois certainties disappeared before the emergence of
European modernism, which Peter Watson has described as 'a response
to the new and alienating late-nineteenth-century world of large cities,
fleeting encounters, grim industrialism and unprecedented squalor'.[25]
Nineteenth century Britain had seen various attempts to rebuild a sense of
lost community (for example, in the work of Pugin and William Morris),
but what is evident in the work of all these individuals is an element, however limited, of fear about the new modern world. That fear was to find
an expression in literature (for example, in the work of Arnold Bennett
and H.G. Wells) and a growing fear of 'society' itself, a world of increasing

complexity where individuals might find it increasingly difficult to find a place in a world, which appears distant and beyond control. This culture of late-nineteenth century angst, in which the rational and instinctive seem so much at odds, gave rise to the great work of Picasso and Freud – work in which the artist or author attempts some reconciliation between what seems to be two divergent, and inherently hostile, attributes of the human person. In the social sciences, the social distance between the individual and the emergent urban world created a new literature, in the work of, for example, Tonnies, Weber and Durkheim about alienation, the loss of community and disenchantment.[26]

'Detection' in this context thus comes to be not just a narrowly defined attribute of a particular individual who is hunting for a guilty person but a generalized social concern with the meaning of the 'reality' of social life. In various ways, detection becomes a general form of intellectual life, a search for what lies beyond (or beneath) the appearance the ordinary and the taken-for-granted. Sherlock Holmes, thus, could not be an 'ordinary' person, in the form of Dr Watson, because that very quality of ordinariness itself involves a general acceptance of the world as it is. Holmes, with that magic white powder, which he takes to give him an even greater psychic distance from banal existence, is the perfect 'detective' of the modern world – the man outside society, and the man for whom the social order as it is has no particular appeal or meaning. Jane Austen, as suggested earlier in this chapter, was as sceptical as Holmes about the integrity of the appearance of the conventional social world. Yet, unlike Holmes, Austen had wished to integrate intelligence and understanding with the social world; child of the Enlightenment as she was (and as are some of her heroines), she did not reject the possibility of creating a social existence and a social world in which the rational and the instinctual, even the spontaneous, could live side by side. For Holmes, and many others of his generation, there was little or no point in this exercise: the given world, with its pomposity, its moral strictures, its banality, demands not integration but only revelation.

Conan Doyle's stories about Sherlock Homes were a literary part of those years at the end of the nineteenth and beginning of the twentieth century, which have become known, variously, as the years of *fin-de-siècle* despair or the years of cultural transformation. In Britain, the figures associated with this period are, most famously, such figures as Oscar Wilde, Audrey Beardsley and Joseph Conrad, all of whom developed a critical and occasionally savage view of what passed at the time for the bourgeois convention. In this context, what these – and others – did was to pursue a similar intellectual quest as their contemporaries Sigmund Freud or Max Weber – a quest, which was essentially concerned with the detection of what lies behind the normative order. As Freud was to recognize early in his work on emotional disturbance, the surface of the social world may appear calm and orderly, but it is often interrupted by small eruptions of chaos and disturbance. In the case of Freud's patients, 'disturbance' took the form of emotional torment; however, in the case of Conan Doyle, it was in various forms of crime. In this same historical period, the sciences were beginning their own path of discovery: there can be few more apt examples of literal 'unmasking' than the development of x-ray technology. In this procedure, the body of the human person was laid bare in exactly the same way that others were attempting to understand human motivation and understanding.

To understand this new world of explorations in science and technology, which were to transform medicine, communications and the theoretical building blocks of physics, a new sort of person was also required. A person not unlike the 'six honest serving men' described by Rudyard Kipling in the so called 'private eye's' character'.[27] If we look back at the detectives of the nineteenth century, we can see how – for example, in the case of Inspector Bucket or Inspector Cluff – they were people who were fully integrated into the social world in which they lived. But once that world had become one that was seen as a world of prejudice, greed and often ridiculous patterns of behaviour, a new kind of person was needed to 'detect' it. In this context, therefore, Holmes was the perfect detective of the modern: a social outsider, a man with no strong social or emotional ties of his own and a person wedded, metaphorically, to his own intelligence. His own valorization of his intellect, his preening narcissism about his intellectual powers made Holmes a difficult detective to love. Yet, at the same time, these qualities made him popular with readers and subsequent generations since Holmes seemed to embody all that that the modern world valued in human terms: a machine-like intelligence, which never failed to analyse correctly any given situation. When Max Weber wrote of the 'technical rationality' of modern capitalism he might have been writing of Holmes; certainly this is a person who is the puzzle solver *par excellence* of the everyday world.

In the British children's comic the *Eagle,* published in the 1950s, there is a wicked character called the Mekon who has no human form (he moves around on a machine shaped like a saucer) but with a furious intelligence. The hero who defeats the Mekon every week is a man called Dan Dare, who has a human, if somewhat chiselled, form. The Mekon, we are led to believe, does not win because he has no values, no sense of right and wrong. This tension, between moral values and intelligence, was passed onto children every week and the appropriate moral lesson was always recognizable as the superiority of 'values' to 'intelligence'. The *Eagle*, published with a commitment to teach children Christian values, was in many ways fighting exactly the same battle as was being fought in the 'cultural wars' of the 1890s and 1900s, a battle about the moral quality, indeed the moral meaning, of intelligence and the capacity for innovation and change. That tension, which was to take such furious form in the battles over sexuality and gender in the same decades, is fought with such determination because capitalist society actually depends upon innovation and change in order to maintain itself. Those values, which romantic conservatives have often praised (of patriarchal families and a hierarchical social order), have often been values of socially stagnant societies. Intelligence and curiosity about the world and the willingness to entertain ideas about difference and development were precisely the ideas that motivated Freud and others. In the world of fiction, Sherlock Holmes. Holmes, like his contemporary Oscar Wilde, was prepared to see that the social world is made up of different layers, a surface layer and other disguised layers where disruptive and challenging ideas and relationships are placed.

But Holmes is not the perfect detective of the modern world merely because of his intelligence and intellectual capacity, which, like that of the Mekon, are not complicated by human values. He is also a perfect detective of the modern because he has all those qualities which had been identified in the mid-nineteenth century as those of the '*flaneur*', the semi-mystical figure, beloved of Baudelaire and Walter Benjamin, who observes and yet is not part of the world in which he lives. It is this particular form of relationship with the social which marks out Holmes and later private detectives. As David Frisby points out, the essential characteristic of a modern detective is that the person should be '. . . an independent young gentleman of independent income, which ensures impartiality and the leisure to pursue investigations'.[28] Holmes is not particularly young but he has all the personal qualities through which he can manifest what has been described as 'imaginative spectatorial dominance'. That concept, derived from the work of Walter Benjamin, further develops the suitability of Holmes as the definitive 'modern' detective.

There are, however, a number of final comments to be made about Holmes and his part in the detection of the modern. We need to note that Holmes, while a person of the male sex, claims for himself little of conventional masculinity. Holmes does not attempt to present himself as particularly physically courageous (except in so far as he often seems unaware of danger) or anxious to display any form of vigorous heterosexuality. Holmes is in no sense a fine figure of a man with the desired empire-winning characteristics of British middle-class men at the end of the nineteenth century; if anything, it is Dr Watson who embodies these characteristics. Holmes is, above all else, cerebral and in this context, he presents a real challenge to those bourgeois *mores*, which would have intelligence disguised rather than explicit. Watson is what the French social theorist Gilles Deleuze would describe as the 'recognisable' figure in Conan Doyle's work: Watson is the person in whom we see conventional tastes and habits.[29]

At the same time, the relationship between Watson and Holmes sets a pattern for many later detectives: that the intelligent detective should have a colleague who is less intelligent but better integrated into the social world. The function of this splitting allows the reader to be reassured that intelligence can be domesticated, and that it can be put to good use. Thus, Watson stands at the beginning of a long tradition of detective 'couples' (Morse and Lewis, Poirot and Hastings, Maigret and Lucas and so on) in whom the coupling allows pursuit of the 'banality of evil' (in Hannah Arendt's phrase) but also access to the banality of everyday life. The symbols of this everyday banality change as the culture changes (Lewis with his enthusiasm for home decorating and Hastings with his romantic enthusiasm for pretty young women are just two examples), but they provide a foil for the distance of the other partner's distance from the 'ordinary'.

In his *Central Park*, Walter Benjamin remarked that 'For people today, only one radical shock remains – and it is always the same: death'.[30] Benjamin was writing in the early twentieth century, but the remark is no less pertinent when applied to the late nineteenth century. As aspects of the daily life of the urban world of the west became ever more predictable, and seemed to offer ever more personal choice, so the onset of untimely death became increasingly 'unnatural'. Thus, murder became the challenge to the modern world, the act that disrupts the certainties of the modern and requires a return to the skills of pursuit and hunting. The people best equipped to do this 'hunting' are the people best able to travel alone, to take on the risks of the chase without the constraints of domestic life. Holmes is this perfect 'hunter', but his very construction asked questions about the modern, which other voices chose to answer in different ways. As we shall see in the next chapter, women writers of detective fiction begged to differ from Conan Doyle and his male contemporaries. They did not see the domestic as a challenge to the cerebral; on the contrary, they came to celebrate this very quality, sometimes read as a challenge to the emancipation of women.

Chapter 3

Detecting the Modern

The relationship between women, the feminine and the modern has attracted a considerable literature. Much of that literature points out that, in various ways and in various contexts, the world of the twentieth century had much to offer women. It 'gave' women (although in no case without a considerable struggle on the part of women themselves) education and contraception; it very gradually (and grudgingly) shifted the power relations within marriage and the civic and public order. The central British figure of literary modernism, Virginia Woolf, is often read as typical of privileged women of her time, able to take advantage of the new freedoms offered and yet at the same time critical of both the limitations of the 'modern' and in particular the continuing power of the masculine and of men. Woolf's *Three Guineas* remains as powerful an indictment of the male 'order' in the early years of the twenty-first century as it was at the time of its initial publication in 1936.[1]

This brief paragraph cannot do justice to the many battles (both personal and private) that took place around the questions of gender and gender appropriate behaviour in the first years of the twentieth century. The general consensus of historians is that the First World War was the major factor in accelerating the actual growth in the employment and the participation of women in the public world although all acknowledge the various fault lines of argument about the 'battle of the sexes', which existed long before the war.[2] Those fault lines covered such central areas of personal, individual freedom and questions about how to dress, who to marry and, most crucially, the terms and conditions of marriage. Yet, even in writing this agenda, it is crucial to recall the class differences of British society, the degree of poverty and personal insecurity and the generally impoverished lives of many in the population. As Alison Light has made clear in her account of the relations of Virginia Woolf and her servants, there existed an uneasy truce between the classes as much as the genders.[3] The 'upper' class may have mourned the loss of servants (a social change for which the First World

War was directly responsible), but for those who were the servants, the war brought with it the opportunities for work in contexts other than the homes of the rich.

Thus, for women, the modern world offered different opportunities for women from different classes. For many middle-class women, and especially those women who had some education, it would have been difficult not to be aware of the social changes surrounding them. The 'new woman' of the world after the First World War became immediately visible, for example, in the way she arranged her hair: short haircuts ('the 'shingle') immediately spoke of the modern and of a different attitude to the world. Literature of all kinds (fiction, biography and autobiography) belonging to the years after 1918 is full of the furious reactions of fathers and husbands to women who cut their hair in this new, 'modern' way. The haircut was, of course, for many women a symbolic act, a 'sign' of different values rather than an explicit commitment to a new way of life. But it nevertheless spoke of division between generations and in its very classlessness (short hair was fashionable and desirable across class lines), an indication of the democratization of consumption, which was to become so much a feature of the west in the twentieth century. The years between 1918 and 1939 saw a marked expansion of relatively classless consumption for women; the heights of fashion remained as exclusive then as now, but what became available to more (although, certainly not all) women, was the chance, literally, to buy into the modern.

But to do this, women had to have money, and having money, again then as now, has been rather more complex a matter for women than men. Before the First World War (1914–18), relatively few middle-class women would expect to be in paid work at any time in their lives even if the 'middle class' is a broad term and encompasses both the daughters of the very well heeled upper middle class to the daughters of the lower middle class. It was from this latter group that the majority of women workers in offices and shops came; the new infrastructure of a more complex, more consumerist capitalism in which women stayed in paid work generally only until marriage. Marriage (unlike later years in the twentieth century when the birth of children had a more determining impact on the lives of women) put an end to the employment of most women, whether by law (as for example in the case of the employment of married women in the English Civil Service) or by custom and convention. At the same time, the majority of the female population, the working-class women who seldom appear in fiction as either authors or subjects, lived lives which did not immediately benefit from the various forms of emancipation available to the middle classes.

To defend the idea and the possibilities of the modern was, therefore, more immediately viable to middle-class women. What they had to lose was considerable: a chance to extend their horizons and their agency outside the domestic world. Some women had never refused agency but what was novel about the world offered to women at the beginning of the twentieth century was that this new world was potentially for all women, rather than those of particular fortune or inclination. Not least in the possibilities offered were opportunities of writing, designing and teaching specifically for women. Precisely as it became expected that women might occasionally be employed or entitled to money of their own, so goods were created for those women. Since women had always played a large part in the reading public, and since crime and detective thrillers were becoming a major part of fiction-publishing, it was inevitable that women authors should recognize a space for their own talents and for their own view on the question of crime.

The path of women from the drawing room to the writing table (or to the writing table in the drawing room) is a well-worn one. Woolf took the needs of women writers further when she demanded a separate room for women to write in, but for many women writers (including some of the most famous names of the nineteenth century such as the Bronte sisters and Elizabeth Gaskell), this was a demand which they never made. Nevertheless, these women, and others who achieved various degrees of fame and fortune, all became professional authors and established the acceptance of the idea that literature belonged to women as much as it belonged to men. It was this sense of ownership which allowed the women writers of crime fiction in what has become known as its 'golden age' to be accepted rapidly by both publishers and public. Symptomatic of the degree of this acceptance was the way in which these women authors (for example, Agatha Christie and Margery Allingham) published immediately under their own names unlike the various disguises of the Brontes or George Eliot.

Between the last cases of Sherlock Holmes (the full-length novel *The Valley of Fear* of 1915 or the short stories *His Last Bow* of 1917), there is only the briefest of pauses before the publication of the first novel, in 1920, of Agatha Christie, the most famous member of the group of women crime writers of the 'golden age'. Between those years, there are various authors who attracted wide audiences (most notably G. K. Chesterton, the author of the Father Brown stories and Baroness Orczy, author of the detective stories in which the detective was 'the Old Man in the Corner') but neither of these authors, or indeed anyone else previously or in the future, was to achieve the kind of worldwide sales of Christie and the iconic status of her

most famous creations Hercule Poirot and Miss Jane Marple. Hercule Poirot
appears, as a grateful Belgian refugee, in Christie's first novel, *The Mysterious
Affair at Styles*, published in 1920. The novel is dedicated to Christie's mother
and that sense of continuity (which has been noted about Christie in Alison
Light's *Forever England*) is continued in the dedication to her daughter,
Rosalind, which appears in the novel *The Murder at the Vicarage*, which
introduces the second of Christie's famous detectives, Miss Jane Marple.[4]
Christie is, of course, only one of the famous women writers who are associ-
ated with the 'golden age', an age, which is generally assumed to be the
period of the 1920s and 1930s and to encompass work by Dorothy Sayers,
Freeman Wills Croft, Anthony Berkeley, Ngaio Marsh, Margery Allingham
and Gladys Mitchell (among others) in Britain with (again, among others)
Ellery Queen and John Dickson Carr in the United States and Georges
Simenon in France. Of these authors, it is Christie and Simenon who continued to write for decades and it is also these two authors whose books sold
millions of copies across the world. By the time that Christie was enjoying
the first years of her extremely successful career, the genre of detective
fiction was only about 100 years old; yet it had captured the imagination of
the reading public and – while often denied 'serious' literary attention –
was an important element in sales of books.

The 'golden age' of detective-writing did not, as the lists of authors above
suggests, in any way belong only to women authors. Nor was the genre
of detective fiction regulated by women; indeed, it was the male Roman
Catholic cleric, Ronald Knox, who set down 'The Ten Commandments of
Detection' in 1928, two years before the Detection Club in Britain, founded
in 1930, demanded of its members that its members should write books in
which detectives would carry out their business 'without reliance on Divine
Intervention, Feminine Intuition, Mumbo-Jumbo, Jiggery-Pokery, Coincidence or the Act of God'.[5] This demand, with its explicit overtones of both
racism and sexism, made it clear to authors that 'detection' should be about
the methodical construction of a case and a argument; detection is being
written here as a quasi-scientific exercise. This method ruled out of order
some of the more gothic flourishes loved and used by Conan Doyle and, in
an earlier context, Wilkie Collins. One point on which the Detection Club
and Ronald Knox agreed was that 'clues' should be honestly presented; the
detective novel was not supposed to proceed like a conjuring trick, with
vital information appearing, like a rabbit, at the whim of the conjuror. But
this emphasis on making the material reliable has other implications; the
material clue, like the bread and water in the Christian communion service
has a symbolic purpose. It is Roman Catholics who, unlike Protestants, believe

in the doctrine of transubstantiation, but in both versions of Christianity, what is passed onto the more general culture is the sense of the symbolic possibilities of the material. 'Clues' in detective fiction have much the same function: by themselves they are nothing, but put them together with other 'clues' and other events and they become, if not a fully fledged belief system then at least an explanation on which, at one point in the history of western criminal justice, depended life and death. The links between the Christian narrative of the death of Christ and the inherited symbols of His existence are thus part of the parallel between the explanations of detection and the beliefs of Christian religion.

The 'hidden' narratives of religious belief, which remain part of our modern worlds have been at odds with claims for more 'scientific' or secular accounts of the world since the Enlightenment. Thus, although the plea for quasi-scientific detection was entirely at one with many of the self-consciously modern attitudes and policies of both society and state in Britain and the United States in the 1920s and 1930s (for example, the enthusiastic take-up by better off classes of the population of domestic appliances of various kinds, not the least of which was artificial contraception), there was also a sense, among sections of the population, that the 'transformatory' potential of the modern was becoming too great. In certain crucial aspects of the social world (for example, attitudes to gender and to history), this suspicion of where the modern might take the world underpinned aspects of European fascism, with both its attempt to return women to the domestic space and its valorization of mythical readings of history. Hence, the modern world held different messages and possibilities for different people; for some women, there were new freedoms while for other women there were suspicions that old forms of the patriarchal order, through which women could sanction other women, might disappear. It is this sense of both the fear and the hope of the modern for women which is played out in the context of detection fiction in the work of various women writers of detective fiction. At the same time, it needs to be recognized that male authors often took their own stance on the perils of the modern: some retreated in their fiction to the closed world of the Oxbridge college, and others continued to write the male detective as something of a social outsider.[6] Entirely conventional police detectives appear in the fiction of Wills Crofts and Simenon and other aspects of the entirely conventional are also maintained in much of the work of both these authors in the distinctions they make between 'good' and 'bad' women.

Against this, it often the case that women writing in the 'golden age' allow their female characters that individual autonomy and capacity for agency which is accepted for men. It would be highly surprising if this was not the case, since the women authors were earning their living through writing and, while doing so, would all have experienced the kind of prejudice and scepticism about the professional work of women which had, and has, a long tradition. Yet, between the authors, there is considerable difference in terms of their views about the position of women in the modern world; that the world changed after the end of the First World War was impossible to ignore, but those changes did not come accompanied by any agreed schema about the part that women should play in this new world. The mothers (and even more so the grandmothers) of the women writers of detective fiction would have grown up in a world in which women could not vote and if married, could not own property and also – most crucially because it affected all sections of the population – effectively question the domestic authority of husbands and fathers. It is, in this context of both the social and psychic control of fathers over women, that the death of the father allowed various forms of emancipation for both Virginia Woolf and Agatha Christie. Had Leslie Stephen, the father of Virginia Woolf, not died when he did, then the Miss Stephens might never have moved to Bloomsbury, and the Bloomsbury Group might never have existed. Equally, Christie wrote of the death of her father:

> Life took on a completely different complexion after my father's death. I stepped out of my child's world, a world of security and thoughtlessness, to enter the fringes of the world of reality. I think there is no doubt that from the man of the family comes the stability of the home . . . You accept it all unquestioningly.[7]

Except that Christie did not accept it all 'unquestioningly' and only a few sentences later, she is mentioning that she was never her father's favourite child, the unspoken implication being that now she is freed from that particular sense of inferiority.

Christie, like Woolf, was not left penniless on the death of her father nor was she ever faced with the kind of poverty and absence of material and social support which was the lot of many in the population. But she, again like Woolf, did need to earn money to supplement the tiny amount left to her by her father, and thus, she, again like other young middle-class women of the time, trained for employment and took what was still a rather rare step for many unmarried middle-class women, of taking a job. That experience, of paid work for women, is everywhere in Christie's fiction, and whether it is in nursing or acting or office work, there is also the omnipresent acceptance of paid work, and work which is generally enjoyed, as part of the world of women. By contrast, we might note that T. S. Eliot's *The Waste Land* (written in 1922) offers two vignettes about the place of women in the modern world: the exhausted mother of five and the lonely typist, who 'lays out food in tins'.[8] Eliot's take on the modern world of women is one which has had lasting influence among conservatives in that only the negative consequences of the refusal of further maternity and the choice of a single life are seen; in Christie (and other women writers of her generation), we see a different path being set out for the new realities of the twentieth century. The shift, from the heroines of nineteenth-century fiction whose only work is the work related to marriage and the home, to heroines who faced different possibilities, is one of the great shifts in the social boundaries and expectations of British fiction. Moreover, it is in the pages of detective fiction that some of the implications of this seismic change are worked out.

The two women writers of detective fiction who do most to explore the possibilities of the modern for women are Christie herself and Dorothy Sayers. Certain critical opinion about Agatha Christie sees her as a conservative, an upholder of explicitly British and narrowly nationalistic values and, in various contexts, both racist and anti-Semitic.[9] The case for all these positions is not difficult to make and examples can be drawn from her work, which demonstrate precisely these views. Yet there are others who have written on Christie (most notably Alison Light), who see her as a defender of the modern world, not least in the possibilities that it offers for women and a less than rosy picture of conservative assumptions about the value of traditional hierarchies of class. Indeed, like Jane Austen before her, Christie does not take the rich and the powerful at their face value; she is quite prepared to find the villain among those possessed of wealth and power and, most crucially, suggests to her readers in all her fiction that nothing in the social world is quite what it seems.

This attitude to appearance, to the outward show of the social, puts Christie very firmly in the tradition of those other distinguished writers (contemporary to Christie) about the modern such as George Simmel and Walter Benjamin as well as later writers (such as Jean Baudrillard), who have famously emphasized the extent of fantasy and illusion in the modern.[10] The people who challenge what people would like us to think are those, like Hercule Poirot and Jane Marple, who resist social constructions of various kinds and who have themselves had to resist definitions of themselves as, respectively, a more than slightly ridiculous foreigner and a silly old woman. The very characters of Poirot and Miss Marple are thus forms of resistance against conventional stereotypes and conventional 'readings' of the social world. Poirot never fails to valorize the importance of thought and rational deduction, those famous 'little grey cells' to which

he often refers, are themselves antithetical to many sections of the bourgeois world. 'Thinking', in various British contexts, not least those associated
with the most socially powerful, has often been regarded as somewhat suspicious, if not positively disruptive. Jane Marple, the elderly spinster, is supposed to be the woman who has somehow failed in heterosexual competition,
the woman who has never 'lived'; yet Miss Marple makes it transparently
clear that she can offer a challenge to all taken-for-granted understandings
of the proper order of social life.

The first appearance of Hercule Poirot is in 1920, in *The Mysterious Affair
at Styles*. In this novel, Poirot is brought in to help solve a rather nasty (and
fatal) case of poisoning in a country house. Poirot is, of course, able to out-
wit the local police force, and in this book, his first introduction to readers,
he follows the same path that he is to follow in subsequent adventures. But
one comment which Poirot does make is particularly interesting; at the end
of the novel, when all the characters are being assigned to their right place
in the social world, Poirot comments that 'The happiness of one man and
woman is the greatest thing in all the world'.[11] This somewhat astounds the
stolid Hastings, who might, presumably, have expected Poirot to invoke
perfect domestic order, or French cooking, as the greatest pleasures in life.
Instead, Poirot refers to a value, a goal, which is far more usually associated
with the feminine and women than with masculinity and men. In making
this comment, we see that from the first Poirot is, in various ways, going
to be something of a transgressive figure in the pages of detective fiction,
a man who asserts the primacy of the private world and the world of the
emotions.

Both Miss Marple and Poirot are, in different ways, as enthusiastic about
happy endings being happy marriages as Jane Austen, Elizabeth Gaskell or
George Eliot ever were. But how this might come about, has, by the 1920s
and 1930s, become more problematic, although Christie is, from her earliest novels, permissive in the characteristics, which make for a happy, heterosexual marriage. In 1930, in *The Murder at the Vicarage*, the inhabitants of the
vicarage are a thoughtful and liberal clergyman, with a beautiful and engaging but domestically incompetent wife. Christie does not suggest that the
husband is unlucky, or that he should make more demands of his wife; on
the contrary, the novel makes it clear that marriages can work without perfect home cooking or other manifestations of domestic skills. What the
novel also makes plain is that male judgement can be entirely wrong. Here,
for example, is Miss Marple abolishing male claims to universal authority in
the space of two pages:

'He has always struck me as rather a stupid man', said Miss Marple, 'The kind of man who gets the wrong idea into his head and is obstinate about it'.[12]

and, only a few paragraphs, later:

'Dear Vicar', said Miss Marple, 'You are so unworldly. I'm afraid that observing human nature for as long as I have done, one gets not to expect very much from it. I dare say that idle title-tattle is very wrong and unkind, but it is so often true, isn't it?'[13]

As Christie then says, 'That last Parthian shot went home'.[14]

In the passages quoted above, what Christie has done, and has done throughout *The Murder at the Vicarage*, is to valorize those ways of thinking and speaking which are always associated with women: chatting, gossiping and the observing of neighbours and friends. Anthropologists have often seen these forms of human communication as means of the social control of the local, but what it has taken the emergence of a more explicitly feminist anthropology to suggest is that local gossip by women is often *for* women, in that it allows the exchange of information and some coalitions of interest and sanction against unwanted actions. Nevertheless, elderly unmarried women like Miss Marple have sometimes been suspected, not just of gossiping, but of those more socially dangerous activities, which have then labelled them as witches. Christie may or may not have known and worried about this; whatever the case, what we see in the fiction is that Miss Marple is kept strictly on the path of well-behaved convention and middle-class normality, living a personal life of the utmost probity and discretion. Indeed, Miss Marple's attendance at her local Anglican church never fails, her home and garden are kept with immaculate attention and scrupulous care and she clearly has little personal taste (unlike her creator) for the exploration of the foreign (either literally or metaphorically) or the bizarre. In a century which has often explored with considerable public energy the more extreme shores of human existence, Miss Marple's iconic stature is a tribute to the lasting appeal of consistency and stability.

But, just as Miss Marple has created for herself a life of rural predictability, so she shares, with Christie, and millions of other people in the twentieth century, a keen sense of the unreliability of the apparently normal and the conventional. What is so distinct about Miss Marple's way of looking at the world (and indeed that of Poirot) is that she sees the unruly, the unstable and the insecure behind the façade of bourgeois and petit-bourgeois life.

This is not to suggest that Christie was the first English writer to put into print the various subterfuges adopted by people anxious to disguise their poverty and need (Elizabeth Gaskell's account of the various evasions of the transparency of poverty by the ladies in the village of Cranford is definitive of this vein of fiction), but Christie saw the implications of the absence of money for those without the means or inclination to secure it. In this context, what can be observed is that Christie acknowledged the sense of agency (and urgency), which money (or its absence) gave to individuals. While the ladies in Cranford might have accepted their poverty with resignation and a degree of passivity, the majority of women (and the shift from ladies to women is an essential ingredient of the twentieth century) had come to realize that earning money was a task for them as well as their brothers and fathers. This, as Christie's novels, demonstrates, very much widens, in fact doubles, the number of likely suspects in murder enquiries: women need money as much as men, and thus, one of the two main motives for murder is as likely to be found in women in men.

Miss Marple's world, which stretches from 1930 to 1965, is thus a world in which men and women are both likely to be murderers or complicit in murder. When, in 1884, Marx and Engels wrote about a core prerequisite of the emancipation of women being their entry into the world of paid work, they forgot to mention that once women did this (and certainly by the time Christie was writing, this had become the reality for many more women than in the nineteenth century), then women would acquire and learn some of the more negative attitudes to money already possessed by men.[15] This is not to imply that women had not always been capable of greed for money (and possibly mean about spending it), but that entry into a world in which women had both to work as hard as men and yet still accept traditional patterns of male authority, started to create the fault lines which would later radicalize generations of women. Christie's Miss Marple, who lives on a private income, has never taken part in this new world; yet she has observed the financial needs and aspirations that women have and which in many ways are created by new forms of consumption specifically involving women. The expression 'a rod for your own back' is not, perhaps, one, which Miss Marple might use, but it does express something of the way in which economies that rely heavily on individual consumption also rely heavily on the suggestibility of women to the transformative powers of various forms of fashion and beauty industries. Christie recognizes, in 1942, that women are, not just metaphorically, but also literally, the victims of what Richard Hoggart was to describe, in *The Uses of Literacy*, as 'the candy floss world'. Christie writes of a murdered woman in *The Body in the Library*:

> And across the old bearskin hearthrug there was sprawled something new
> and crude and melodramatic. The flamboyant figure of a girl. A girl with
> unnaturally fair hair dressed up off her face in elaborate curls and rings.
> Her thin body was dressed in a backless evening dress of white spangled
> satin. The face was heavily made-up, the powder standing out grotesquely
> on its blue swollen surface, the mascara of the lashes lying thickly on the
> distorted cheeks, the scarlet of the lips looking like a gash. Finger-nails
> were enamelled in a deep blood-red and so were the toenails in their
> cheap silver sandal shoes. It was a cheap, tawdry, flamboyant figure – most
> incongruous in the solid old-fashioned comfort of Colonel Bantry's
> library.[16]

As it turns out, this unfortunate young woman has been murdered (like
another similar young woman in Christie's earlier novel, *Death in the Clouds*,
published in 1935 and with Poirot as the sleuth) because she seems to
threaten an inheritance. What Christie is using here is a particular aspect of
the ancient sexual 'double standard'; the general assumption which allows
men sexual activity but denies it, except within the confines of marriage, to
women. But the aspect of that double standard, which Christie is exploring,
is that of class: of the refusal of upper-class men to marry women from lower
classes with whom they might have been 'involved'. Such cross-class romance
has never been a general, empirical feature of Britain (or indeed other
western societies), but as Christie's novels suggests, the fantasy that it might
be real has had a long history.

It is not, of course, the case that all young women who are entranced by
the appeal of pretty (inexpensive) dresses end their days a murder victim.
But Christie, through the eyes of both Miss Marple and Hercule Poirot, sees
some of the problems which that particular aspect of the modern raises
for women. The first is that rhetoric of gender equality and female emancipation that becomes part and parcel of British and North American politics
from the middle of the nineteenth century onwards. The second is the
transformation, after the end of the First World War, of the relationship
between women and paid employment: in the space of a few years, this had
changed from an exceptional and aberrant reality for middle-class women
to an ordinary reality. The history of women and employment, throughout
the west, is one which differs from country to country (in countries such as

France, which remained primarily agricultural until after the Second World War, women were much more likely to remain part of a domestic group of producers), but in Britain there is a slow transition throughout the twentieth century (much accelerated, in different ways by two World Wars) towards the normalization of paid employment for all women. Again, as elsewhere, the pattern was different for different social classes: for working-class married women, for example, paid work was often impossible outside the home but occasionally viable within it. Third, but no less important, is the shift in constructions of gender and gender identity, which were both the results and causes of other social changes. What has been described as 'gay modernity', the flourishing of sexual ambiguity at the end of the nineteenth century, heralded a public departure from more rigidly defined gender stereotypes. By the time Christie (and other women writers of the 'golden age') had begun their careers, men, and previous normative versions of masculinity, have begun to change. It is therefore no accident that Dorothy Sayers's famous detective, Lord Peter Wimsey, should be both athlete and aesthete. This fantasy man united what had, by the 1920s, emerged as a new set of expectations for middle and upper middle-class men. Femininity, as a transsexual capacity, had become as welcome in men as a version of masculinity (independence and autonomy) had become in women.

Inevitably, and few recognized it as well as Christie, this new (or at least changed) world was, like all new worlds, deeply disturbing for many people. Christie's novels are full of rather stupid men who cannot recognize female competence (whether in the form of Jane Marple or other competent women) and who regard with great suspicion any woman who does not pay her dues to male superiority. For example, in *A Murder is Announced* (published in 1950), faced with Jane Marple, Detective Inspector Craddock says to himself of her, 'Completely ga-ga'. By the end of the novel, Miss Marple has made it clear that her 'methods' of detection are considerably more effective than those of Craddock; rather than rely on 'science', Miss Marple observes what we now define as 'body language' and considers the general situation of characters who might be suspected of murder. Thus, at the denouement of *The Body in the Library*, she explains to another lumbering male policeman:

'You haven't had as much experience with girls telling lies as I have. Florence looked at you very straight, if you remember, and stood very rigid and just fidgeted with her feet like the others. But you didn't watch as she went out of the door. I knew at once then that she'd got something to hide. They nearly always relax too soon. My little maid Janet always did.

She'd explain quite convincingly that the mice had eaten the end of the cake and gave herself away by smirking as she left the room.'[17]

Miss Marple's particular strength is to take what might be described as 'domestic' knowledge and use it for wider, social reasons. In every novel in which Miss Marple appears, a man or men and sometimes a women will make the mistake of assuming that nothing can be learned by observations of the private world of the household, and that it is never a place in which people acquire understanding of the social, public world. What has been described as the 'femininisation' of the twentieth century has often been seen in terms of the greater public discussion of subjectivity and the acceptance of the lack of correspondence of the characteristics of masculinity and femininity with the biologically male and female. Yet many institutional worlds, these same worlds that Virginia Woolf observed in *Three Guineas*, actually often refused the implications of 'feminine' understanding. Woolf died at the beginning of the Second World War, but Christie continued to set Miss Marple against the rigidities of the professional world and by 1957 was so confident of her judgement about the lack of fit between the 'feminine' and the modern world that she was able to invent a character, who embodied every characteristic of emancipation with a full understanding of its possible limitations. That character was Lucy Eyelesbarrow in Christie's *4.50 from Paddington*.

The *4.50 from Paddington* is a particularly interesting example of Christie's lifelong engagement with the gendered imagination and the modern world. First, it is in this novel that Miss Marple has to 'create' the murdered corpse. Rather than the corpse being discovered in a room in a country house, this body does not even publicly exist until Miss Marple forces its discovery. A friend of Miss Marple reports to her that she has seen a man strangling a woman in a train. Not only does Miss Marple pay her friend the supreme compliment of believing in this slightly unlikely story, she actually sets in progress an investigation. To do this, she engages Lucy Eyelesbarrow:

The name of Lucy Eylesbarrow had already made itself felt in certain circles. Lucy Eylesbarrow was thirty-two. She had taken a First in Mathematics at Oxford, was acknowledged to have a brilliant mind and was expected to take up a distinguished academic career. But Lucy Eylesbarrow, in addition to scholarly brilliance, had a core of good sound common sense. She could not fail to observe that a life of academic distinction was singularly ill rewarded. She had no desire to teach and she took pleasure in contacts with minds much less brilliant than her own. In short, she had a taste for people, all sorts of people – and not the same people the whole time. She also, quite frankly, liked money. To gain money one must exploit shortage.[18]

Lucy Eylesbarrow is, of course, a figment of Agatha Christie's imagination. But Lucy is, compared, for example, to Ian Fleming's James Bond (who was coming to life at about the same time), an interesting example of the way in which women had rather different patterns of accommodation with 'the modern' than men. Christie herself had lived through years which had seen the granting of the vote to women (in 1919), the greater access of middle-class women to higher education and the passing of a Divorce Act (in 1936 and through the work of A. P. Herbert), which did a great deal to equalize formal legal relations in marriage between men and women. Christie herself, in her divorce from her first husband (who left Christie for another woman), would have experienced that stigma about divorce which was still manifest in all sections of British society. But at the same time, Christie would also have known (and certainly by 1957) what the social historian Ross McKibbon has described as a new 'social peace which enthroned the middle class'.[19] Hence, Lucy Eylesbarrow is allowed to be both highly educated and autonomous but without any kind of deference to class codes, which might have disallowed a 'lady' from taking up domestic work, however well paid. Ian Fleming's James Bond, with his obsession with expensive (and named) possessions and an absolute distance from any kind of domestic task more demanding than ordering meals from room service, is, by contrast, an anachronistic character, more sexually adventurous certainly than Lucy, but even in that a Don Juan of the most ancient mythology.

The qualities of Christie's heroine Lucy are not long in being recognized by many of the other characters in the *4.50 from Paddington* and by the conclusion of the novel, Lucy has received several proposals of marriage. Even though this might appear to be the most conservative of endings, Christie makes it clear that Lucy herself will choose her husband and that the internal dynamics of marriage are not seen by either Christie or Jane Marple as a matter of constant amicable contentment. As Miss Marple remarks:

'So you see', said Miss Marple, 'it really turned out to be as I began to suspect, very, very simple. The simplest kind of crime. So many men seem to murder their wives'.[20]

This bold statement had as much basis in fact in 1957 as it does today: women are most at risk of serious harm from their male partners, and Christie is stating here what many people, then as now, would rather not consider. What this allows us to consider is the way in which detective fiction, and particularly here in the case of Christie, has a constant radicalism in the way that it allows us to see inside the privacy of marriage and what has long been constructed as the sacred place of hearth and home. The early detective fiction (of much of the nineteenth century) took murder and/or serious crime to the streets and the cities. In the twentieth century, in detective fiction written by both women and men, the domestic space became the location of murder and evil intent. Christie, throughout the years of her career (from 1920 and *The Mysterious Affair at Styles* to the late fiction of the 1960s), continues to place the emotional struggles of her characters very firmly in the domestic world. This continuity of Christie's considerable output (the list of the Agatha Christie Collection in the front pages of Christie's novels names eighty novels) remains considerable: even though sexual and social mores are allowed to change (Miss Marple observes these changes but is too shrewd an observer of human beings to pine for a rosy past), Christie consistently asserts the powers of greed and social disclosure to provoke lethal feelings and acts. *Mrs McGinty's Dead* (published in 1952) is perhaps the best example among Christie's work of a plot which revolves around the importance for an individual of maintaining secrecy about aspects of their past.

In all of Christie's fiction, it is made apparent that woman can be the moral and intellectual equals, for good or bad, of men. Women can be bold and intelligent – and entirely trustworthy – in the form of Lucy Eyelesbarrow, or they can be mean and vicious, as in the case of Josie Gaskell in *The Body in the Library*, Marina Gregg in *The Mirror Crack'd from Side to Side* or Mrs Tanios in *Dumb Witness*. In the case of all these, and other, women, what makes them kill is either the fear of unflattering aspects of their lives being discovered or the desire for money and the escape from either likely or actual poverty. In both cases, the reasons women kill are inherently social and it is this which makes Christie so much part of a modern, Enlightenment tradition in which human beings are perceived as capable of command of their feelings and of understanding and controlling the world in which they live. These characters are, further, not the villains so beloved of crime fiction later in the twentieth century, when it is individual pathology rather than amoral reason, which creates murderers. The people who kill in Christie are invariably 'ordinary' people making extraordinary choices.

Christie's world, and her main characters Jane Marple and Hercule Poirot, seldom move far from a white, British world. But although Christie is consistent about the confined racial boundaries of her fiction, she is much more pluralistic about the way in which she presents class. Indeed, like many other women writers of the 'golden age', she is highly sceptical of the idea that superior social position is to be equated with an elevated moral standing. In a fictional tradition, which stretches from Austen to the twentieth century, there is no automatic veneration for the upper class or the aristocracy in Christie, any more than there is in Allingham, Marsh or Mitchell. Aristocrats in Christie are likely to be as venal as any in previous fiction. In this context, fiction accords precisely with that public scepticism towards the sagacity of the ruling class which was, in Britain, part of the legacy of the First World War. The 'century of the common man', as Evelyn Waugh put it, may have been a historical exaggeration by a writer with personal aspirations towards inclusion in the aristocracy, but the comment does reflect that democratization of culture which became part of the twentieth century.[21]

Nevertheless, among British writers of detective fiction in the interwar years, there is one, Dorothy Sayers, who stands out as an embodiment of the wish to continue not merely conservative but virtually feudal traditions. Unlike Christie, Sayers does not present the modern world as one which offers much to women, and the series of detective novels, which Sayers wrote featuring her most famous sleuth Lord Peter Wimsey, all do their utmost to uphold the socially conventional. Lord Peter himself, with his faultlessly establishment background (Eton, Balliol, a 'good' First World War and membership of a ducal family) offers readers a fantasy of the social transcendence of class, because Wimsey eventually marries the daughter of a 'country doctor', a woman called Harriet Vane who was saved, by Wimsey, from the charge of murder. In Sayers's world, this marriage is possible because Harriet is (almost) as intelligent as Wimsey. She too has her first-class degree and has made a living by writing detective stories. Sayers does not subvert the gender order of the time by making Harriet cleverer than Wimsey; indeed the marriage between Wimsey and Harriet is finally agreed in Sayers's novel *Gaudy Night*, in which the possible harm to women of academic work is an important part of the plot.

The world of *Gaudy Night* is a world of Oxford colleges , a London 'Establishment' and the distant ducal estates of Peter Wimsey and his family. It is, of course, a world which only a tiny minority of the British population have ever had any contact with, except as servants. The traditions of social exclusion and the ruthless pursuit of its own interests of the British upper class were never lost on large sections of the British population, but until the Second World War there was, as Ross McKibbon suggests, a degree of esteem and deference for the aristocracy and the upper class. Peter Wimsey certainly has a sense of social responsibility; indeed, he belongs to that tradition within English fiction in which moral worth is indicated by the care, which a person (although generally a man) takes care of his estates. Mr Knightley in Austen's novel *Emma* is, in this, the forerunner of Wimsey. Although Knightley has none of Wimsey's flamboyance and intellectual flair, both men share that highly Protestant sense that care for both material property and the property of the self is a virtue. In this context, we see, again, the way in which detective fiction continues traditions developed in other forms of fiction: Wimsey (for all his metropolitan lifestyle) is essentially the conscientious landed squire.

Dorothy Sayers does, however, have to 'modernise' Wimsey enough to make him credible to readers in the early decades of the twentieth century. She does this in a way which is, as with Christie, part of that hugely important contest in the twentieth century over the meaning of masculinity and the relationship of men and women to the modern. But in contrast to Christie, Sayers suggests a rather different resolution of the issues confronting men and women in the interwar years. As we have seen, Sayers allows Wimsey to marry a woman who has lived by her own pen, which might in itself suggest that Sayers is sympathetic to the idea of female independence. Yet the version of female autonomy presented here is one to which only a minority of women could ever aspire; earning a living through writing fiction was as perilous and as unlikely in the 1920s and the 1930s as in any later decades. But Harriet Vane does manage to provide for herself in this way, and it is matter of fierce pride to her that she has managed to do it; part of the long, five-year courtship between Harriet and Peter Wimsey involves Harriet's struggle to relinquish this hard won independence and accept the comfort of Peter's wealth.

However, finally, in *Gaudy Night*, Harriet makes the transition from courted to caught. Readers are asked to consider that this shift comes about because Harriet has come to acknowledge that Peter Wimsey has a number of qualities (intelligence being foremost) that make him her superior. Harriet, in fact, has to ask Peter Wimsey for help, and that finally forces her to acknowledge how much she needs him. But she is also brought to this realization by living in an all-women Oxford college: an institution, which might, in many ways, be seen as entirely 'modern' but which is seen by Sayers as destructive and 'abnormal'. The plot of the novel involves a number of unpleasant and damaging incidents at the college; unusually, for a detective novel, there is no corpse, although there are one or two near fatalities. The explanation for these events is the bitter fury felt by one of the college servants against one of women dons. This latter person had shown that an academic article written by the servant's husband had been built upon evasion and deceit. The husband had been disgraced, had died, and the wife had been forced into service, eventually in the same college as the woman who had exposed her husband. Thus, here are brought together questions about the value of higher education to women, the moral responsibilities of husbands and wives, the different rights of men and women to paid work and the appropriate 'natural' place of men and women. As such, the novel is rich in ideas about social transformation.

The case against social transformation is most violently put by the woman, Annie, whose husband was publicly disgraced. For her, the women dons are taking away jobs which should belong to men and the women are, in their academic preoccupations, turning their backs on 'real' life and love. When her criminal activities are finally exposed by Peter Wimsey, Annie attacks the women dons thus:

> 'Don't you know what you're doing? I've heard you sit around snivelling about unemployment – but it's you, it's women like you who take the work away from the men and break their hearts and lives. No wonder you can't get men for yourselves and hate the women who can . . . There's nothing in your books about life and marriage and children, is there? Nothing about desperate people – or love – or hate or anything human . . .'.[22]

These quotations, taken from Annie's diatribes against the women dons at the conclusion of *Gaudy Night*, are presented as the voice of a distraught and cornered woman. Nevertheless, what Annie says contains much that has been said throughout the past 200 years: a general social fear about 'blue-stocking' women, the fear (on the part of women themselves) that being seen to be 'clever' will alienate men and the long social (and political) assumption that access to employment belongs to men. That couplet once found on birthday cards for girls ('Be good sweet maid, and let who will be clever') might now be derided as part of an ancient culture, but the various forms of both private and personal reservation about gender equality which still persist might suggest to us that the idea is not quite so dead as some of us might wish.

Sayers is clearly far more sceptical than Christie about the possible resolutions of gender difference which modernity offers. Thus, while Christie offers us happy and self-sufficient women (most typically Miss Marple), Sayers cannot take that step and Harriet Vane never becomes as much the heroine of her novels as Peter Wimsey is the hero. Throughout the saga of the Harriet Vane/Peter Wimsey novels, it is made plain that Harriet is the sounding board for Wimsey's ideas: she might be the object of his desire (although perhaps an unconvincing one since she seems to lack anything close to charm), but her role is largely to demonstrate the degree of Peter's intelligence. Casting Harriet in this role is to follow that model of male and female relationships in which women provide narcissistic confirmation for men. Miss Marple does not in any general sense challenge men (let alone, more dramatically, using her intelligence as a way of undermining their potency), but neither does she exaggerate their abilities. In this sense, she takes that step forward into the gendered order of the modern in a way which Sayers does not. Not for Miss Marple the role of being the mirror which allows men to see themselves as double their actual size.

Peter Wimsey and Harriet Vane remain, however, firmly in the land of fairy story and fantasy. There is now a considerable literature on the subject of novels which are essentially 'rescue fantasies'; tales of young women being 'rescued' from difficult and/or taxing situations by male others, literally the prince on the shining charger, who gallops to the rescue of the maiden in distress. These stories, usually associated with the famous English romances published by Mills and Boon, have passed through various forms of cultural re-invention (from virginal heroines to the more explicitly sexually active), but all suggest that it is a rather bad idea for women to be on their own. This is less an idea, in the Mills and Boon account, about the general value of social life, intimate relations and social community and rather more about the importance of that 'compulsory heterosexuality', which Adrienne Rich defined in 1980 and that can be seen, throughout the twentieth century, as a defining (if often contested and resisted) order in sexual relations.[23]

Harriet Vane is thus not allowed to remain 'alone' and being alone, or being more accurately an unmarried female, is shown to be, in *Gaudy Night*, a thoroughly bad idea, which at the very least will make a woman unbalanced by pedantry and obsessed with the details of the past. But, set against not just Christie, but also other writing by women in Britain in the 1920s and the 1930s, we see in Sayers a very determined endorsement of the possibilities of heterosexual marriage. The theme of female 'disappointment' in the writing of such authors as E. M. Delafield and Margaret Kennedy provides what Susannah Radstone describes as 'the sexual politics of nostalgia'.[24] But what these writers spoke about was, in the view of many critics, the various disappointments which women faced, the realization that achieving that desired state of heterosexual marriage did not bring with it happiness and fulfilment. As the literary critic Lauren Berlant has suggested, what women were (and are) offered is the promise of a 'normative optimism' but that this optimism is itself an 'opiate', designed to obscure the endless repetition of structural inequality.[25]

In Berlant's work, the structural inequality to which she is referring is largely that of gender relations. But in this context, the discussion of crime fiction in Britain between the two world wars, the form of structural inequality which was at least as important was that of class inequality, and it is here that Sayers, again like Christie, is at her most imaginative. When Wimsey marries Harriet Vane, he does something which is not just remarkable in fiction but is equally remarkable in real life: whatever else was being transformed in the culture of the interwar years, in Britain as across Europe, it was not relations between the classes or social mobility between them. Yet the attraction between Wimsey and Vane is constructed and articulated by Sayers in a way which remains unconventional: it is Harriet's intelligence which attracts Wimsey, her ability to listen patiently to his lengthy sentences and to make sense of his Latin quips. To the modern reader, Wimsey's conversational mode may be less beguiling than it clearly is to Harriet, but what is important is that the erotic tension between the pair is seen as made with the mind as much as the body.

This scepticism about the importance of the body, and physical appearance, in sexual attraction and gender relations is a tradition which has long been present in writing by women. Indeed, it is arguably a major defining feature of female, rather than male, fiction that women writers do not see it as necessary to embody their heroines with striking good looks. Despite the veneration for female beauty that has been part of western traditions for centuries, women writers, in the creation of their heroines, have often ignored the need to conform to this assumption. Physical beauty in women is thus seen by women writers, from the end of the eighteenth century onwards, as highly problematic, inviting as it does, they often suggest, narcissism in the beautiful women themselves and false expectations in others. Agatha Christie, in making Miss Marple elderly, removes her from conventional discussions about her appearance. It is a strategy followed by a contemporary of Christie's, Gladys Mitchell, who creates her powerful female detective (Mrs Beatrice Bradley) in the form of another elderly woman; this time, one whose appearance is generally agreed to border on the bizarre. Both Miss Marple and Mrs Bradley have a considerable knowledge of the ways of the world, even if that knowledge has been rather differently acquired; both of them are superbly effective as detecting the identity of murderers.

The dead bodies which often constitute the subject of the attention of Miss Marple and Mrs Bradley (and indeed of Peter Wimsey) are frequently those of women who are young and pretty. The gender distribution of the dead in crime fiction has not yet been quantified but what is noticeable is that young and attractive women (across cultures and throughout the twentieth century) are often the victims of murderers. In this context, crime fiction identifies one of the schisms of western culture: its veneration for female beauty but the ancient fear of its disruptive possibilities. Thus, young women get themselves killed because they are sexually seductive and because this may disrupt patterns of inheritance and/or social convention. Elderly and middle aged women are much less vulnerable and then largely because they learn something which endangers others (Mrs McGinty for example in Christie's *Mrs McGinty's Dead*). Women's beauty is written as embodying the potential for agency; a consistent theme suggesting throughout crime fiction that female beauty can both provide women with social and personal confidence and inspire men to exceptional actions. Part of the genius of Christie was to make her male detective, Hercule Poirot, the antithesis of conventional expectations about masculinity. Poirot sees no reason (and reasons are important to him) for action per se, and he regards much of the movement of the modern world as potentially ridiculous and unnecessary. He knows no reason why he should demonstrate his masculinity by the pursuit of animals or uncomfortable travels; the very possibilities that modernity offer, of physical variety and changes of location, mean nothing to him.

So here are two characters, Poirot and Miss Marple, who offer their own versions of challenge to the modern world. Towards the end of her life, the eminent academic Gillian Rose wrote that she hoped that she would not be deprived of old age. 'I aspire', she wrote, 'to Miss Marple's persona: to be exactly as I am, decrepit nature, yet supernature in one, yet equally alert on the damp ground and in the turbulent air'.[26] Sadly, Gillian Rose was to be deprived of old age but she had found in Miss Marple a kind of solace in the way in which Miss Marple lives in the world on her own terms, yet with a comprehensive understanding of it. This is the achievement of perfected knowledge, not merely the gaining of qualifications but the ability to comprehend human motivations and actions, without sitting in judgement on them. In this sense, we find that Miss Marple, and to a significant extent

Hercule Poirot as well, achieves the status of a secular God: she (and he) can know all but does not aspire to direct or judge it; both Poirot and Miss Marple are quite content to let the law take this responsibility.

What we can find throughout Christie's work, directed as it is to the detection of human evil, is a robust articulation of the many optimistic possibilities of the modern. Christie is not a pessimist about any aspect of the modern; even in her novels written after the Second World War (by which time the promise of modernity and in particular its technological achievements had acquired highly negative associations), she maintains optimism about human achievement and human relations. She does not, like other authors (male and female of general as well as detective fiction) become disappointed in the modern or even resistant to its very existence. Miss Marple may regret the passing of certain aspects of the past, but she is able to see positive aspects in change and does not resort to the kind of 'miserabilism', which overtook others of her generation. This may be, cynics might observe, because of the enormous success which Christie had with her writing and with the evidently happy and secure private life which she was able to build for herself. But apart from this personal capacity to enjoy success and live in comfortable and consistent relations with others, there are certain features of Christie's understanding which suggest that the second half of the twentieth century remained for her as optimistic as the first. These defining features, all of which are aspects of the modern world, are Christie's sense of the complexity of meaning in language, her attitude to money and her sense of the value, especially for women, of autonomy and agency. Christie, in short, did not find in the modern a problematic world for women. In this view, she established two important traditions for other women writers of detective fiction: she allowed women to exist comfortably as single women (an acceptance of a way of life that the later generation of women crime writers, which included Val McDermid, Sara Paretsky and Sue Grafton, were to enjoy to the full), and she was to assert the value of a particular, female intelligence, an intelligence located in knowledge of the local and the domestic (again to be repeated in the generation of McDermid et al.) rather than in the world of science and technology that is the forensic world of Patricia Cornwell.

Christie, as has been suggested earlier in this chapter, had no objection to young women exploring the world and earning money for themselves. In that view, she fully embraced the changing needs of consumer capitalism and yet at the same time she recognized, as did those male detectives who were created by Christie's contemporaries on the other side of the Atlantic, that the language through which we become part of that everyday life is rich with contradictions, evasions and deliberate misreadings. In this context, Christie's novel *Mrs McGinty's Dead* is rich in suggestions about the ambiguities of language, from the very names and titles which people have (the gender-bending first name Evelyn for example) to the ways in which commonplace descriptions can be both entirely inaccurate and entirely meaningless. As Poirot himself remarks, ' "Oh my friend, consider, Very nice people". That has been, before now, a motive for murder'.[27] As Christie showed us, social convention and a moral code are two different things. In her work, she found ways of upholding the latter; in the United States, as we shall see, the possibility of that achievement was thrown into greater doubt.

Chapter 4

Illegal and Immoral

While Miss Marple, Lord Peter Wimsey and their contemporaries were maintaining aspects of the social and moral order in Britain, two traditions of detective-writing were developing in other parts of the west. In that writing (in the United States, the generation that included the writing of Raymond Chandler and Dashiell Hammett and in Europe, the writing of Georges Simenon), there was a much less enthusiastic endorsement of the conventional world and of the clarity of moral boundaries. It would not be true to say that Christie and Sayers (and others) were not well aware of the limitations of the conventional world (there is much in Christie, including the construction of her two central characters Miss Marple and Hercule Poirot to suggest this scepticism about the conventions of the social world), but they maintained, throughout their work, a respect for the institutional order, which was often lacking on the other side of the Atlantic. Most particularly, what is evident in Britain is an assumption that the police and judiciary are above reproach; they might be stupid (and Christie certainly has no confidence in the 'little grey cells' of the police), but they are honest and well meaning.

The period in which crime-writing in the United States (and to a certain extent in Europe) becomes noticeably different from Britain is during the years between the two World Wars. All the countries concerned (Britain, France and the United States) had emerged from the First World Wars as victors; all had taken part in the ruthlessly vindictive prosecution of Germany in the Versailles settlement. In cultural terms, the years immediately after the First World War had seen, in Europe as much as in the United States, an energetic emergence of modernism. Hercule Poirot was the most enthusiastic supporter of aspects of the modernist revolution in design (particularly in his embrace of mechanical and technological forms of domestic comfort and order), but the work of all writers of detective fiction in Europe included, at this time, some form of acknowledgement that whether they liked it or not the world was changing. Experimentation in art and social relations appears throughout British detective-writing; the metropolitan world becomes a place of change and debate in fiction as much as it was in the reality of the artistic and avant-garde circles of Paris and London.

The United States shared much of this enthusiasm for the modernist project and in addition was undoubtedly on the way to becoming the world's major locus of technological innovation and competence. The massive transformations of production, which had been put into place by Henry Ford in Detroit, were bringing to the better off citizens of the United States, a part in a new order of democratic access to manufactured goods. While many citizens of Europe had come to acquire manufactured goods such as clothes, food and furniture in the nineteenth century (and buying them at the department stores of London and Paris), it was in the United States that many citizens first had the opportunity to acquire domestic machinery (refrigerators, washing machines and so on), which ushered in a new world of domestic life and new expectations about it. Participation in this new world depended on a reliable income – for many people extremely unreliable in these years – and access to urban life. Thus part of the continuity between detective fiction in the nineteenth and the twentieth century is that the focus of crime is generally (although not always) on the city and the urban space. Even though critics write of the 'country house' murders of the interwar years, many of the plots of those tales (whether in Britain or in the United States) involve relationships and interests located in urban worlds.

The city (or more precisely some cities) had been a focus for fashion, power of various kinds and many forms of intellectual and cultural life throughout the eighteenth and the nineteenth century. For example, Paris dominates western ideas about fashion from the eighteenth century onwards in the same way that Berlin was to become a place re-known for avant-garde work in various aspects of the visual arts in the 1920s. Fiction and autobiography throughout the nineteenth and the twentieth century bear witness to the various ways in which cities are either fashionable or intriguing; often, the citizens of one fashionable city are themselves in thrall by the delights of another. For example, those committed Parisians Jean-Paul Sartre and Simone de Beauvoir spent much of the interwar period longing to visit the United States (in particular New York) with much the same enthusiasm as others longed for a life in Paris.[1] The pursuit of the mythical cultural 'centre of the world', which has become a feature of late-twentieth-century ideas about all cities, acquired its energy from the hope that in being in a particular place an individual could acquire a sense of immediacy and engagement with a fashionable world.

It was thus that the cities where Hammett and Chandler placed their detectives were worlds in which people were judged by their appearance and consequently were much engaged in the presentation of themselves as identifiable with images and fantasies constructed by the professional makers of fashion. In the novels of both men, women dress to disguise their social origins, just as men dress to emphasize their power and their wealth. It is in this sense that cities offer the people the chance of 'making themselves'; they can choose a surface identity and through access to the goods of the city fulfil all those expectations of a particular persona. In the years when Hammett and Chandler were writing, the United States was home to the development of the first forms of mass entertainment, in particular, the cinema and popular music. Although the celebrity culture of the 1920s and the 1930s did not exist with the same energy as it does at the beginning of the twenty-first century, it had come into existence by this time. *Detecting*, then, acquires a new responsibility and a new form: it is now increasingly about the unmasking of the person, of uncovering the person who is hidden behind some form of social disguise.

In accounts of the work of Hammett and Chandler (particularly in the classic studies of detective fiction), much is made of the role that the private investigator plays in the detection of crime, and the nature of the world and the politics makes this necessary. In Mandel, Symons and Binyon, the point is made that the new urban worlds of the United States grew so quickly that there was insufficient time to put into place those social networks, which might have supported the emergence of honest and incorrupt policing; as it was, the rise of the great North American cities coincided with the rise of organized crime and in many cases, a form of organized crime which was integrated with the police and with the population as a whole. A major part of the tradition of politics in the United States (in cinematic terms the tradition of *Mr Deeds Goes to Washington*) then became the establishment of a political agenda designed to 'root out' corruption and take the values of the honest small town to Washington. It is a tradition that has continued into the twenty-first century, with politicians of both major parties endlessly endorsing the values of the small town and the homestead against those of metropolitan life and urban existence. As corruption became more complex – and more global – it continued to be necessary for the United States to uphold the myth of the honest (usually male) individual, who fights for honour and decency in a corrupt world.

Mandel, Symons and Binyon all refer, with differences of emphasis, to this pattern of detective fiction in the United States. Mandel, for example, writes thus:

Sam Spade, Philip Marlowe, Nestor Burma and Lew Archer may seem hard-boiled characters devoid of any illusions in the existing social order. But at the bottom they are still sentimentalists, suckers for damsels in distress, for the weak confronting the strong. In a classic passage of 'The Simple Art of Murder' Chandler himself describes this combination of cynicism and romanticism:

'Down these mean streets a man must go who is neither tarnished nor afraid. The detective in this kind of story must be such a man. He is the hero, he is everything. He must be a complete man and a common man and yet an unusual man. He must be, to use a rather weathered phrase, a man of honour, by instinct, by inevitability, without thought of it, and certainly without saying it'.

As Mandel somewhat waspishly remarks: 'It is not difficult to detect the naivety of that portrait'.[2]

In that comment, Mandel has used the word 'detect' about the analysis of Chandler's ideas. In this context, Mandel is implicitly suggesting to his readers the value of the process of 'detection', a case in which it is not conscience that makes detectives of us all but only the general need to know. It is that 'need to know' that so dominates the literature of Hammett and Chandler; there is often no particular reason why Hammett and Chandler's private investigators should continue to pursue a course of inquiry (and they are often asked to stop their inquiries by those employing them), but they cannot turn their backs on the partially revealed. Fully aware that 'knowledge is power', they are not to be distracted from their path by either threat or bribe.

Of the two pivotal figures of detective-writing in the United States in the inter-war period, it is Hammett whose life and work perhaps offers the most insight into the meaning and the growth of the process of detection. Hammett was born in 1894 and began his working life as a clerk at the Pinkerton National Detective Agency. The agency, founded by Alan Pinkerton in the middle of the nineteenth century, had the motto 'we never sleep', and indeed, the agency expected its operatives to work night and day in the pursuit of the guilty, be they thieves, adulterous spouses or, most problematically for Hammett's later politics, labour unions. It was in this last context that Hammett encountered in his very first months as a Pinkerton operative a case of 'lynch mob violence' towards a man named Frank Little, who was a Wobbly, a trade union organizer and hated by factory owners in the state of Montana. Hammett was offered what was then the enormous sum of $5,000 to help to murder Frank Little. In the event, somebody else murdered Frank Little before Hammett arrived on the scene, but as his biographer Diane Johnson writes of this event:

> But at some moment – or perhaps at the moment he was asked to murder Frank Little or perhaps at the moment that he learned that Little had been killed, possibly by other Pinkerton men – Hammett saw that the actions of the guards and the guarded, of the detective and the man he's stalking, are reflexes of a single sensibility, on the fringe where murderers and thieves live. He saw that he himself was on the fringe or might be, in his present line of work, and was expected to be, according to a kind of oath of fealty that he and other Pinkerton took.[3]

Hammett lived until 1961 (and thus through the Depression, the Second World War and the emergence of the Cold War), but his greatest work was published in the period between 1929 and 1934: *The Dain Curse* in 1929, *The Thin Man* in 1934 and *The Glass Key* in 1931. (Julian Symons has described *The Glass Key* as 'the peak of Hammett's achievement, which is to say the peak of the crime writer's art in the twentieth century'.[4]) Hammett's novels brought him considerable fame and fortune although the last twenty years of his life were unproductive and spent in various battles: his own personal battle against alcoholism and his shared political battle on behalf of the Communist Party of the United States. For refusal to answer questions about matters related to the Communist Party, Hammett was sentenced to six months imprisonment in 1951; for the last ten years of his life, his health was precarious, and he continued to be subject to various outbursts of anti-Communist fervour.

None of these outbursts, however, affected or undermined the lasting appeal of Hammett's work or the eagerness of film directors to translate his work into cinema. Obituaries and later criticism of Hammett's work have all spoken of its presentation of a new kind of hero, indeed an anti-hero who acts in terms, generally, of making the rather better (or more defensible) choice in a situation where neither option is ideal. Indeed, Hammett's 'heroes' occupy the kind of moral space that has been associated with nihilism and existentialism; the world outside that of the conventional world has long been of great interest to that very world. For example, in the work of Jean Paul Sartre and his protégée Jean Genet, there is a consistent engagement with what the respectable world might define as the 'underworld': certainly, a world beyond the confines of respectable society. Throughout the 1920s and 1930s, Sartre and Simone de Beauvoir sought out the disreputable and the marginal places of the social world since for them their inhabitants possessed an authentic morality. Beauvoir wrote of one such excursion:

> We also visited the music halls . . . At Bobino's we heard . . . Marie Dubas who stirred audiences to wild enthusiasm and laughter . . . we read into these parodies of hers a satirical attack on the bourgeoisie. She included in her repertoire some rousing popular songs, the very crudeness of which we interpreted as a challenge to the police-protected classes; so for us she was an anarchist, too.[5]

The work of Hammett articulates much the same position and all his work contains the outline of a morality, which is *totally at odds* with the apparent dominant normative order of the United States. Hammett certainly did not establish a moral tradition in the United States, but he can be credited with giving a dissenting moral order a voice and a position in the United States that has continued throughout the twentieth and into the twenty-first century. It is part of the cultural history of the United States that the country has made desperate (and often vicious) attempts to outlaw dissent and difference, but these attempts have done nothing to bring about the disappearance of the kind of values that Hammett was attempting to articulate. The tradition of the single figure who takes on the forces of both evil *and* convention continues to this day in detective and crime fiction in the United States; the following passage was written in 2008 by James Burke in his crime novel *Swan Peak*. Reviewing the capture and imprisonment of two wealthy citizens Burke writes:

> The families had been in business together for decades, in the same kind of symbiotic alliance that had existed in the nineteenth century between the street gangs of New York and Boston and the blue blood families whose names have been polished clean by success and the passage of time . . . The faces of the actors may change, but the story is ongoing and neither religion nor government has ever rid the world of sin or snake oil.[6]

Hammett's refusal of, and scepticism about, all that was conventional and culturally enshrined in the United States poses a question about contemporary understandings of the cultural and intellectual history of the twentieth

century, which go beyond the immediate concerns of detective and crime
fiction. It is that in the crime fiction of the 1920s and the 1930s, most clearly
in the United States but in certain contexts in Europe, it is possible to see
a widespread rejection of the social world that is being built after the First
World War. What Hammett suggests to his readers (and Raymond Chandler
and others echo the same views) is that the civic world of the United States
is one that is deeply corrupt and cynically careless about the lives of its
citizens. In other forms of literature in this period, there were many voices
who suggested similar arguments: the pervasive and often idiot consumer
culture was the focus of attack in the novels of Sinclair Lewis just as the
decadence and moral fragility of the rich and privileged was examined by
Scott Fitzgerald. Indeed, a glance at the canonical literature in the United
States in these years would suggest that among the *literati*, there was little or
no endorsement of the normative social world. Corruption, dishonesty,
greed and stupidity were widely found and widely recorded.

This negative portrayal about both the private and public lives of many
citizens (especially rich citizens) in the United States suggests we are mis-
taken if we read the cultural history of the twentieth century in terms of
that disjunction between modernity and post-modernity that has become the
orthodoxy of recent discussions of social and cultural change. In eminent
and well-regarded works such as David Harvey's *The Condition of Post-
Modernity*, it is argued that what is described as the *project* of modernity (the
various ideas about the individual, society and the state that emerged in
Europe after the Enlightenment) was transformed in the 1960s by the collapse of what are generally described as 'grand narratives'.[7] This is not the
context in which to explore those various arguments, but what is both
important and relevant here is that the reading of history that is articulated
through this periodization pays little or no account to the complexity
of views about the world which can be gleaned from another form of reading – that more literal reading, which encompasses fiction and other forms
of narrative.

This second form of reading, however limited, of literature as a whole, and
detective fiction in particular, in the years between 1918 and 1939, would
reveal that the 'modern' world is viewed with various degrees of contempt,
fear and distrust. The previous chapter has discussed the ways in which the
'modern' can be problematic for women; the detective fiction, which takes
as its central character the private investigator, offers us an insight into the
limitations of the modern for men. Christie, Sayers et al. are all very well
aware of the constraints of domesticity; this same recognition is no less an
element in the work of Hammett and Chandler, where much male energy

is devoted to escaping or avoiding what is seen to be the domestic and domesticating world of women. Hammett lived his own life as a single, autonomous person; although he was married and had a long lasting relationship with the playwright Lillian Hellman, he made no concessions to conventional expectations of marriage or sexual fidelity. On both sides of the Atlantic, perceptive authors (Sinclair Lewis in *Babbitt* and George Orwell in *Coming Up for Air*) had noted the coincidence between women, the domestic space and profit, and it is difficult to locate among the literature of the inter-war period a literary work, which offers a positive view of either the modern world or gender relations within it that is unambiguously positive.

Although the growth of a form of capitalism, which increasingly emphasized the growth of domestic consumption, reinforced that form of gender relations in which women barter sexual favours for access to material goods, the major focus of attack in the novels of Chandler and Hammett was elsewhere. Whilst both authors (and their contemporaries in their own country and in Britain) were well aware of the ways in which the new desires and needs created by the market furthered traditional forms of sexual bargaining, it was not 'ordinary' individuals who were the primary focus of the contempt of Chandler and Hammett; it was the rich and the powerful. It was the corruption of power that Hammett attacked, a form of corruption which could refuse evidence, lynch the powerless and make rules without any recourse to public debate or consensus. Accounts of the history of the United States often suggest that the pursuit of dissenters only began in the years of the Cold War, but the infamous House Un-American Activities Committee had existed throughout the 1930s and was active in creating various kinds of difficulty for dissenting voices, among which was Hammett's.

Disillusionment and despair about the fate of western societies was endemic among intellectuals on both sides of the Atlantic in the 1930s, although many were to view the war against Hitler's Germany as just. Hammett was certainly of this view and despite his physical weakness and ill health, he enrolled in 1942 in the US Army in the Second World War. He was unable to take much part in combat duties, but he did find in the comradeship and commitment of his fellow soldiers something of that sense of identity and shared purpose which he had never found elsewhere. Again, he shared this sense of renewed moral purpose with others of his generation: fighting the evils of Nazism gave existence a shared meaning that did not exist in civilian life. Most of Hammett's days in the army were spent as the editor of an army newspaper, but despite this harmless activity (and one much valued by his fellow soldiers), Hammett was still being pursued by the FBI. In a comic example of bureaucratic incompetence, a FBI dossier recorded, at a time when Hammett was a Corporal in the US Army that 'a further check is being made to ascertain whether he is actually in the Army'.[8]

Wars inevitably create chaos (and a rich literature about this chaos), and so Hammett was probably not the only serving soldier in the United States that the FBI could not trace. Just when Hammett was serving his time in the US Army, Evelyn Waugh, on the other side of the Atlantic, was becoming rapidly disillusioned with the army and the 'soldiering', which initially he, like Hammett, had so much wanted to take part in. Waugh's experiences in the British army led not to detective fiction but to the *Sword of Honour* trilogy and the argument that only the values of the past had any real value. Hammett did not endorse this position, but what he did share with Waugh was an enthusiasm for the Allied cause that suggests that on both sides, not just of the Atlantic, but also of the political spectrum, there was now a cause which was worth fighting for. The corrupt and decadent world of 'modern' Europe had suddenly found a way of redemption. The left wing Hammett and the conservative, Roman Catholic Waugh could now take part in a campaign that was identifiable with positive and altruistic values.

The popularity of the Second World War – the sense that unlike the First World War this was a war worth fighting – left a considerable (and still largely underestimated) legacy in making the west a morally defensible world. In the interwar decades, western detective fiction had seldom shown a positive social world; detective fiction might have taken place in country houses (though much less so than is generally supposed), but any reading of this fiction that does not mistake the historical world for the desirable world has to recognize that both personal corruption and institutional corruption were far more general than it was often comfortable to assume. The degree and the extent of this institutional corruption in the United States have been described thus by Mandel:

> Corruption, violence, and crime were evident not only in the periphery of American society, but at its very centre. Where the British civil service was a genuine servant of bourgeois society and the successful British politician was seen as a public sage, the American civil service was regarded as virtually useless throughout the nineteenth century, and successful politicians were seen as crooks. From the outset, then, the American crime story presented crime as far more completely integrated into society as a whole than the British did.[9]

Certainly, there is evidence to substantiate Mandel's view; for example, Leonard Woolf, before his marriage to Virginia, spent seven years as a civil servant in what was then, Ceylon, and clearly worked hard and honestly throughout this time. Nobody would have known (or perhaps even cared) if Leonard Woolf had spent his seven years in Ceylon in complete idleness, but he did not. Miles away from any form of supervision, he worked with conscientious dedication, an exemplary example of a fully developed commitment to his work and internalized values of integrity.[10]

Yet, although Mandel and others make distinctions between crime and detective-writing in the United States and Europe, many follow, with perhaps less emphasis than Mandel on class politics, the comments, which Mandel goes on to make:

> . . . the common ideology of the original and classical detective story in Britain, the United States, and the countries of the European continent remains quintessentially bourgeois . . . It plays a powerful integrative role among all but extremely critical and sophisticated readers. It suggests to them that individual passions, drives, and greed, and the social order itself – bourgeois society – have to be accepted as such regardless of shortcomings and injustices, and that those who catch criminals and deliver them to law-enforcement agencies . . . are serving the interests of the immense majority of the citizenry. The class nature of the state, property, law and justice remains completely obscured. Total irrationality combined with partial rationality, condensed expression of bourgeois alienation, rules supreme. Bourgeois legality, bourgeois values, bourgeois society, always triumph in the end.[11]

What is interesting about this passage is that it contains within it some assumptions about crime and detective-writing that have become generally accepted (for example the view that detective and crime fiction has an integrative social role) with a highly schematic and oppositional account of values and rationality. Mandel wrote the above in 1984, two years after the publication, in 1982 of detective novels by Sara Paretsky (author of *Indemnity Only*) and Sue Grafton (author of *A is for Alibi*). What is remarkable about these books is that they largely refute the assumptions by Mandel that detective and crime fiction actually supports 'bourgeois' values. On the contrary, all the subsequent novels by Paretsky and Grafton have been sharply critical of many bourgeois values. In their different ways, both authors have attacked those 'bourgeois' values of which Mandel is so critical and had little to say about conventional society which is positive. Indeed, the integrity of both the heroines of Grafton and Paretsky is derived from their refusal to condone or collude with the values of the supposedly 'respectable' world.

A more detailed discussion of both Grafton and Paretsky forms part of the following chapter, but their work is mentioned here because they serve as an example of the way in which criticism, such as Mandel's, which is so firmly located within a particular interpretation of Marxism and is also so disinclined to 'see' gender as an organizing feature of the world of the imagination, can misinterpret or disallow the implications of gender in cultural analysis. Mandel, and others, writing about Chandler and Hammett (or Christie or Simenon) do not fail to identify the author as male or female but almost always fail to see the implications that this might have. It is impossible to read Chandler and Hammett (and the other 'private eye' literature of the United States) and not 'see' gender: the private eyes are always men, and this aspect of their social being is entirely taken for granted. Yet, once gender is problematized, what emerges is a rather different reading of the crime fiction of the 1920s and 1930s and one that contributes towards a different understanding of the organizing problem at the core of detective and crime writing of this period: the problem of *the identity and meaning of capitalism*. Indeed, in many ways, exactly who or what capitalism was (and is) is the great mystery of western society: whether this form of social system is 'natural', or the only social system which guarantees human liberties or one which exploits all but a few; these are some of the issues, which were the 'mysteries' of nineteenth century society. When Marx wrote that a 'commodity is a mysterious thing', he was referring to the ways in which the forces of the capitalist market can create the value of goods or services, apparently out of nowhere.[12] Although many others did not (and do not) agree with Marx's analysis of the dynamic of capitalism or his account of class relations, the 'mystery' of this form of society was crucial to the self-examination of the west from this period onwards. Marx and Darwin (later Freud) had introduced self-consciousness to the study of human society and having done this, nothing social remained 'natural'.

The relevance of this to the discussion of crime and detective fiction is that in much of this genre of fiction, authors are trying to introduce their readers to the problem of what this world of western capitalism is actually about and what kind of place the individual has in it. This is very far from Mandel's argument that detective fiction always confirms the social order; on the contrary, what we are shown is the complexity of the social order and the absence within it of any defining set of values and standards. Hammett and Chandler did not write fiction which confirmed the moral order of capitalism; they wrote fiction that suggested that this form of society, within which the west now lived, had very little that was coherent (let alone acceptable or praiseworthy) about either its moral values or its code of ethics. In writing novels that suggested the moral chaos of the west (rather than that agreed moral order which Mandel is suggesting), they arrive at a position that is actually very much more in accordance with the history of the twentieth century than an account of those same years which sees only bourgeois hegemony. A brief glance at the history of the twentieth century will show that capitalism is able to coexist with various forms of fascism (Italy, Spain and Germany in the 1930s) as much as various degrees of social democracy (France, Great Britain and the United States in the same period). While glancing around the western world in the 1920s and the 1930s, any acute observer of that world's politics would find it difficult to establish a single answer to the question of what capitalism, as a moral and cultural system which organizes individual lives, invariably upholds.

There are two further aspects of various literatures, which contribute to the question of the 'mystery' of the social and moral identity of capitalism. The first is that in the books of both Hammett and Chandler, women, just as men, are often morally at fault and as ruthless and cruel towards their fellow human beings as any men. Female evil is no invention of the twentieth century, but what both these authors do is to show that women, in the same way as men, are just as likely to be greedy for money and material goods. Again, there are numerous female figures in both history and fiction who have had precisely that characteristic, but Hammett and Chandler see their female characters not as aberrant individuals but as social 'types'. This is a highly significant step towards that understanding of the world where we are not just individuals but also a part of groups and classes that is derived in part from Marx but also from the emergence in the nineteenth century of those collective social organizations (trade unions being a notable example), which emphasize the possibility of collective rather than individual human action. Hammett and Chandler were both writing of the United States where these forms of collective action had a more restricted history than in Europe, but this only contributes to their sense of the need for a social world to acquire socially agreed values. This is far from upholding bourgeois values; it is concerned rather more with their identification.

So women, in Chandler and Hammett, play out their parts as (occasionally) 'good' women but more occasionally rather bad women, like the character Muriel Chess in Chandler's novel *The Lady in the Lake*.

If Muriel Chess impersonated Crystal Kingsley, she murdered her. That's elementary. All right, let's look at it. We know who she was and what kind of woman she was. She had already murdered before she met and married Bill Chess. She had been Dr Almore's office nurse and his little pal and she had murdered Dr Almore's wife in such a neat way that Almore had to cover up for her. And she had been married to a man in the Bay City police who was also sucker enough to cover up for her.[13]

What Muriel Chess and *her kind* of women do is therefore every bit as bad as that of men; Muriel is capable of murder, deceit and sexual manipulation in order to get her way. Again, it is possible to cite women characters in fiction throughout the nineteenth century who could persuade men to do their bidding (English canonical fiction contains such examples as the strong-willed Rosamond Vincy in George Eliot's *Middlemarch*, not a literal murderess but a woman who effectively demolishes all her husband's plans for his life and work), but the difference between these women and the characters such as Muriel Chess is that the latter are types; greed for money has infected not just one women but groups of women.

It is thus that private investigators in the novels of Hammett and Chandler confront a world in which there are few easy assumptions to be made about the existence of virtue and the integrity of institutions. The various forces of law and order, the large corporations and the rich and the powerful may inhabit palaces and present to the world a public face of order, polite manners and gracious living, but part of the exercise in which Hammett and Chandler are involved is the revelation that these places of apparent virtue are all too often the places of actual vice. Appearance is one thing, reality is quite another, and no one can be sure of what kind of behaviour is to be found behind the imposing doors of the bourgeois world. In this exercise of unmasking, Hammett and Chandler join another western tradition: that of those non-fiction writers about the social world who have, since the nineteenth century, been ever sceptical about the moral integrity and permanence of the social world.

It is the second tradition, that is, the tradition of Marx, Freud, George Simmel, Walter Benjamin and the Frankfurt School, with which Hammett and Chandler share so much. That list of major social theorists working within the western world is far from exhaustive, and although it is largely composed of individuals who would place themselves to the left of the political spectrum, others more often identified with the political right, for example, T. S. Eliot shared the same concern with regard to the changing values of the social world and, in particular, aspects of what all saw as the growing brutalization and commercialization of the culture of the twentieth century. Simmel and Benjamin wrote of the urban life of the twentieth century in ways that are similar to those of Hammett and Chandler, describing a world in which only money has any real value or social agency but also a world in which fantasies about the contemporary world (and the place of the individual within it) hold an enormous sway on human action. The western world, by the end of the First World War, had become a world of ever increasing technological sophistication, but individual understanding of that world, particularly, in terms of the scientific and technological exper- tise that defined much of its existence, became deeply mysterious to many people.

This world, as Europeans were to discover to their hideous cost by 1939, was a world in which fantasies about the world could acquire an all powerful political impact. But, for Europe in the 1930s, one particular fantasy about this world had an appeal which gave strength to fascist politics: namely, the fantasy of the possibility of the recovery of a vanished, but once glorious, national past in which conquest and domination over others was apparently possible. Mussolini's Italy and Hitler's Germany both drew on versions of past history that marginalized the technical competence of empires such as those of Ancient Rome and instead invoked theories of racial power and magnificence. In a very important sense, fascism, although capable of con- siderable feats of social transformation and organization, was at its heart, an irrational enterprise; one that did not care to examine or consider too closely the actual means through which empires were made and sustained. Thus, as many historians of Hitler's Germany (and to a lesser extent, Italy at the time of Mussolini) have pointed out, there were various examples (for example the refusal to integrate women into the work force and the commitment of scarce resources to the Final Solution), when these regimes acted entirely irrationally. In the twenty-first century, the term 'rational' has come to be taken as synonymous with the good and the positive; in the context of this discussion about the politics of the early and mid-twentieth century, we also need to remember that, in fact, the word has no such moral implications.

It is on the question of the meaning of 'morality' that Hammett, and to a lesser extent Chandler, is such a powerful writer. For Hammett, formal morality, the normative order as sociologists would describe it, is something that is to be examined critically and provides no necessarily useful guide to personal (let alone general) questions of how to act. Hammett knows, and communicates this knowledge, that convention is not morality. Convention may be a useful way of making social relations more pleasant and conve- nient, but it is not in itself any substitute for moral understanding or engage- ment. What we notice about the private eyes in Hammett and Chandler is that they are almost always conventionally polite and what might be described as 'well behaved'; they do not abuse women or become violent for no reason; they dress respectably and are perfectly able to hold their own in what is sometimes referred to as 'polite' society. They could pass for what the British, at this period, might have described as 'gentlemen'. At first glance, they accord perfectly with the expectations of white, middle-class, urban men.

But what Hammett and Chandler do with these figures is make them powerful, individual judges of the social world in which they live. These men could have lived out the conventional life of the suburbs (wife, house, children and so on), but for various reasons they chose not to. Two aspects of this refusal are important: the first is that from the first years of its construction, very powerful voices in the imaginative world of the United States condemned this new version of social nirvana. (It was to take another 30 years before Betty Friedan, in *The Feminine Mystique*, wrote her devastating critique of the American suburbs as a place where thousands of women were going quietly – and subsequently not so quietly – insane.) The second is that along with this tradition of refusal and contempt for the American Dream was the suspicion that it was based on corruption, exploitation and deceit. Corruption was to be found in the deals about land and resources that effectively stole them from their owners; exploitation was the use of the poor (both Afro-American and white) as cheap and insecure labour; and deceit was the endless performance of ritualized manners and social behaviour. This was not, felt many writers in the United States in the interwar years, a country in which they found much to praise.

It is thus that we do not find that Hammett and Chandler are alone in their critique of the United States in the 1930s. Other, equally well-known names such as Sinclair Lewis, Ernest Hemingway, John Dos Passos, William Faulkner and Scott FitzGerald all share a very vivid disenchantment with the society in which they live. For all of them, behind the technological achievement and the achievements of science lies a world empty of moral reason and understanding. It is precisely that disenchantment with the modern world that Max Weber saw as a central tradition in the modern and in modernity: the world is more obviously subject to human control, but with it goes a longing for those years when spontaneity and meaningful relationships between individuals had a place in the social world. Karl Marx may well have shrugged his shoulders and pointed out that subservience to the cash nexus was never likely to bring with it human happiness, but many other social scientists in the early years of the twentieth century recognized the melancholy and the sense of loss that technological and organizational mastery can bring with them. Civilization, as Sigmund Freud, pointed out, is both socially necessary and psychically disruptive: we live more ordered and creative lives because of it, but at the same time we do not lose our longing for the spontaneous and the expressive.

In this context, women, and more precisely a specifically feminine form of sexuality, occupy the possible space of a kind of 'last frontier' of the unchained and the unsocialized. The shift in the ways in which women and men have been presented in the literature of the twentieth century as opposed to the literature of the nineteenth has been the subject of many studies in the years after the writing of Hammett and Chandler. But, at the time, the difference was also noticed; in a passage from her autobiography, published in 1937, Gertrude Stein reported a conversation between herself and Dashiell Hammett:

> I said to Hammett there is something puzzling. In the nineteenth century the men when they were writing did invent all kinds and a great number of men. The women on the other hand never could invent women they always made the women be themselves . . . Now in the twentieth century it is the men who do it. The men all write about themselves, they are always themselves as strong or weak or mysterious or passionate or drunk or controlled but always themselves as the women used to do in the nineteenth century. Now you yourself do it why is it. He (Hammett) said it's simple. In the nineteenth century men were confident, the women were not but in the twentieth century the men have no confidence and so they have to make themselves as you say more beautiful more intriguing more everything and they cannot make any other man because they have to hold onto themselves not having any confidence.[14]

On this occasion (if Gertrude Stein's reporting is correct), Hammett spoke with that wonderful clarity which was a feature of so many of his public pronouncements about the world. But, the issue that he described as 'simple', that of the collapse of male confidence, is one that has now generated a considerable academic and more popular literature. The 'collapse' of masculinity, the 'femininisation' of society and the wicked emasculating effects of feminism have all been the subject of both scholarly and popular debate. Far from being 'simple', the question invites debate and examination.

If we turn, for an examination of the question that Stein has raised, to the novels that Hammett wrote, it is possible to see how much his male characters correspond to Stein's definition. The characters, in all of Hammett's novels, are versions of Hammett himself: curious about the truth, willing to follow an investigation to its ends and in many ways complicit with the culture from which they are so apparently detached. Alcohol and endless movement structure the stories, in much the same way as they provided a background to Hammett's life, a life lived between places, in hotels and only for relatively brief periods in settled circumstances. We can explain some of the features of Hammett's life, as we can explain those of any human being, in terms of his personal circumstances and the dynamic of the relations within his family. But, at the same time, we have to recognize that Hammett shared with millions of other men of his generation the condition of living in an increasingly wealthy society but a society in which the wealth was very unequally shared and in which in some cases (notably the Afro-American population), millions of people were entirely excluded from any share in prosperity. Hammett, like Chandler, seldom raises questions of race in his novels; there are few people in his fiction who are not white, urban and with some degree of education. Excluded from this picture of the social world are of course those millions of poor citizens of the United States: people who were largely illiterate and lived out their lives in extreme rural poverty.

Hammett, however, is not writing in order to convey a picture of the United States as a whole. He writes, in the years of his great productivity, about a central moral problem of the United States: that of how this diverse and rich society can order itself without recourse to the gun and violence; the rule of two forms of thuggery, one that of officially sanctioned law and order and the other that of the professional criminal. It is a question, which is eerily prophetic in terms of the later development of the United States: a country, which 'turned' to both fundamentalist religion and repressive politics in the years just after the Second World War, just at that point where Europe was becoming increasingly secular and sanctioning (for example in the landslide victory of the Labour Party in Britain in 1945) new political interests. Indeed, with the single example of the British attempt to retake the Suez Canal in 1956, much of Europe, in the years after the Second World War, has been consistently more liberal and progressive (certainly in its domestic politics) than the United States. Yet, part of the paradox of Hammett's writing is that while he, a self-defined social radical is writing stories which suggest the widespread corruption of both legal and illegal forms of enterprise in the United States, he is also, through the isolated, entirely singular central characters that he creates, perpetuating the mythical figure of the lone moralist, the one 'good' person among webs of deceit and greed.

Stein's conversation with Hammett (which took place long before there existed an academic literature on the collapse of masculinity or the femininization of society) is important in that it shows how conscious Hammett was of the moral vacuum in the United States, not just in terms of the country as a whole but equally in terms of the authority of the male. Writing in 1934, in an introduction to *The Maltese Falcon,* Hammett said of his central character, Sam Spade:

> Spade had no original. He is a dream man in the sense that he is what most of the private detectives I worked with would like to have been and what quite a few of them in their cockier moments thought they approached. For your private detective does not – or did not ten years ago when he was my colleague – want to be an erudite solver of riddles in the Sherlock Holmes manner; he wants to be a hard and shifty fellow, able to take care of himself in any situation, able to get the best of any-body he comes in contact with, whether criminal, innocent by-stander, or client.[15]

Here is precisely that twentieth century man who had been the subject of the discussion between Stein and Hammett: a man lacking in both social and sexual confidence and hence having to exaggerate, for both effect and purpose, a sense of his isolation from relationships with others, his refusal of feeling and his aggressive and essentially entrepreneurial ('get the best of anybody he comes in contact with') in his attitude to the social world. This is the character who has dominated much of Hollywood, the archetypi-cal 'hard man' in a tradition, which stretches from John Wayne to Arnold Schwarzenegger – the man who is always alone and who is never to be corralled by the demands of domesticity or the ties of affection. Of course, this same 'hard man' is a great believer in the conventional arrangements of the domestic space, but such ways of life are not for him. This 'dream man', as Hammett describes him, was to have a huge hold on the American psyche. Yet, at the same time as this isolated 'hard' man was being con-structed in the novels of Hammett and Chandler (and countless imitators) as well as in the films of John Ford, the United States was also building (in this case quite literally) a suburban world, which was to become a proto-type for cities across the globe.

While these new suburban cities demanded, in the individual dwellings which were part of them, space and money for their construction, they also demanded two central characters, one of whom was the husband and pro-vider, the other the American version of that well-known character – the angel in the house. While the first angels in the houses of the British bour-geoisie (and other rather more lowly households) had been able to rely on servants for the performance of most household tasks, the new suburban homes had to rely on machinery and the willing participation in domestic life of both adult participants: the wife as the user of household machinery and the husband as its provider. This equation, as already suggested, did not sit any more easily with many Americans (both male and female) than it did within the imagination of American writers and film directors. The United States, in the 1920s and 1930s, was arguably moving in two different directions as far as models of masculinity were concerned: the one of the lone male, the bringer of moral order to a lawless society and the other the integrated, domesticated male who was a willing participant in the purchase and support of the American house and home.

Perhaps inevitably, one of the characteristics of the United States in the first part of the twentieth century (and indeed since that time) was that it had a divorce rate which was significantly higher than in other parts of the world. To fit the mythical lone male in the 'little boxes' of suburbia was not always successful, and the distance between the man who was supposed to be provider and figure of strength and the actual male human being was always considerable. By the 1930s, many men had decided that women were to blame for what was perceived as emasculation: women, male writers argued, only saw men as providers, and men were forever chained to the demands of the domestic space. The Second World War allowed a greater space for traditionally male pursuits, but once that conflict was over, male voices returned to the thesis of demasculinization. Little wonder, perhaps, that the most famous male stars of Hollywood in the 1940s and 1950s made their names playing either literally the heroes of Chandler or Hammett or some version of the same person. Humphrey Bogart is just one example of the construction of a mythical cinema presence via Hammett and via the refusal of an individual man to be corralled by female demands.

Hammett, a friend and lover to many women, would no doubt be appalled to find himself described in terms of participation (however unwitting) in the sex and gender 'wars' of the United States. Hammett gives women a central place in his fiction, although he stops short of allowing women that central moral space that later women writers of detective fiction were to claim for their characters. But Hammett, like writers of detective writers on both sides of the Atlantic, allows women to be bad, and bad in ways that are often more than simply complicity with male deviance. In this context, Hammett shares with Agatha Christie, Georges Simenon and many other famous writers of detective fiction the acceptance of 'evil' as a gender-free quality. There is, however, one qualification to this assertion. Hammett's women characters are quite capable of murder (usually with rather ladylike but nevertheless ruthlessly effective small hand guns), and they murder for much the same reasons as men, usually greed and social gain of some kind. But women, in both Hammett and Chandler, 'use' men for their own ends, and what is striking about the work of both men, in the context of a society that was attempting to uphold its own version of the 'angel in the house', was that men, in the pages of the most famous and best-selling detective fiction of the age, saw women as anything but angels.

The domestic ties that could bind men to house, home and women did not sit easily with other aspects of ideologies about men and masculinity in the United States in the years between 1930 and 1950. In Hammett's *The Thin Man*, a gloriously happy heterosexual couple (Nick and Nora Charles and their famous dog, Asta) are the central characters, and here, in hotel rooms and in a constant round of drinks, readers are given a glimpse at a male version of a successful heterosexual relationship. Yet, what is significant about this relationship, both in print and when translated to the screen, is the way in which Nora and Nick communicate: part banter, part shared jokes and always with a sense of openness about what can be said between men and women. After a burst of minor affray in the Charles's hotel room, one of the hastily summoned 'official' detectives says of Nora, 'admiringly', 'there's a woman with hair on her chest'.[16]

This aside suggests that while the ideological construction of women in the first half of the twentieth century contained much that sought to emphasize the passivity, the helplessness and the general irrationality of women, there were other, equally important cultural strands, which publicly praised women with intelligence and determination. Again, this would suggest, *contra* Mandel, that far from its constant allegiance to conventional values, the writers of detective fiction often expressed different and dissenting views about human relationships and indeed the moral order of the social world. Hammett and Chandler (and their fellow citizen and fellow writer of detective fiction Ed McBain) positively endorse female agency and have very little time for dependent and passive women. These views were in direct opposition to much of the culture of the domestic and the domestication of women, which prevailed in public life in the United States in the period just after the Second World War. One particularly successful publication of these years, *Modern Women: The Lost Sex* by Ferdinand Lundberg and Marynia Farnham (published in 1947) was unequivocal on the proper state of womanhood. The goal of female sexuality, proclaimed the authors is:

. . . receptivity and passiveness, a willingness to accept dependence without fear or resentment, with a deep inwardness and readiness for the final goal of sexual life – impregnation.[17]

Those unhappy women who do not accept this concept of femininity will
be 'miserable, the half-satisfied, the frustrated, the angered'.

Lundberg and Farnham's book was a bestseller in the United States, even
though just a few years later Simone de Beauvoir's *The Second Sex* (whose
views about women were rather different) was also to be widely read. Two
issues are important here: the first is that detective fiction, particularly in
the case of the most esteemed and the most popular writers in the genre
did not endorse or replicate a passive female/active male binary of human
agency. The second is that what is made clear by the diverse views of the
time about gender appropriate behaviour is that tensions and differences
of opinion of the place of women and men in the social world was an issue
in every decade of the twentieth century and not only in those decades,
most prominently the 1970s, when it is usually assumed that feminism was
influential. There was always, if not a woman's movement, then at least, and
among both women and men, a commitment and discussion about sexual
equality.

The period just after the end of the Second World War was a period in
which, in both Great Britain and the United States, there were both ideological and institutional attempts to persuade or more explicitly direct,
women to give up those jobs which they had held during the war.[18] It was
also, for all the Allies, a period in which they could bask in the sense of a
task well done, the awful spectre of a Nazi victory defeated and a war fought
and won that had general political and public support. The Second World
War, unlike the First, became (and has continued as such in the mythology
of the west) a *good* war, a justified war. Inevitably, this created moral problems for readers of Hammett's work: here was a man who seemed to be
suggesting that this valiant society, which had just defeated a wicked enemy,
was a place of moral confusion and chaos. This view was put very clearly
in a review of Hammett's work in the *Times Literary Supplement* of December
1950.[19] Hammett was berated by the reviewer for the 'nihilistic intransi-
gence of his heroes'. Hammett was pleased about the review (he said in
correspondence that the review was 'awfully stuffy and pompous, of course,
but I guess its still the most influential publication in the world') but did
not see his heroes as nihilistic.[20] For Hammett, his characters Sam Spade
and Nick Charles showed the world up as the confused and contradictory
place that it was and tried to restore a little order to it.

'Order' and especially ideological order was to become a central concern
in the later years of Hammett's life, and it was in the final years of his life
that he found himself prosecuted by the US government for his political
views. The moral authority, which the outcome of the Second World War

had given to the United States, allowed it to suggest to its own citizens that the political order that defeated Hitler was the only legitimate political order in the world: the Cold War had begun. It is thus in the 1950s that there is an increasing coincidence in the writing of detective fiction in the United States of moral authority in the conventional forces of law and order: the private eye becomes the marginal character, and the moral torch is passed to detectives such as those who make up the staff of Ed McBain's fictional *87th Precinct* – an urban location in an unnamed city, albeit one, which bears a close relationship to New York.

Ed McBain (also known as Evan Hunter or Richard Marsten or Hunt Collins) published his first novel in 1956 and over the remaining years of his life (he died in 2005) wrote a series of books about the various detectives of the 87th Precinct. From the first book, McBain did not shy away from presenting the impact and the reality of crime in the twentieth century city: his writing takes something of an imaginative leap from the focus on those dynamics between individuals that lead to murder to the wider dynamics of the social origins of crime. Equally, the novels about the 87th Precinct, while they do not entirely conform to what later became known as the 'police procedural novels', do emphasize that much of the work of detection is not about the intelligence and the determination of one man but about the work of teams of people, working together with considerable assistance by various forms of technology. It is thus that detective fiction makes something of a rather overdue technological leap, as well as making a step towards the recognition, in print, of the reality of much of police work. The early works of many previous writers of detective fiction (Christie, Simenon, many 'golden age' writers, Hammett and Chandler) acknowledge the importance of such evidence of criminal activity as finger prints and types of bullet, but they are generally much less concerned with this than the excellence of the 'little grey cells' possessed by their various detectives. It is always, in the work of these writers, human *intelligence* that leads to the unmasking of the villain. The form that the intelligence takes can vary from the more or less sedentary (although far from inert) *personae* of Miss Marple and Hercule Poirot to the more visibly athletic characters of Wimsey and Sam Spade. Furthermore, all these characters are essentially (or actually in the case of Miss Marple) amateurs in that they have received little or no training in detection.

For Hammett and other writers (on both sides of the Atlantic), the evidence of crime plays a part less in its detection than in ensuring that should a crime (and criminals) come to trial then they will be convicted. Getting a conviction has long been a major concern of democratic police forces

throughout the world and to this end forensic science has been developing
since the end of the nineteenth century. It was at this point that fingerprint-
ing was first developed, initially for the identification of possible criminals
in the countries of the British Empire rather than in the cities of Britain
and the United States.[21] Various forms of the detection of possible poisons
in the body became known in the early twentieth century, and the art of
the autopsy became increasingly sophisticated as the century went on.
Nevertheless, confession of a crime by its perpetrator remained much
favoured by the majority of authors until well into the second half of the
twentieth century. Often provoked by some kind of verbal trickery (Agatha
Christie remained particularly enthusiastic about this form of denouement),
many authors chose to close their novels with human recognition of human
transgression. The perpetrators of evil, suddenly outwitted by detectives
would confess all, thus absolving the police force from the tedious business
of collecting evidence and taking evidence from countless individuals.

What becomes clear, and hence in part the title of this chapter, is that in
the detective fiction of the United States of the 1930s and the 1950s, there
is a relationship between detection (and particularly private detectives)
and the law which is at best difficult and at times positively antagonistic.
Hammett's politics were such that he was well aware of the coercive power
of the state and the lengths to which the rich and powerful would go to
make sure that their version of events dominated the social and political
worlds. Yet, although the politics of both Chandler and (later) McBain did
not belong as closely as Hammett's to the left of the political spectrum,
both these authors suggest dissatisfaction and a distance from the formal
legal system and from the explicit political values of the United States.
Indeed, the picture painted in the novels of all these writers (and McBain
continued to write from the 1950s to the 1980s) was of a social world in
which the moral boundaries between crime and the forces of law and order
were often, at best, murky.

We can read this perception of the moral ambivalence of detectives (be
they employed by the state or acting as private investigators) in various ways.
First, the fictional pictures of the moral (or immoral) collusion between
criminal and detective in the United States could be read as an accurate
picture of crime everywhere, rather than in one society. Second, we might
consider that the British refusal to recognize possible corruption in the
police force was part of a British delusion about the probity of all institutions of the British state; on the British side of the Atlantic, it was simply
impossible (prior to the novels, for example, of Ian Rankin), for publishers

and public even to consider that policemen might take bribes, cover up evidence, and in various other ways act at least as badly as the villains they were supposed to be bringing to trial. A third possibility is more empirically based: that corruption in the police forces of the United States, particularly in the years after Prohibition and during the post-1929 Depression was a product of a society fractured by both rigid forms of moral censure and widespread poverty and insecurity. In this context, it was perhaps not surprising that policemen (and lawyers) were often willing to take bribes and, in acting savagely towards criminals, act out their own guilt as much as those more obviously guilty.

The question which confronted writers of detective fiction in the United States in the 1940s and the early 1950s was less about how their heroes might catch villains and rather more about how they might communicate a sense of moral order to their readers. A way out of this impasse, since many readers were unlikely to be convinced by simple assertions about the integrity of police forces was the path taken by those fictional police forces described by Ed McBain in the United States and Georges Simenon in France. Simenon (born in Belgium but living for much of his adult life in France and later Switzerland) had started to write his detective stories in 1931 and in all, he was to write 76 titles in the Inspector Maigret series. From the first, many of these accounts of Maigret's various cases had dwelt upon (in the same way as Hammett and Chandler), the difficulty of establishing clear moral lines between the worlds of 'respectable' society and the world of the criminal. For example, in the *The Man Who Watched the Trains Go By* (first published in France in 1938), the plot involved a hitherto upstanding, conventional citizen who had turned to murder when his firm had become bankrupt. In his characteristically economical style, Simenon describes the way in which financial collapse changes the character of this man's world. After his arrest, the murderer tries to explain this to a visiting doctor:

> You cannot imagine how simple everything became, one I had come to this decision. No more reason to worry about what so-and-so might think, what was forbidden or permitted, proper or improper.[22]

The doctor interviewing the murderer finds him hard to understand; yet this is part of Simenon's argument: that those within the normative moral order of bourgeois society are unable to comprehend understand both the fragility of its morality and its relationship to a material order. Take away the material prosperity and the apparent certainties of the ownership of wealth and little is left. The final words of *The Man Who Watched the Trains Go By* are spoken by the murderer: 'Really, there isn't any truth, is there, doctor?'

Simenon, like many other Europeans of his generation, was to discover after 1939 that the 'total war', which broke out would sweep away many expectations of an ordered moral universe. But in the years after the war, as a consensus emerged that the Second World War had been a war 'worth fighting', a new set of alliances between the state and the detective became apparent. It was, after all, the Allied states that had taken on Nazi Germany and in doing so, had suggested that a bureaucratic order was not necessarily corrupt or incompetent. This point was not lost on the writers of detective fiction: no longer was there quite so much need for the hero to be the lone hero fighting evil, there was now a possibility that institutions could possess, and exhibit, moral qualities and that in the internal relationships of these various bureaucracies there could be (as Simenon and various other writers of detective fiction were to suggest) warm and affectionate friendships and patterns of cooperation.

If the defeat of Hitler had given detective fiction a new sense of the moral possibilities of the institutional order, it was destined to be a relatively short lived view. It was not the case that after 1945 detective fiction turned back to the lone detective pursing the criminal but that the difficulties put in the way of detectives began to assume a different form. This led, as the following chapters will suggest, to two developments in detective fiction: first, the emergence of the female private investigator: the women who took up the mantel of Sam Spade and his colleagues and pitted their wits against the forces of both crime and law and order. The second development was that male policemen, no longer the individual entrepreneurs of the fight against crime but men employed by the state, with pensions and promotions to worry about, were increasingly beset less by corruption than by a new bureaucratic order of form-filling and 'correct' procedure. Without exception, the widely read (and televised) male detectives of the 1960s onwards are men who are deeply uncomfortable within the world of the police force turned corporation; they systematically subvert managerial expectations and are constantly at war with the expectations of an audit culture.

Simenon was among the first to recognize this aspect of police work. In one of the more remarkable book of the series of the Maigret novels (*Maigret and the Idle Burglar*), Simenon allows Maigret to take two moral positions, which have various implications for police work in reality. The first of these positions is that in the novel, Maigret, unlike some of his fellow officers, refuses to dismiss the murder of a burglar as of little or no importance. To Maigret, the burglar was a murdered human being and as such this man has a right to have his death investigated and the perpetrator of the crime brought to justice. For police forces all over the world, the social status of the victim was, and continues to be, an issue of some importance: the police procedure in Britain at the time of the 'Ripper' murders in Yorkshire was a vivid example of how the police could choose to ignore the murders of those individuals deemed socially inferior. The public outcry at the incompetent and half-hearted investigation of the murders of prostitutes was precisely the kind of public response that Simenon wished to encourage.

The second particular interest of Simenon's *Maigret and the Idle Burglar* is Simenon's account in the novel of the transformation of the police force in which Mairgret works and the impact of new recruitment and regulatory systems within the force. Here is Maigret (being attended, as ever, by the loving Madame Maigret) but depressed at the way the police force is developing:

> The place was being reorganised, as they called it. Well-educated gentlemanly young fellows, scions of the best French families, were sitting in quiet offices, studying the whole thing in the interests of efficiency. Their learned cogitations were producing impractical plans that found expression in a weekly batch of new regulations. To begin with, the police were now declared to be an instrument at the service of justice. A mere instrument. And an instrument has no brain . . . What was more, the orders were no longer to be carried out by the old-fashioned type of policeman, the traditional "flatties" such as Aristide Fumel, some of whom didn't know how to spell.
>
> Now that it was nearly all paperwork, what was to be done with such men, who had all learnt their jobs in the streets, the department stores and the railway stations, getting to know every drinking den in their own districts, acquainted with every tough and every tart, and able, if need be, to argue with them in their own language?
>
> Now they had to sit for exams and obtain certificates at every step of their career, and when he needed to organise a raid, Maigret had nobody to rely on except the few survivors of his old team.[23]

The passage could be the elegy of many people who have worked in public or private institutions and found, that throughout the twentieth century, there was a gradual increase in the size of many organizations but something of a decrease in the flexibility of working and employment practices. Maigret (and/or Simenon) might be more inclined to see this in a negative sense than those who would argue that many of the innovations in work-place conventions (equal opportunities quotas, health and safety at work regulations and so on) have a positive value for all employees. Maigret (in the same way as latter British detectives such as Morse, Frost and Rebus) loathes and despises paper work, and those who generate it: as a genre detective fiction speaks more than any other as the voice of those oppressed by over-regulated employment. (Nor is it the case that it is only in detective fiction set in the contemporary west that we can observe this dislike of the bureaucratic: in Boris Akunin's detective fiction set in Tsarist Russia and Leonardo Padura's novels set in Castro's Cuba the heroes express similar feelings.[24]) If at least some crime remains the most perfect form of individual entrepreneurship, then it is mirrored by the affection with which many policemen hold for the idiosyncratic, individual form of detection.

There is, in detective fiction after the years in which Chandler and Hammett wrote, little that suggests that police forces are anything but imperfect institutions, only able to correct the worst excesses of human behaviour rather than prevent them taking place. This emphasis, which runs counter to many of the 'mission statements' of police forces and ever hopeful governments that the police will prevent crime, suggests that in point of fact (at least as far as the 'fact' of fiction is concerned) that the work of the detective has advanced little since the days of 'hue and cry' and other forms of the entrapment of villains. Yet, at the same time because fictional detectives (and their creators) remain deeply sceptical about the institutional response to crime, there remains a sense in which a certain hope about moral order is still maintained, even if that hope – very clearly – does not depend upon better management or organization. But, in this scepticism, detective fiction perhaps speaks for one of the major lessons, which the twentieth century west might have learned from its own history: that bureaucratic order is not 'good' in itself; it is only good if it is put to work for commendable principles. The lessons of the persecution of various dissenters, for example, political minorities and Jews in Hitler's Germany speaks to the moral neutrality of bureaucratic order: there was 'order' in this persecution, and it was certainly 'rational' (in the sense of being extensively considered) but it was immoral in the fullest sense.

The individuals who wrote detective fiction in the 1930s, 1940s and 1950s all saw the various tragedies of the Second World War unfold. But, they also recognized that these tragedies came about not through the absence of public order but through the reverse: of a sense of order, which marginalized differences and could only hate those who seemed in some way to challenge the new orthodoxy. The internal, personal chaos of those individuals most responsible for various diasporas of 1939–45 has been the subject of many psychoanalytic works: however literally disordered are the lives of fictional detectives, one characteristic that they do not share with these individuals is a wish to impose order on the world. Indeed, the political tradition of detective fiction, which emerges in the west in the latter years of the twentieth century, is in many ways, anarchic. Detectives have no wish to see murderers roaming the streets, but other than that they have no ambitions to mould the world in their own created image. Despite the moral fervour that the media can sometimes exhibit about crime (and this fervour, as the case of the Yorkshire Ripper illustrates is not necessarily a fervour of simplistic revenge), detective fiction, read by quite as many people as those who regularly read the newspapers, is generally free from crusading impulses about the 'defeat' of crime and criminals even if, as David Peace's novels suggest, there are certainly crusades to make the police more effective.[25]

The detective fiction of the latter part of the twentieth century acts, therefore, as something of a corrective to the idea that the western public views crime (and criminals) as a terrifying social phenomenon and one to which vast, retributive resources should be directed. Although the past decades have seen campaigns, throughout Europe and in the United States, for more police and harsher penalties for criminals, this public feeling exists alongside what can be read as a degree of accommodation with crime, at least insofar as crime is directed against property rather than the person. Part of the reason for this may well be that although in Britain (again as in Europe) the population as a whole no doubt regards itself as deeply and consistently law abiding ,the biography of more or less every person involves some minor criminal act, be it adolescent shoplifting, petty thefts from the workplace to tax dodging of some minor kind. If misusing the resources of an employer became a criminal offence, then it is likely that the entire British work force might be arraigned on criminal charges.

The ongoing battle between employed and employee, between the rich and the poor, is seldom fought at the barricades or in explicit class warfare. But, it is fought in terms of the endless day-to-day negotiation between the public and the police, policemen and other policemen and between the powerful and the less powerful about what can be allowed, and what is termed unacceptable. This constant guerrilla activity is something which the writers of detective fiction often understand rather better that most politicians or other figures of public authority might care to admit. Indeed, in the past decade, we have seen, in Britain, the case of one prime minister,

Tony Blair, making himself ridiculous by the idea of on-the-spot fines for minor acts of civic disturbance. The impossibility of enforcing this rule, let alone the problem of defining exactly what constitutes a 'minor' act of civic disorder, epitomizes a refusal to recognize both the accommodative possibilities in the social world and the persistence of certain patterns of behaviour. The ability of the public to tolerate degrees of disorder and to change the boundaries of their toleration is visible in any historical account of the twentieth century. For example, dress codes change and – more importantly perhaps for the lives of many people – changes in attitudes to race and sexuality have reorganized the boundaries of the socially acceptable.

Many detectives, like many people, mourn the passing of certain kinds of codes of manners and socialization. But these same people recognize that they cannot change these shifts in public values. It brings many fictional detectives (as it must many real life policemen) to the point where they come to question the value of their work. A belief in the importance of a retributive state and a police force committed to this ideal is not an ideal that remains intact throughout the twentieth century. Indeed, as the century went on, there are an increasing number of fictional voices challenging the real value, except as ever in those few cases of premeditated and persistent murder, of police work and the vast edifice that defends it. It is more effective, as many writers suggest, to call individuals to correct the harmful excesses of other individuals.

Chapter 5

Are the Times a' Changing?

In 1963, two books were published in the United States that suggested that certain social assumptions (black people are inferior to white people; a woman's place is in the home) were about to be radically challenged. In neither case was the nature of the challenge novel; in both cases, there were long traditions of dissent and often furious rebellion at dominant views about the prevailing social orders of gender and race. But what was about to be unleashed (at first in the United States but rapidly across the west) were assertions about the social order which demanded wide-ranging structural and individual change. The two books, one fiction and the other non-fiction, were Betty Friedan's *The Feminine Mystique* and *The Expendable Man* by Dorothy Hughes. The title of Hughes's book, in the light of what was about to be said by sections of the women's movement about men, was especially prescient: the need for the independence and the autonomy of women was to become a central argument in western feminism in the 1970s and the 1980s.

Friedan's book, an immediate bestseller and often cited as one of the key books of what is known as Second Wave Feminism, was a non-fictional account of white, college-educated women, married and with children, going slowly crazy in their suburban households. Hughes's novel was about another potentially explosive current in the life of the people of the United States: in this case, not its sexism but its racism. *The Expendable Man* is about a black doctor who, on returning to his family home in the south of the United States, becomes a suspect in the murder, after an illegal abortion, of a teenage girl. In a wonderfully apt cover note to the recent Persephone Press edition of the novel, the editors note that 'in the 1950s domestic responsibilities led her (Dorothy Hughes) to concentrate on journalism'. Dorothy Hughes was, in fact, one of those women about whom Friedan was writing: an educated and successful woman who found that marriage and children closed the doors to creative work and access to the wider world.

Except, of course, that rather than going the way of many of those subjects of Friedan's work, Hughes maintained her professional life as a writer
and then wrote a novel which captured both the ordinary fears of black
people in the southern United States and the much greater fears, indeed
terror, of those people should they come into contact with the formal institutions of white society. In the same year that *The Expendable Man* was published, George Wallace had attempted to prevent racial integration at the
University of Alabama, and Medgar Evers, the head of the Mississippi branch
of the National Association for the Advancement of Coloured People, had
been shot dead outside his home. Race was, literally, an explosive issue, and
when the fictional hero of Hughes's novel, Dr Hugh Densmore, is taken to
the police station for questioning by Venner, the investigating detective, he
is, as his creator suggests, rightly terrified:

> Venner took westbound Washington across town. There were few other
> cars abroad. Even when they reached the downtown section. When they
> passed the courthouse without reducing speed, Hugh knew fear. He
> spoke up. 'Where are we going?'[1]

As it turns out, the party is on the way to the morgue to see the body of
the dead girl, the very same hitch-hiking girl to whom Densmore had given
a lift. Eventually, the story ends happily (at least for Densmore and his
family), but at the conclusion, there is also a despairing note about race
relations in the United States. The young black woman, to whom Densmore
is attracted, is asked by him if she would marry another, white, suitor. 'No,'
she replies, 'It's too soon. I'm not that strong'.

'Being strong' would have involved transgressing those unwritten (and
in some states of the United States, clearly written) laws about interracial
marriage. In this sense, *The Expendable Man* does not challenge all the normative boundaries around race, but what the novel does do, with great
effect, is give the reader a sense of what it might be like to live in a world
which makes instant (and usually negative) judgements about individuals
on the basis of their skin colour. People, being 'out of place', is one of the
great themes of social anthropology, and it is this refusal of being assigned
a social world and a social place that is common to both Hughes and
Friedan. Friedan's book does not address the question of race (indeed, her
subjects are more or less exclusively white) in the same way that Hughes
partly addresses the question of gender; but in their different ways, as much
as both address various forms of social segregation, they are also raising
the question of women and/or black people subverting and transgressing
social rules.

It was these possibilities of transgression that became so essential to the politics of the 1960s throughout the west. Transgression is itself no new aspect of western life, but the various forms of transgression that emerged in the 1960s and the 1970s had one significant difference from their previous manifestations: they were democratic, in the sense that transgressive forms (be they of appearance, behaviour or politics) became part of the worlds of entire, cross-class generations, rather than the preserve of a privileged few. In an article written in 1998, the sociologist Elizabeth Wilson had pointed out that at the beginning of the nineteenth century, 'The combination of aristocratic outlawry and underworld associations marked the emergent bohemian out as quintessentially anti-bourgeois'. In the same context, she also suggested that:

> We no longer believe in self control and sublimation, nor do we believe that familial duty must always triumph over wayward desire. The 19th-century bourgeoisie attempted to domesticate Gautier's 'modern love', but today liberal Western society has gone much further in adopting what is essentially a bohemian belief in the transcendent value of erotic passion as the touchstone for the authenticity of relations between the sexes . . . To the bohemians we partly owe the liaison between romanticism and consumer culture in which transgression, excess and the triumph of feeling and sensation triumph over more traditionally Enlightenment values . . . In this sense . . . we are all bohemians.[2]

It was not so much that the new values of the 1960s, as described by Wilson, took root across the west (many of the values were, as she suggests, already implicitly present in certain aspects and contexts of western culture), and became part of the everyday culture. Clothes, codes of manners, all kinds of consumer goods gave a material form to values that, once transgressive, rapidly became part of the conventional world. Many young people, across cultures and continents, began to discover that what had once been, if not outlawed, then at least the subject of widespread disapproval, had become possible and increasingly acceptable.

But this new cultural world was not achieved without hard-fought battles, in both personal and social worlds. Individual social rebels invariably had various forms of difficult times (although the enforcement of convention has differed widely across place and historical time), but in the 1970s, western societies began to legislate to transform the institutional world in ways that reflected changes in attitudes and expectations. In the United States, race relations became the subject of civil rights legislation, and across the west (although at different times and with different degrees of enthusiasm),

packages of legislation changed the law about many aspects of sexual relations, the various rights of husbands and wives within (and after) marriage
and about the relation of the individual to the state. The 'permissive' society,
as it was called with loathing and hatred by some and with enthusiasm by
others, began to allow a greater degree of freedom in the public expression
of those forms of personal behaviour – for example, homosexuality – that
had been publicly unacceptable.

This cultural transformation was to become, by the end of the twentieth
century, a western way of life, which has been both replicated in other cultures and at the same time, often passionately resisted. The extent of the
social space, in the west, for the diverse transformations of the 1960s and
the 1970s was considerable; in many ways, aspects of the cultural transformation went hand-in-hand with the constant needs of capitalism for new
markets and for the social creation of new consumer needs. For example,
the emergence of a specifically youth culture opened up vast new markets
and at the same time, made it dysfunctional to refuse to allow women full
access to the workforce and the use of consumer credit on the same terms
of men. Women, like youth, were new domestic markets, which carried
fewer risks and difficulties than markets in other countries.

Into this new world came, as certain aspects of human behaviour were
decriminalized, new forms of crime and new ways, both fictional and non-
fictional, of fighting crime. Most remarked upon was the 'new' woman
detective, the heroine of the novels by Sue Grafton, Sara Paretsky, Val
McDermid and others – women who happily embraced aspects of the permissive society (sexual freedom, autonomous ways of life and a refusal of
domesticity) and yet took up arms against crime. In some ways, the novelty
of the lives of the heroines of these writers is more apparent than real: the
heroines of the novels of Agatha Christie, Margery Allingham and Dorothy
Sayers had often been successful professionals, had lived alone and had
somewhat less than rosy views about the possibilities of domestic heterosexual bliss. But the imagination of readers in the late twentieth century was
seized by the 'new' women detectives, all of whom, at least in the United
States, had one entirely novel characteristic – they carried guns and were
quite prepared to shoot to kill.

This particular form of emancipation was part and parcel of an attitude
towards crime in the 1960s that increasingly saw it as part of a more general,
socially threatening, culture. In certain quarters, crime and especially what
seemed to be an increase in crime, was associated with the new youth and
permissive culture. In opposition to this, but as much part of the loss of
moral hegemony in western morality in the 1960s, was what became known

as the 'new criminology'. This new criminology, which had its origin in academic work on crime, took a view of crime that was highly sceptical of both policing and many of the boundaries drawn between the illegal and the legal. Thus, for example, new criminology argued that stigmatization through arrest and prosecution, particularly for socially disputed crimes such as the possession of 'soft' drugs, only created more criminals and more resistance to police work in general. At the same time, this new criminology, particularly in the work of Steven Box, emphasized the different degrees of police energy devoted to white collar and corporate crime as opposed to crimes against property. (Within the same tradition, Belinda Morrissey has discussed those traditions which always assume that women are the victims of crime).[3] 'Crime' became a contested term and what was – or was not – criminal became (and has remained) a matter of intense public debate. What was also part of this contestation was an increasingly widespread recognition of the collusion of aspects of the apparently criminal and the non-criminal world. In the worlds created by Paretsky, Grafton and McDermid, there is a scepticism about the behaviour (and the morality) of the conventional world, which is as great as anything in the work of those other great twentieth century sceptics about the morality, both personal and social, of the bourgeoisie, Brecht and Thomas Mann.

In the histories of the 1960s and the 1970s (be they autobiographical accounts or more dispassionate academic histories), there is something of a tendency to assume that, as Philip Larkin put it, 'sexual intercourse began in nineteen sixty-three' and to write as if no homosexual relations or heterosexual relations outside marriage had existed before this magical, transformatory year.[4] Any glance at fiction in the past 200 years will demonstrate that this is not the case, even if the nature of certain relationships is a matter of implicit rather than explicit discussion by the author. No such inhibitions affected the writing of the women writers of detective fiction in the years after 1963: all of them gave their heroines active (and varied) sexual lives, and all of them had attitudes towards the police that suggested a very high degree of continuity and agreement with the heroes of Chandler and Hammett. This, perhaps, is the first most important characteristic of many contemporary women writers of detection, even if these young women who dissent from respect for formal policing exist in the same library spaces as those women writers (such as P. D. James), who are consistently positive and supportive about the police.

The question of women (and gender) and the police is an area in which there is no overall authorial agreement. In the work of Paretsky, Grafton, McDermid, the central characters (V. I. Warshawski, Kinsey Millhone, Lindsay

Gordon and Kate Brannigan, respectively) view the police with some scepticism not least because, in the view of the heroines, the police are all too eager to accept the view of the powerful and the conventional. The police will not, in these novels, think 'outside the box' in terms of the possible identity of both the murderer/criminal and the nature and motive of the crime. In Paretsky, in particular, whose work, both fictional and non-fictional, has become an increasingly determined attack on the values and the policies of corporate America, the police are all too willing to accept the view that wealth and virtue are always related. Although the fictional V. I. Warshawski (the daughter of a policeman) has not abandoned all respect for many ordinary policemen, she has also come to question the ethical standards of the police force and lawyers and in particular that Protestant view which suggests that the accumulation of worldly goods is a sign of a search for possible redemption. This most Protestant of Protestant views is contested, appropriately enough, by a woman from a Roman Catholic background. V. I. Warshawski has long abandoned the beliefs of the Catholic Church; yet she nevertheless retains a sense of the different religious communities of the United States and the different social and political experiences that have followed from this. Warshawski's social radicalism does not come, Paretsky makes clear, from Roman Catholicism itself but from the social marginality of Catholic immigrants into the United States. Faced with representatives of white Anglo-Saxon Protestant communities (who are, in Paretsky's work, more than likely to be the employees of exploitative corporations), Warshawski speaks as a representative of the underprivileged in the American dream. Thus, for example, she confronts a man who has been complicit in ensuring that workers do not get adequate health insurance from their employers:

> I was too appalled to speak. His words came out so glibly that they must have been spoken hundreds of times at committee meetings or before the board of directors. Let's just see what are work-force costs will be if we know that X percent of our employees will be sick Y Fraction of the time. . . . run different cost projections tediously by hand in the days before computers . . . The enormity of the whole scheme made me murderous with rage.[5]

The strength of the passage, and the extent of V. I. Warshawski's/Sara Paretsky's fury is not disguised here, nor is it just a fictional rage against a fictional phenomenon. Millions of people in the real world of the United States do not have health insurance, and both in the United States and in other parts of the world, many corporations (and smaller employers) have records that are far from unsullied in terms of the forms of health and safety protection that is offered to employees.

That same kind of political rage about aspects of the organization of the social and political world informs the fiction of Sue Grafton and Val McDermid. What is interesting about these writers (and others, such as Katherine V. Forrest and Sarah Caudwell whose work can be described as highly politicized detective fiction) is that this group of women authors explicitly make use of the genre of detective fiction in order to further what they present as political agendas. Among those agendas are the general heartlessness and lack of concern about individuals of the corporate world, the complicity of many western states and their institutions with those worlds and the various forms of deceit which are practised in order to disguise diverse forms of malpractice. None of the authors mentioned are particularly (or only) censorious of police forces; as frequently guilty of deception and corruption are white-collar professionals (lawyers and doctors in particular) and those women who are dependent upon the earnings of their male partners for a privileged lifestyle. Indeed, these women are often described with particular venom by women authors, as if their own hard-earned independence (and that of their heroines) is affronted by the parasitic existence of the 'kept' wives. Yet that theme, of the lengths to which women are prepared to go in order to make financially advantageous marriages is reiterated in the fiction of Grafton, Paretsky and McDermid. These women, all of whom grew up in a world changed by the arguments and ideas of Friedan and the later feminist authors, make detective fiction a place in which those battles between conventional and radical expectations of gender are played out. The idea of a 'female eunuch' seems to have been particularly influential. For example, in Sue Grafton's *S is for Silence* (a Kinsey Millhone novel published in 2003), conventional values about marriage, and the determination of a young woman to marry 'well' provide the motive for murder. The 'silence', which is referred to in the novel's title, is the silence of the community about what happened: a form of silence, which, while censorious of murder, is not prepared to acknowledge the extent of its complicity in the values that led to it.

Grafton, Paretsky and McDermid are all part of a generation which grew up within the various cultural transformations of the 1960s and the political sympathies of all these novelists are with various forms of left-wing politics. But, far more important than these politics (which are evident enough), all the writers share a commitment to the idea that women should be able to live independent lives, choose the form of their sexuality and escape that domestic imprisonment which they see as the lot of previous generations and those unable to avoid it in their own. The values of *The Feminine Mystique* are alive and well throughout the work of this group of writers. However, while their work might be seen as innovative within the confines of detective fiction, there is perhaps less real difference with previous fiction than is often supposed. Undoubtedly, these women (Paretsky et al.) are women with guns, and they are women with their own homes, bank accounts and highly developed sense of personal autonomy. At the same time, while the form which their agency takes (varied sexual partners, freedom of movement and so on) is undeniably part of the late twentieth century western world, there is also a sense in which they share with their male fellow detectives of the 1930s and the 1940s (the generation of male private detectives), all the traditional characteristics of the individual moral agent. These women are, just as much as Sam Spade or Philip Marlowe, determined to take action – sometimes, virtually a form of revenge – on individual acts of wrongdoing. Women detectives thus become less 'angels in the house' and more appropriately described as 'avenging angels'. The values that inform Warshawski, Millhone and others are in many ways exactly the same as the values that inform their male predecessors: this is less a revolution in detection but rather the continuity of retribution. Indeed, by 1995, Val McDermid had allowed one of her heroines Carol Jordon to become a police officer. Here, Carol explains her reasons for joining the police force to a colleague:

> It all started when I read sociology at Manchester. I specialised in the sociology of organisations, and all my contemporaries despised the police force as a corrupt, racist, sexist organisation whose sole role was to preserve the illusory comfort of the middle classes. To some extent I agreed with them. The difference was that they wanted to attack institutions from the outside, whereas I've always believed that if you want fundamental change, it has to come from inside.[6]

Not, perhaps, a view, which Marlowe and Spade would have entirely endorsed, but one which certain male writers of detective fiction (for example Michael Malone) were endorsing at the same time, with the added intention, in the case of the characters in Malone's novels, of rooting out not just financial corruption in the police force but sexism and racism as well. Yet at the same time as Malone's heroes were re-moralising the police force, the parallel tradition of male private detectives continued in novels such as John MacDonald's Travis McGee series.[7]

Across the years between Marlowe and Spade and the 'women with guns' of the 1970s onwards, there lies an ongoing narrative of individual attempts to make good the failings and the disappointments of the social world. Both groups of detectives share the attitudes of outsiders and the socially marginal to the conventional world; yet, at the same time, there is a consistent refusal of anything approaching collective action. Two questions are important here: the first is that in these continuities of detective fiction, we can see, written very clearly, an aspect of the moral assumptions of the twentieth century west: although there is definitely such a thing as society (which is, according to all the authors, generally negative in its social implications), it is only in the individual that a moral sense can be fully developed. The social, in fact, more generally negates morality since it is in the social (in convention, the greed for money and/or power) that the motives for murder lie. The question that can be asked of detective fiction is that of the degree to which this form of fiction is explicitly restorative; that is, whether or not detective fiction takes as its unwritten theme the idea of restoring order, justice and honesty to a world which has lost sight of these characteristics. Yet in that, and certainly in the human characteristics of the various detectives, there remains a degree of adolescent angst and that form of adolescence, which refuses, like Peter Pan, to engage with adult life. Like the children of warring parents, many detectives wish to heal disunity; yet, that healing is also about maintaining a safe space in which they can remain as adolescents. Thus, the problem of growing older besets many of the fictional characters of detective fiction: long midnight chases after villains and endless nights without sleep may be possible for those characters in their twenties. The ordinary process of ageing, however, suggests that the career of detection cannot last for long, in the same way as the child or adolescent cannot endlessly seek to repair the problems of their parents.

Female detectives with guns (rather than female murderers with guns) constitute a central innovation in detective fiction, even if the degree by which this is valuable is debateable. On the one hand, it has been observed (for example by Simone de Beauvoir) that respect is given 'not to the sex, which brings forth but to that which kills' and in this sense, women detectives with guns represents an equalizing shift.[8] On the other, the generalization of a gun culture might not seem to epitomize social progress. Although the novels and authors already mentioned all concern women who glory in their solitary state, and in their solitary action, there is another sense in which women and 'the feminine' come to inform detective fiction from the 1960s onwards. It is that various authors, writing in the same decades as Paretsky and others either 'feminise' their male detectives or give male detectives a female colleague (or colleagues). Masculinity as such, alone (or partnered by another male) begins to be something of a rare trait in the detective fiction of the late twentieth century. This shift is accompanied by two other recent organizing themes of detection: the first is the theme of the detective at war with institutional order; Inspectors Morse, Frost and Rebus, are the British trio who embody this theme. The second is the alliance of women detectives and/or forensic scientists with the technology of detection – a genre of detective fiction made famous by Patricia Cornwell.

The 'feminisation' of the twentieth century has long been a theme in both social and cultural history. The idea was first most comprehensively outlined by Ann Douglas in her work about the culture of the United States.[9] Although it is difficult to accept the thesis as a whole, given the extensive militarization of the twentieth century, there is also the sense in which we might interpret the excessively brutal and extravagantly vicious military activity of the past 100 years as less a symptom of the hubris of the masculine and rather more as its reaction to fears of the feminine and the possible inherent emasculation. The destabilization of the certainties of gender identity together with the literary voice of subjectivity in European modernism, while unlikely to have been the sole inspirations for the emergence of the all-conquering masculinity of European fascism, did pose, and has posed, a long-term question mark over what are often rigidly constructed certainties of gender. For writers of detective fiction, this has brought to greater prominence the question of how guilt, and the guilty party, is to be discovered. In the 1920s and 1930s, the great majority of detective writers, male and female, made considerable allowance for what they variously discovered as 'instinct' or 'feeling'. Both these qualities, traditionally associated with women and the feminine, were seen as in opposition to those masculine versions of police work, which put great emphasis on the existence of 'facts' and 'evidence'. Indeed, we might conjecture that the socially marginal qualities of those famous detectives Miss Marple and Hercule Poirot are essential to their unique blend of qualities; both have an astute intelligence and a willingness to refuse to accept the authority of the socially orthodox. Thinking across the conventional lines and demarcations of gender has always been socially transgressive; during the same time as societies have sanctioned and allowed it (for example the cross-dressing of the Elizabethan theatre and more recently, the rich comic and visual traditions of 'camp' sexuality), there has also always been a rigorous determination to maintain gender certainties.

By the 1960s and 1970s, however, many sections of western society had come to accept, for a variety of reasons, that rigid distinctions of gender were as much socially dysfunctional as they were of use. Various forms of public campaigns attempted to shift those social divisions (particularly in education and the work place) that seemed to perpetuate 'male' and 'female' worlds. In practice, many gender divisions, in various social contexts, stayed in place. But, in detective fiction, the feminine, either in terms of male interest in 'feminine' pursuits or in the form of female human beings, came to play a significant part. It is in this sense that the feminized male detective is arguably more modern and more innovative than the lone female detective: the latter continues a tradition, which dates back to Sherlock Holmes, while the former is more at home with the gender uncertainties of the late twentieth century.

The archetypical 'feminised' detective of the late twentieth century is Adam Dalgleish, the fictional detective created by P. D. James. Dalgleish is a senior policeman, working in London, a widower whose wife died (with their baby son) in childbirth. So far, so conventional: the difference is that Dalgleish is also a published poet, with personal tastes that demonstrate a consistent interest in the arts and high culture. Yet, as unrepresentative as Dalgleish might be assumed to be (both in fiction and in reality), it is important to recall that Lord Peter Wimsey, albeit an amateur sleuth rather than an employee of the state, was a man of the same highly developed sensibilities as Dalgleish. Indeed, it is arguable that Wimsey only became a detective because he was exposed, in the First World War, to traditional masculinity in its most aggressive form. The experiences of the trenches gave to Wimsey what the tragedy of his personal life reinforced in Dalgleish, a sensitivity to both human suffering and to the extent of the human capacity for evil. Here is Dalgleish musing about the suffering of a woman condemned to death:

> Dalgleish was silent. Ever since, as an eleven-year-old, he had read of that distraught and drugged woman being half-dragged to her execution, the case had lain at the back of memory, heavy as a coiled snake. Poor dull Percy Thompson had not deserved to die but did anyone deserve what his widow had suffered during those last days in the condemned cell when she finally realised that there was a real world outside even more dangerous than her fantasies and there were men in it who, on a precise day at a precise hour, would take her out and judicially break her neck? Even as a boy the case had confirmed him as an abolitionist[10];

At the same time as various shifts in the representation of gender took place in the late twentieth century, and as tempting as it might be to assign these to developments in twentieth century culture, it is also important to recall that social definitions of both masculinity and femininity have always been complex and have never wholeheartedly refused sensitivity for men or intelligence for women. It is an inadequate view of human history, which assumes that until the various feminist movements of the late nineteenth and late twentieth century, there was no female autonomy or male sensitivity. But as far as detection is concerned, there are patterns of gender alignments, which suggest that in detective fiction, as much as in other form of work of the imagination, there remains a considerable debate about how to 'do' gender, and, in particular, how to relate gender to the process of discovery.

Dalgleish is therefore given, through his poetic gifts, the cultural 'sign' of sensitivity. At the same time, and in many of the novels about Dalgleish, P. D. James introduces a female detective, Kate Miskins, who is, in both class and gender terms, a foil to Dalgleish. Kate Miskins has had to fight her way out of poverty and deprivation to reach the ranks of detective; she has a consistently sharp (and vocal) awareness of class privilege, and she is often made the fictional locus of James's conservative politics. Here, women are useful, but they are also inherently subordinate. Kate is not at all the subaltern who does not speak (to borrow from the terminology of Gayatri Spivak); indeed, she is often vocal.[11] But, as a character, she is often disallowed by James, since Kate is taken to represent that 'partiality' of social inequality, which is presented as redolent of social unrest, envy and hostility towards those who are richer or more powerful.

The relationship between Dalgleish and Miskins, the sensitive man and the less sensitive woman, captures an alternative reading of gender relations in the late twentieth century west, which suggests that rather than society becoming feminized, masculinity has learned, to its own advantage, how to 'do' femininity. In a detailed study of the workings of the City of London (an environment not unlike the senior police force in its male culture and pattern of recruitment), Linda McDowell has described the way that femininity is a disservice, and socially (and professionally) negative for women but positive for men.[12] In this sense, Dalgleish embodies precisely that late twentieth century phenomenon of which McDowell is writing: the powerful and successful man who is made even more so by his public avowal of certain aspects of what is traditionally supposed to be femininity. Dalgleish, like the men in the City of London whom McDowell describes, is authoritative and determined in his actions; he has no hesitation in exercising his rank and status. But at the same time, he is also written as the man with an appreciation of what are often described as the 'finer' things of life, a description which suggests that 'life' (and particularly aesthetic appreciation) can be neatly compartmentalized into those things, which are 'fine' and those, which are less fine. Dalgleish, as a policemen, has to deal with a great deal of the rather less fine in his work; yet, in many of P. D. James's novels about him, the plots turn upon those whose professions (in the arts, literature and publishing) are much involved with the apparently 'finer' aspects of the world and most specifically high culture.

In the work of P. D. James, there is perhaps an attempt to resolve the various fissures of the social world (most specifically of class, morality and gender) through a central character who seems able to transcend these divisions. Through his intellect and his peripheral engagement with the world of the arts, Dalgleish suggests to readers that a traditional figure of authority in British (and indeed much of western) society can produce reconciliation and the restoration of social harmony. In order to do this, it seems to be important that Dalgleish is presented as a somewhat solitary figure; only in the most recent novels is Dalgleish given a personal life. Social relationships, and particularly intimate relationships, remain difficult to achieve, it would seem, for cerebral, authoritative white middle-class men. The problems of achieving (and maintaining) a personal and private life are set out by P. D. James; on more than one occasion, Dalgleish has to put his work first and in doing so, he disappoints the woman whom he loves. It is those instances, where Dalgleish does put his work over his personal life, that it is suggested to readers that important men in important jobs have no other choices; although Dalgleish has been 'modernised' to the extent that he is both able, and willing, to express his sensitivities in literature, what remains is a world in which professional commitment is, for men, uncritically allowed. As readers, we are never allowed to suppose, for example, that Dalgleish resents the demands and constraints of his job, whereas in the case of Kate Miskins, we are allowed to see that Kate often feels driven by the strains of her job and the extent to which it interrupts both her personal life and the claims of others (in her case, her grandmother) upon her.

The novels by P. D. James have attracted a considerable, world wide audience, although the plots are always set in the United Kingdom. The cultural diversity of the world appears, in the novels, within, rather than outside, Britain and to this extent again, there is an apparent sense in which James has 'modernised' the traditional figure of the sensitive male detective and his world: a tradition, which might be collectively referred to as 'The Wimsey Tradition'. Yet, in James's books, cultural difference and cultural variety is generally seen in terms of the meeting of essentially very different cultures; what is not suggested is that all cultures might be open, rather than sealed and derived from different strands and historical and social roots. In passing here, since this is the subject of later discussion, we might note that while 'modern' male detectives can, in certain senses, be 'modernised' (a modernization, which takes place largely through the association of a conventional white man with a capacity for sensitivity and aesthetic appreciation derived from an association with high culture), these men remain largely centred in homogeneous and largely closed white cultures.

Although P. D. James's creation Dalgleish remains perhaps the clearest example of the 'feminised' traditionally authoritative male, there are two other detectives, again the creations of popular writers, who articulate the ways in which 'modern' masculinity remains deeply conservative. The two examples are the novels by Elizabeth George (with the central character of Inspector 'Tommy' Lynley and Sergeant Barbara Havers) and the Brock and Kolla series of novels written by Barry Maitland, which feature Inspector David Brock and Sergeant Kathy Kolla. (Other writers who replicate this pattern include the British writer Elizabeth Corley, creator of Detective Chief Inspector Andrew Fenwick and Sergeant Louise Nightingale.) All these series of novels replicate the pattern in the work of P. D. James: the sensitive, conventional, middle-class man (in the case of Tommy Lynley, not just middle class but a titled aristocrat) is accompanied in his work of detection by a working-class woman who nurses a degree of class antagonism and personal bitterness about the circumstances of her childhood. George (perhaps because she was born, brought up and has always lived in the United States) has a somewhat more romantic vision of class relations in Britain than Maitland, but in both cases, what informs the novels is the sense that the perfect coupling in detection is that of a highly intelligent man (with a considerable degree of emotional awareness) and a woman who combines determination with what has often been described as 'feminine intuition'. This association of certain personal characteristics with male and female human beings has never been as rigid or as all-encompassing as has often been argued. But in the second half of the twentieth-century west, there has been a movement away, in popular culture, from that form of masculinity (again, never as dominant or as uncomplicated as sometimes suggested), which was sometimes portrayed in film, archetypically in those characters played by John Wayne and others. Nevertheless, there remains a considerable resistance on the part of male characters to expressing emotion, even in the most extreme circumstances. Here, for example, is Tommy Lynley's reaction to the death of his wife:

'What the hell else do I have to regret?' His voice broke horribly and he hated the breaking and what it revealed about how he had been reduced.

Man no longer but something like an earthworm exposed to salt and to sun and writhing, writhing, because this was the end this was surely the end and he hadn't expected . . .[13]

An account of terrible grief, but notable because of the picture of internal fracture which is produced: either man or earthworm, a transformation into the animal.

Both Elizabeth George and Barry Maitland, in common with P. D. James, see contemporary Britain in terms which suggest a world of social breakdown and constant random violence. In George's *With No One as Witness*, for example, Lynley's pregnant wife is shot and killed in an apparently motiveless crime; in all the Maitland and George novels, all the detectives face considerable danger in the face of their work; indeed, in the first Brock and Kolla novel of the series (*The Marx Sisters*), Kathy Kolla is almost written out from any other part in the later novels as a result of an attack by the murderer. Although Maitland and George go to some pains to reproduce the endless tedium of police work, and the many hours spent pouring over a computer screen and taking telephone calls, the cavalier way in which they expose their female characters to violence suggests, perhaps, a certain underlying suspicion about the propriety of women's involvement in serious crime. (At the same time, this also demonstrates a scant regard for the reality of police work, since the experience of such danger and risk is seldom a feature of real life detection.) Even though Kolla and Havers are always rescued, it would seem that women are still those people whose actions are likely to be impetuous, little thought through and dangerous for themselves. At the same time, there is another, equally long-lasting tradition at work in these examples of detective fiction – the idea of the strong personal and erotic attraction, which can exist between a cerebral, middle- or upper-class man and the working-class women, the person who performs 'dirty' work. This dynamic, most vividly and lucidly explored in Liz Stanley's account of the relationship between Arthur Munby and Hannah Cullwick, suggests the possible strength of the bond between those for whom the 'dirty' work of life (emotion, domestic work, children, disease and so on) is disallowed and those for whom these concerns are paramount and indeed their very livelihood.[14] To emphasize this point about the supposed dichotomy between the clarity of the male mind, and that of the confusion (or even chaos) of the female mind, George, James and Maitland all give their female characters either bleak or physically messy or unattractive places in which to live. The moral of this part of the characterization of female detectives (at least in Britain) seems to be that women who work (and work long hours) are the kind of person who cares little about her domestic environment. Women, it would seem, are not to be allowed to have it all.

It is hardly surprising perhaps, given the ways in which women are assigned to the place of the perpetually junior and the inherently inferior in both certain detective writers' books and many actual police forces, that women such as Paretsky, Gafton and McDermid choose to place their female detectives entirely outside the police machine. But, there is another recent tradition, involving women and detection, which takes a rather different view of the possible alliances and relationships among those professionally involved in the detection of crime. That tradition is the tradition of the alliance of women forensic scientists and police forces, a tradition established by Patricia Cornwell but later developed, across the west, by other writers such as Kathryn Fox. The first novel by Patricia Cornwell, *Postmortem*, is an account of the way in which the female forensic scientist, Dr Kay Scarpetta, discovers the identity of a serial killer through technical expertise and in the face of determined resistance from members of the police force. Some of the dynamics of the novel are suggested by the cover of a British version of *Postmortem*. This features the back of the body of a naked woman, being photographed by what looks like a male photographer and looked down on by a uniformed policeman with a rather mournful and dishevelled Scarpetta in the background. The visual pattern of this cover says much about both the characters and the plot in this particular novel and of popular images of crime in the late twentieth century: women are the typical victims; it is women who are the mourners for victims, but it is men whose agency and technical expertise is capable of identifying the murderer.

Many, but not all, of these assumptions are overthrown by Cornwell's work and by those later writers whose work allows the same connection between women and technical expertise in the detection of crime. Fifty years before Cornwell's work, Agatha Christie had challenged the assumption that it was only men who could detect crime. But, Miss Marple did so by the feminine methods of intuition and a wide circle of friends and acquaintances who provided her with considerable amounts of social information. Kay Scarpetta detects villains by expertise in the laboratory and by the authority which science and technology have acquired in the late twentieth century. As many people have remarked, we all live in a world in which the majority of us have no understanding of the technology which makes our lives possible (for example computers and various other forms of communication). Nevertheless, we have implicitly agreed to trust this technology and accept the authority of its judgements. This has been particularly important in the detection of crime where forensic evidence (in particular, the kind of physical contact between murderer and victim, which can be established through DNA testing) has come to be accepted as often uncontroversial evidence in court. Although there have been cases in actual criminal trials where this has been contested, in Cornwell's fiction, this suspicion is negated by the technical skill and sympathy of an honest woman. Here, for example, is Kay Scarpetta's niece Lucy speaking for Scarpetta's values (in Cornwell's novel, *Predator*) and resisting over-rapid police judgements:

> She is careful how she words it. Marino (a policeman) hadn't been told about PREDATOR. Benton doesn't want him involved, fearing Marino wouldn't understand or be helpful. Marino's philosophy about violent offenders is to rough them up, to lock them up, to put them to death as cruelly as possible. He is probably the last person on the planet to care if a murderous psychopath is really mentally ill as opposed to evil, or if a pedophile can no more help his proclivities than a psychotic individual can help his delusions. Marino thinks psychological insights and explorations in structural and functional brain imaging are a crock of shit.[15]

It is apparent, throughout her many novels, that Cornwell is on the side of those who wish to avoid hasty decisions about, and punitive sanctions towards, criminals. But as a whole, her work to date offers a number of complex, and often contradictory, insights into questions about the relationship of both science and crime to gender. Thus, while Cornwell challenges some of the common sense understandings about women and science (in the most simple instance, for example, that it is not a discipline for women), in a more complex way she also helps to rewrite that script about women and science that Mary Shelley established in 1817 in her masterpiece *Frankenstein*. In that work, Mary Shelley allowed science to take the ultimate step of allowing culture (as in Frankenstein's command of science) to take on the role of nature and produce life (the Creature of the novel). But, at the same time as Frankenstein was allowed to do this, Shelley also took him, and a particular form of dominating, colonizing and entrepreneurial masculinity, to task. Frankenstein was no supportive father and guide to the Creature; on the contrary, he was a careless and thoughtless parent who abandoned his child to the very Nature which had been robbed of its task of procreation. In the final pages of the novel, the Creature and Frankenstein are locked into a mortal struggle: the product of science facing the man who supplanted Nature.

Shelley's vision, of the negative possibilities of science, has remained part of popular culture about science; the creation of the stock figure of the 'mad' scientist replicated Frankenstein as the man who cannot properly understand or appreciate the ways of the social and the emotional world. In the years after 1945, in which science had demonstrated its most radically destructive possibilities, science became both 'good' in the public mind as the discipline, which could do much to ease human suffering and the conditions of our existence and at the same time, the form of knowledge, which can ultimately destroy it all. Second wave feminism took up many of the arguments of those who had been critical of science; arguments about, for example, the medicalization of childbirth and male control of women's fertility emphasized the scientist as a latter-day Frankenstein. Other more complex critiques, notably from Donna Haraway, Sarah Franklin and others, have emphasized the ways in which science has made 'cyborgs' of us all.[16] While women remain marginal in the professional community of science itself, there are many feminist voices that have made crucial contributions to our understanding of the gendered dimensions of science. To these debates, Cornwell (and later women writers about women and forensic science) has arguably contributed a positive role model for those who wish to challenge the idea (in part inherited from Mary Shelley) that science is a highly problematic place in terms of the different gendered moralities and assumptions that are brought to it.

The argument against this is that while Cornwell has given us, in the imagined character of Kay Scarpetta, a woman scientist with highly developed professional skills, she also makes that character, and the victims in the novels, endlessly vulnerable to male attack and appalling cruelty. Thus, while Cornwell gives to women the fictional space in which they might achieve considerable scientific prowess (and Kay Scarpetta is almost never incorrect in her professional judgements), she also takes away from women both reliable judgement about sexual partners (a characteristic, which Cornwell shares with other women writers of detective fiction about women forensic scientists and indeed private detectives) and a confidence in the safety of the social world. Women, in Cornwell's fiction, are often vulnerable; despite the apparent safety of their homes and workplaces, they can, apparently, be set upon by ruthless serial killers who appear (happily) very much more frequently in detective fiction than they do in reality. At the same time, what these killers do to their female victims is exceptionally sadistic, involving very much more than death from a single bullet or strangulation, generally the fate of previous victims. No author of detective fiction has ever pretended that murdered people are anything other than a horrifying sight. Even those who are poisoned may not slip easily into sleep but die deaths of horrible pain; but in the novels of Cornwell (and some of her peers), the horrible, tortured deaths of the victims are described in explicit detail. What is done to the body in this fiction often brings together ancient human sadism with modern technology; a pattern in crime which replicates much of what can be done to the body in the course of 'ordinary' medical or cosmetic surgery and intervention.

One of the complexities of Cornwell's novels is that while providing the reader with more than they might wish to know about an individual's untimely death, she is also often apt to domesticate other contexts of her fiction. Thus, while murder becomes more violent, work involving detection (and the places where that work takes place) is often domesticated. Here is a description of a laboratory in the novel *Postmortem:*

> Several doors down was the computer room, clean, almost sterile, and filled with light-silver modular hardware of various boxy shapes and sizes, bringing to mind a space-age Laundromat. The sleek, upright unit most closely resembling a set of washers and dryers was the fingerprint matching processor, its function to match unknown prints against the multimillion fingerprint data base stored on magnetic disks. The FMP, as it was known, with its advanced pipeline and parallel processing was capable of eight hundred matches per second.[17]

And later on the same page:

> Vander seated himself with the deliberation of a concert pianist about to perform. I almost expected him to flip up his lab coat in back and stretch his fingers. His Steinway was the remote input station, consisting of a keyboard, a monitor, an image scanner and a fingerprint image processor, among other things.[18]

Against this 'domestication' of science, there are two other consistent themes in Cornwell's work, which are suggestive of a certain ambivalence towards forensic science and its possibilities. The first is that although Cornwell will often use domestic objects and situations to personalize the laboratories where forensic science takes place, she also emphasizes the distance between the reader and the understanding of science by sentences which are rich with a technical jargon. Hence, the findings and the processes of science might be domesticated in terms of descriptions of its machinery and its context but the complexity, and highly technical vocabulary of science, which puts science into a rarefied part of the world, is in stark contrast to the actual simplicity of the social judgements made by Scarpetta and her colleagues. This juxtaposition, complex science versus simple society, is part of contemporary mythology about science and society, a mythology, which continues the assumption that somehow what happens in society is almost natural, whereas science represents all that is difficult and cultural. In *Postmortem*, after the discovery of what turns out to be the first victim of a serial killer, one of Scarpetta's colleagues remarks about killings across racial divides:

> 'But we're getting more of them these days. That's the trend, an increase of sexual slayings in which the assailant is black, the woman white, but rarely the opposite'.[19]

That particular comment was made in 1990, a year in which (as indeed was the case for subsequent years), there was no evidence in any western society that the particular trend referred to was actually occurring. But again society, and the social, is made apparently straightforward, not to say racist, since the explanation given by Cornwell (via her detectives) is that such slayings are the work of serial killers, who are a consistent part of all populations. Nature, it is suggested, simply ensures that such people always exist:

> It has been conjectured that at least one per cent of the population is psychopathic. Genetically, these individuals are fearless; they are people users and supreme manipulators. On the right side they are terrific spies, war heroes, five-star generals, corporate billionaires and James Bonds. On the wrong side, they are strikingly evil: the Neroes, the Hitlers, the Richard Specks, the Ted Bundys, antisocial but clinically sane people who commit atrocities for which they feel no remorse and assume no blame.[20]

In statistical terms, or even the terms which make it possible to walk the streets with some sense of security, the just mentioned assertion of the numbers of psychopathic individuals in the population is somewhat alarming. In the current British population, this would indicate that there are approximately 60,000 psychopaths at large. Even if we assume that some of them are those 'terrific' 'corporate billionaires' whom Cornwell cites, that still allows for considerable numbers of people with somewhat malicious intentions roaming freely among us.

Cornwell's view of the social world, like that of later authors who replicated her interest in forensic science and women's involvement in it, provides a vivid picture of a certain late twentieth century view of the world. It is a world which, for all its apparent scientific sophistication, is simple to the point of banality when faced by the complications of the social world and the individuals within it. There is, in Cornwell's world, no attempt to understand the intricacies of human motivation or the ways in which individual identity is constructed through class, race and gender. What we are like, and particularly what 'dangerous' people are like, is put down to a form of genetic malfunction. It is an extraordinary paradox that in a society such as the United States, where industries around self-improvement and counselling make billions of dollars and are based on the assumption that human beings can both remake and change aspects of themselves, that there is also, it would seem, such a profound inclination to believe in the 'natural', unalterable existence of evil.

The narcissistic engagement with self that has been identified as part of the culture of the United States in the late twentieth century is not, however, a form of culture which is confined to that country. Throughout that part of the world, which is generally described as 'the west', it is also possible to identify those authors whose work follows a similar pattern to that of Cornwell: a fervent embrace of science and technology and an equally fervent rejection of the idea that the social world might be part of the understanding of crime and murder. Even though aspects of Cornwell's account of the world are flatly contradicted in the novels of certain of her contemporaries, a general pattern persists: killers are (to rephrase Simone de Beauvoir's remark that 'women are made, not born') born, not made. It might, however, be reassuring to recall that other authors do not always speak with such assurance as Patricia Cornwell of the universal existence of serial killers or ignore with such confidence the social and the cultural in their individual psyches. A forensic scientist in the novels of Jo Nesbo (writing of Scandinavia) states that: 'However, the most characteristic trait of the serial killer is that he's American'.[21]

Among those other authors who have followed the association of women and science, which Cornwell made so powerfully, have been Terri Gerritsen (also writing in the context of the United States with novels about the forensic scientist M. J. Novak), Kathryn Fox (writing about the Australian Dr Anya Crichton, a forensic physician) and another American, Kathy Reichs, whose central character is Dr Temperance Brennan, a forensic scientist who appears in narratives, like those of Cornwell, replete with scientific terminology. In all these novels, a consistent theme is the difficulty, for women, of maintaining a domestic life in the face of the demands of their work. There are long-term relationships, for example between Scarpetta and Benton in Cornwell's novels, but this relationship, like those of the other women characters, is endlessly interrupted and disrupted by the demands of work. As Benton says when he is feeling lonely in Cornwell's novel *Predator*, 'He wishes she

were here. As usual, something came up'.[22] It is only in the novels of Kathryn
Fox that there is anything approaching a feminist understanding of the
demands placed on women by the world of work (and Anya Crichton is
alone among these fictional detectives in having a child). It is not that the
other women characters do not fight passionately for understanding, professional appreciation and recognition of their work but they write of
the prejudice which women face in individual rather than collective terms.
Crichton is a-typical in being prepared to recognize that there is, perhaps,
a structural problem in the contemporary organization of work, which produces gendered pattern of exclusion and discrimination.

The women in Cornwell et al. in much the same way as the women private
detectives in Paretsky et al. have chosen lives that are, in the main, both
single and singular. It is striking that in many of the novels, it is ties of affection (for children, friends, relatives and partners), which are the cause of
danger and threat for the central character. Women, it would seem, would
be well advised to avoid close, lasting relationships. But this is only half of
the story about detectives and intimacy; a glance at the other side of the
story (what is the picture for male detectives) suggests that in much the
same way as for women, the detection of crime is also seriously disruptive
of an ordered and consistent domestic and personal life for men. It is not
the case, therefore, that women, professionally associated with crime, suffer
more than men. What is the case is that women are more often assigned a
specialist function in relation to crime and that women, at least in the latter
part of the twentieth century, are more likely than men to be self-employed
than those male characters in detective fiction who have taken a particular
hold of the public imagination. It is also the case that, despite the best
efforts of British crime writers such as McDermid, Ruth Dudley Edwards
and Veronica Stallwood, in the latter part of the twentieth century, the
United States remains the global headquarters of the private investigator,
be they female or male. With a glance, perhaps, at those amateur traditions
of British detective fiction, many authors of crime novels about female
detectives make crime a secondary concern (and certainly not the source of
income) for their heroines. The 'day job' remains crucial to the economic
survival of many British women detectives.

The male detectives who have taken a particular hold , at least of the
European imagination about crime and detection, are men who work
within state police systems. The most popular figures, in Britain, are Morse,
Rebus and Frost, the creations, respectively of Colin Dexter, Ian Rankin and
R. D. Wingfield. They share, like the women forensic scientists, a number of
characteristics. Like the women, these men live by themselves, in situations

of various degrees of domestic confusion, both physical and emotional. Of the three men, Rebus and Morse drink rather more than is good for them, Rebus and Frost have untended homes and all three men eat little and badly. All three make various attempts at sustaining relationships with women, and about all three, there is never a suspicion of anything other than heterosexual sexuality, even though the relationship of Morse to Sergeant Lewis suggests a degree of autocratic paternalism. In Scandinavia, Henning Mankel's character Kurt Wallender shares all these characteristics. In this pattern, Donna Leon's character Inspector Brunetti (employed in the police force of Venice) is a somewhat exceptional model of domestic happiness and order. Brunetti is a detective who goes home to lunch, a meal that there is never any suggestion that Rebus, Frost or Morse have taken for years, except in a liquid form. On the other hand, Michael Dibden's Italian detective Aurelio Zen has a complicated personal life although he is not always badly fed. Barbara Nadel's Inspector Cetin Ikmen of Istanbul is happily married, although seldom at home.[23]

But what unites all these men, across countries and cultural tastes, is a contempt for their senior officers and for the world of bureaucratic policing. The degree of contempt is not entirely uniform, nor is the reason for the contempt. Rebus is most obviously, and publicly, at war with the establishment within the police force, although it is made perfectly clear that given the degree of corruption and collusion with crime that apparently takes place in the Edinburgh police force, this is the only possible reaction of an honourable man. This unity of dislike for the order, the assumptions and above all the values of the bureaucratic world of state policing is a remarkable feature of late twentieth century detection, since it suggests both a radical separation between individual policemen and the normative order of policing and an equally radical alienation of individuals from the social world in general. For Rebus, Frost and Morse, there is little comfort or sense of unity and reconciliation in any part of the social order. The bourgeois world of Edinburgh (to which Rebus, in his view, is all too frequently exposed) appears, in its own way, as dishonest and destructive as that of the career criminals. The latter is more likely to be physically violent, but what Rankin suggests to his readers is the sense that the two worlds are linked in chains of dependence and mutual support. Both Morse and Rebus work consistently in cities (Oxford and Edinburgh respectively) where there are considerable concentrations of rich and powerful people. Part of Colin Dexter's theme about Oxford is that its famous and beautiful colleges are just as replete with various forms of the seven deadly sins as the world outside. This theme, the hypocrisy and the moral corruption of the apparently respectable, is echoed in Rankin's account of Edinburgh. Although both Rankin and Dexter are typical of what John Sutherland has described as the 'hyperlocality' of crime-writing, the choice of the cities of both Edinburgh and Oxford suggests more than the geographical familiarity of the authors with these places.[24] Oxford and Edinburgh are important in terms of the civic and cultural values which they are supposed to represent; the deformations of these values are the concern of Rebus and Morse, and both detectives pursue these defamations with the intensity of those Weimar critics who were so scathing in their attacks on the German bourgeoisie. Indeed, the pictures, which Dexter and Rankin paint of the worlds of Oxford and Edinburgh, share many of the actual pictures of the German artists Georg Grosz and his contemporaries, in which corpulent bourgeois are pictured hand-in-hand with worlds of crime and vice. The lethal ambitions in Oxford are often trivial except to those academics maddened to the point of murder by desire for academic promotion; ordinary financial greed is more typical of Edinburgh.

Against these corrupt worlds, Morse, Frost and Rebus fight their lonely battles. They do not do so, like the women in Patricia Cornwell or Kathryn Fox, with any great faith in either science or technology. Morse, Frost and Rebus are not actually technophobic, but their use of technology (and forensic science) is strictly utilitarian. They know that they need forensic evidence, but they also suggest to the reader that human beings, being the creators of science, are also capable of evading its grasp. All these men are perfectly able to recognize that many criminals are fully aware of forensic science; for them, no case is fully closed until the murderer has admitted their guilt. In this pattern, so different from those detective novels in which science becomes both the basis for proof and the explicit form of pursuit, there is an intellectual battle between pursuer and pursued, a gladiatorial conflict in which, for the most part, the major weapon on both sides is the human brain rather than the microscopic or the tools of the laboratory. The attempt to modernize the process of detection, and of the pursuit of crime in general, is met with scorn by Morse, Frost and Rebus; they systematically avoid training courses and any suggestion that their performance might be enhanced by an extension of what are described as their 'skills'. Morse resists such terminology (and such agendas) from the standpoint of the patrician gaze of high culture; Rebus sees these agendas as the arena of the politically subservient, while Frost is simply convinced that these exercises are a waste of time. A similar viewpoint, of a professional's refusal to be taught his or her job by those possessed of generic (or 'transferable') rather than specific skills, is that of Superintendent Andy Dalziel, in the

Dalziel and Pascoe novels by Reginald Hill. Of the male British detectives who have, like Morse, Frost and Rebus, become part of the public imagination, it is only Ruth Rendell's Wakeford and Peter Robinson's Alan Banks who have a degree of ease with their senior colleagues, and then largely because in one case (in the Alan Banks novels), the superior officer is of what is described as the 'old school'.

Although there are many professionals besides those in the police force who might well sympathize with Frost and others about the intrusion into a particular specialist space of those without either specialist knowledge or professional credibility, there is also a sense in which this group of detective writers (all, with the exception of Ruth Rendell, male) are writing not just detective novels but also a form of *resistance* novel against modern working practices. The rejected and loathed practices generally include excessive form-filling and paperwork, together with the idea that various forms of non-specific 'training' can nurture professional skills. But the new codes of workplace practice also include some form of acknowledgement (including modifications in the use of language, a particular problem for Dalziel) of the rights of those who do not belong to the world of white, male professionals. In this sense, therefore, aspects of current detective fiction, at least as far as Britain is concerned, constitute a certain resistance to that world of paid work in which ideas (if not practices) about equal opportunities are part of the workplace and in which there is an acknowledgement of different ways of conceptualizing the world than that of the more traditional aspects of British culture. Although Banks, Morse, Rebus and Wakeford have cultural tastes that are wide-ranging and eclectic, they all share a degree of suspicion towards those professionally engaged in higher education and the arts; it would seem that professions which demand imagination and a degree of separation from the business of ordinary life, are also professions in which that very necessary imagination can too easily take a criminal turn. This group of men do not quite match the fervour of Pope Pius X, who in 1907, in his encyclical *Pascendi Domenici Gregis*, condemned all forms of modernism, but they have something of the same fervour in their scepticism, if not actual hostility, for both the world of science and those who refuse possibilities for good and bad in all human beings. Yet, at the same time, as this might imply a certain moral rigidity in this group of detectives, it is also important to recognize that their judgements, while invoking a clear sense of right and wrong are not legal judgements: none of these detectives take the view that the law, or the judgements of the population as a whole constitute morality, a capacity and a form of judgement that in their collective view is more complicated and derived from other sources. What those sources are sometimes remains somewhat obscure, although we can surmise that neither religion nor concepts about 'good citizens' are foremost. Most importantly, all these detectives voice a late-twentieth century concern that the agreed morality of the social world, institutionalized by the state through the law, is neither a sufficient nor a necessarily justifiable morality. This is not to say that any of the individual detectives is neutral about murder or violence towards others; but they all acknowledge the hidden 'crime' (in terms of other forms of the physical, material or emotional abuse of the person) that can form part of the context of murder.

In reviewing the various traditions of detective-writing from the 1960s onwards – the women writers of detective fiction about female private detectives, the women writers about (also female) forensic scientists and the male, British writers about male professional policemen – it would appear that the major differences are those of culture and nationality rather than of gender. The accounts of the various murders in the novels are consistently, although not exclusively, more detailed in the violence of their descriptions in the United States than in Europe. At the same time, the nature of the relationship between the hunted and the hunter follows the same pattern: it is far more likely that the relationship between detective and culprit will involve physical force in the United States. V. I. Warshawski, for example, seldom escapes danger in any of Paretsky's novels; in the same way, Kinsey Millhone often has to put her excellence at shooting (and shooting to kill) to the test. Wakeford and his British colleagues are seldom involved in such exploits. Morse would no doubt regard any investigation which ended in this way as an indication of failure rather than success. Rebus is no stranger to aspects of the gun culture of the darker side of Edinburgh, but he does not, any more than any of the other detectives, carry a gun as a matter of course or regard it as part of his job to do so.

If women and men are not fundamentally divided by their attitudes to crime, and its detection, it would seem, as Donna Landry and Gerald Maclean have suggested, that:

> In terms of a politics in which traditional identities founded on essentialist notions of gender, class, sexuality, and race or ethnicity are put in question, Paretsky, Grafton and Forrest have produced texts whose liberal progressive effects would be hard to deny. Oddly enough, though their feminism comes through loud and clear, and all three address class and racial prejudices as well as gender ideology, Grafton and Paretsky are less bold when it comes to questioning contemporary notions of gender and

sexuality than one might expect. Both construct a fundamentally straight world in which the definition of one's identity as a gendered and sexed person as such is not at stake.[25]

This comment highlights the important idea that sexual identity, at least in the west at the beginning of the twenty-first century, is losing much of its social importance. Or, to put it another way, sexuality has become (or is becoming among many individuals and groups) less politicized than it was in previous epochs. As gay marriage, gay rights and a degree of gay presence in various social arenas such as the media and politics have all become part of the day-to-day culture of the west, there remains relatively little political impact in the literary representation of homosexuality or unconventional forms of heterosexuality. What Jeffrey Weeks has described as *The World We Have Won* is a social world in which there is much greater (although not universal) tolerance for the public acknowledgement of diverse sexualities and forms of sexual relationships.[26]

So while the women detectives of the late twentieth century pursue their various quarry with fervour (and in order to pay their bills) there is, perhaps, little that is novel about these women other than their somewhat idiosyncratic lifestyles. In Grafton and Paretsky (and in many other British and North American female detectives), the only characteristic, which they all possess, and which is largely irrelevant to the pursuit of criminals, is that in various ways they are all anxious to opt out of the traditional rhetoric about 'love and marriage'. The enjoyment of (largely) heterosexuality is to be had without the accompanying baggage of romance, a shared home and commitment to monogamy. For all the women, again on both sides of the Atlantic, there is a very strong sense that what these ideological forms of heterosexual relations will do is to make women subservient to men. The most agreeable men, apparent liberals and supportive of armed female detectives following their careers, will evolve into strict patriarchs once they become part of a heterosexual relationship. It is not, in the case of women detectives, that these characters will necessarily find themselves, in the words of the Spare Rib tea towel 'Once you fell into his arms, now you are up to your arms in his sink', but male control, dominance and authority can too easily become part of a domestic sexual relationship. The women will continue to refuse to cook or housekeep with any enthusiasm, but there will also be a male person who now expects them to be accountable for their actions.

In this, it would seem that although the world of detection is far more violent (and far more pessimistic in its expectations of crime, particularly

pathological crime) in the United States than in Europe, there is another
sense in which the experiences and expectations of the genders coincide.
It is that in the work of detection there is also a considerable tradition of
resistance and dissent. The individuals involved in the process of detecting
the murders and the criminals who inhabit the social space are also individuals who are anxious to make another kind of claim about the contemporary social world, namely that the conventional world is only conventional
in the sense in which it wishes to maintain a normative dominance on the
population. It is not 'conventional' in the sense of wishing to uphold certain positive values; indeed what seems to unite much of late-twentieth
century detective fiction is its scepticism and its personal refusal of the
world in which many people, and most especially people in authority, live.
Again, we might refer to those traditions of critique of the bourgeois world:
traditions which did not see the bourgeois world as a world of positive
values but, on the contrary, a world of hypocrisy, evasion, deceit and greed.
Recognition of this long-lasting critique of bourgeois society might remind
us that contemporary debates about what is sometimes referred to as the
'broken society' have been made in every year since the beginning of the
nineteenth century. As soon as 'society' is recognized, it would appear that
it becomes essential for critics to suggest its disappearance.

Detectives, however, do not, on the whole, accept the view that society has
in some sense been broken or destroyed by the modern world. The factor,
more than any other, which in the view of many detectives seems to be fatal
to social cohesion is the need for the powerful to maintain both their moral
and material hold on the social order. The 'powerful' are not necessarily
any one social group; they are just as likely to be those individuals who have
achieved some form of social 'power' (be it an advantageous marriage or a
financially rewarding position) and are then determined to hold onto to it.
Murder and serious crime, therefore, are seen to be about maintaining,
rather than making a social space and a social position. What detectives
(be they male or female) recognize is that there are links between these
individual aspirations and the wider order of the social world, a world,
which their seniors and their various allies in management, are determined
to uphold. For Morse and others, it is a matter of sadness and regret that
individuals are infected by corrupt social values and that the motives, which
support murder, are part of the fabric of the social world.

This reading of crime stands, as suggested, in a long tradition of critique
of 'polite' society, a tradition, which has informed both satire and politics.
The satire, from Hogarth to Grosz, now hangs on the worlds of art galleries;
the politics continue to evolve in terms of political agendas about 'halting

decay', 're-establishing the family', asserting 'Victorian values' and so on. There is little evidence that detectives feel that it is their mission to 'clean up' the social world, but there is evidence, and Patricia Cornwell is most clearly part of this trend, of a movement towards the explanation of crime and the criminal in terms of 'evil' and the sensationally evil individual. This, in itself, furthers agendas which refuse the complicity of aspects of bourgeois society with crime and the criminal and attempts to 're-naturalise' the causes of crime.

Responsibility for this contemporary enthusiasm for explanations that rely on ideas about 'evil' lies in aspects of the history of the twentieth century. Hitler and Stalin are the archetypical figures who are generally assumed to represent 'evil' on a scale, which, although not unknown in human history, was supposed to have disappeared in the twentieth century. Although Hitler and Stalin are the most usual examples of the embodiment of 'evil', they are not alone in attracting this description: whenever a crime is committed that is assumed by the public to be particularly dreadful, it is more often than not that the term 'evil' is yet again produced. This suggests that consistent failure of the public imagination in the ability to understand the significantly dreadful in any way other than that of ancient judgements about innate moral qualities. In Britain, in the past decades, the 'Moors Murderers' as Myra Hindley and Ian Brady were described, have attracted the definition of 'evil'; so did the killers of the toddler Jamie Bulger and, in 2008, Karen Matthews, a woman who was not a murderer but was found guilty of a plot to fabricate the kidnap of her daughter. Reviewing the Matthews case, the journalist Tim Adams wrote:

> The police officer in charge of the case Detective Chief Superintendent Andy Brennan branded Matthews as 'pure evil' when the verdict was announced. It seemed a lazy, populist thing for a senior police officer to say, and whatever it might mean, the description didn't fit.[27]

In this quotation, the words 'whatever it might mean' are oddly evocative of Prince Charles remarking, on his engagement to Lady Diana Spencer, that of course he was in love, 'whatever that might mean'.

It would appear, to link these two uses of the English language, that certain of the most potentially powerful words, love and evil, no longer have secure meanings. There was no real need to label Karen Matthews as 'evil' since her actions, a mixture of fantasy, greed and infantilism, are all explicable in terms of ordinary human habits and vices. It may well be the case that Karen Matthews possessed what Gillian Rose described as the common mindset of the twentieth century ('we have become endlessly sentimental about ourselves and ruthless towards others'), but it is not difficult to locate her many, evident failings both as a mother and as a human being in her own biography and in the degraded and highly sexualized popular culture which was her predominant form of relationship to the outside world.[28]

Very much to its credit, most detective fiction (with, as already suggested some notorious exceptions such as Cornwell and Kathy Reichs) do not explain murder in the same terms as a real-life policeman. But this explanatory model about human behaviour, that acts of extreme violence that can only be described in terms of 'evil', challenges the view that the twentieth century west has become steadily more enlightened and educated about the nature of the human psyche and the possibilities of human behaviour. The world of the twentieth century is supposed to have been one, which, post-Freud and the generalization of the ideas of psychoanalysis, became more familiar with the idea that as much as human beings could love, so they could also hate. Indeed, this division in ourselves was not a characteristic of exceptional individuals but of all of us. Our relations with our parents and the outside world, we came to understand, would be crucial in defining the extent to which we could resolve our feelings of fear and hostility to the world. Yet, just as a society such as the United States embraces billion dollar industries of self-improvement, therapy, individual realization and individual perfection so an equally consistent public voice maintains a simplistic account of human actions. Most visible in the political reactions to violent attacks on civil society, the term 'evil' effectively halts debate, discussion and understanding about the roots of human actions.

Within this parody of the very idea of explanation differences between male and female writers are perhaps less significant than the differences arising from different politics and different cultures. The recourse to the explanation of 'evil' is, in the broadest sense, political, since it both narrows the discursive boundaries of the social world as much as it can come to justify extreme and vicious punishments. Detective fiction, on the whole, has resisted this form of both individual and social limitation. Yet it has often left detectives, Morse and his colleagues, fighting lonely battles against misunderstanding and banal judgements. In the case of the majority of British fictional detectives, it still remains the case that the pursuit of the criminal is both worthwhile and necessary. Certain aspects of the social world are still worth defending. In Scandinavia, we shall see, there is less certainty about this function of the social democratic state.

Chapter 6

The Dream That Failed

The fault lines that can be perceived between detective fiction in the United States and Europe are largely those about violence (by the murderers and the police) and the reliance on forensic science for the identification of murderers. No one professionally involved in crime (whether in writing fiction or being in a police force) could deny that both the new and the less new technologies of crime have resulted in the arrests of the guilty. But the very sophistication of the technology now available (particularly in DNA testing) suggests a vision of the detection of crime in which it is only necessary to have a sample of DNA from a crime scene, feed it into a computer and wait for a match with either those with a criminal record or – a very much more nightmare scenario – the entire population. Given the recent assaults on human rights and privacy that have taken place in parts of the west in the name of a defence against 'terrorism', it may not be entirely pessimistic to suppose that at some point in the future, this form of detection might become the norm.

At which point the writer of detective fiction will become redundant as will the entire genre of detective and crime fiction. Once detection becomes a matter of computer-generated pursuit, there may be little of interest for either readers or writers. The only possibility at that point might be to reverse the process of detection in fiction, so that readers always know who has committed the crime, the only question to be answered is how to demonstrate to the murderer her or his guilt. The political scientist Slavoj Zizek has noticed that in the television series *Columbo*, the act of murder is shown in detail; we know 'who did it' at the beginning of the programme. As Zizek writes:

In the TV series Columbo, the crime – the act of murder – is shown in detail in advance, so that the enigma to be resolved is not that of whodunit but of how the detective will establish the link between the deceitful surface (the 'manifest content' of the crime scene, to use the term from

Freud's theory of dreams) and the truth about the crime (its 'latent thought'): how he will prove to the culprit his or her guilt. The success of Columbo attests to the fact that the true source of interest in the detective's work is the process of deciphering itself, not its result . . . This strange reversal of the normal order has theological connotations: in an authentic religious belief, I first believe in God and then, on the ground of my belief, become susceptible to the proofs of the truth of my faith; here also, Columbo first knows with a mysterious, but nonetheless absolutely infallible certainty, who did it, and then, on the basis of this inexplicable knowledge, proceeds to gather proofs.[1]

This comment is interesting for two reasons: the first is Zizek's account of *Columbo's* method, a method that is not, in point of fact, all that radical, but is an excellent example of the form of detective fiction, labelled 'police procedural', a tradition that many authors who write about and of detective fiction, trace to the novels of Ed McBain, and in the more distant past, Freeman Wills Crofts. The second is the reference in the quotation to dreams and their difference from reality. Both these comments are useful in examining not a television series but detective writing in Scandinavia and most particularly, Sweden. Among the many popular Scandinavian writers of detective fiction, three stand out: the Swede Henning Mankell (the author of the series of novels about Detective Inspector Wallender) and the Swedish wife and husband writers Maj Sjöwall and Per Wahlöö (authors of the series of ten books about Inspector Martin Beck).

In both these cases, the detective concerned follows much the same pattern as those male British detectives (Morse, Frost et al.) who live lives of some domestic and emotional discomfort. Police work (apart, it would seem, from work in the police forces of Venice and Istanbul, the locations of the fiction by Donna Leon and Barbara Nadel, as well as in those detective novels set in the very distant past, such as the Brother Cadfael novels by Ellis Peters) makes a happy private life difficult, and none of the authors disguise the fact that as much as the detective himself is sometimes quite miserable, so are members of his family.[2] But what the novels of Mankell and Sjöwall and Wahlöö are organized around is not the psychic or social reality of the lives of the detectives (although this certainly plays a part in many of the narratives) but the account of the nature of police work. Not for nothing are the novels of Mankell and Sjöwall and Wahlöö described as police procedural novels. This form of detective fiction is not an invention of these Scandinavian authors and as various writers on detective fiction have pointed out, the form of 'police procedural' novels about crime has a long history, which dates back to the 'Golden Age' and the novels of Ngaio Marsh, Freeman Wills Crofts and the more recent novels, about police work in the United States, by Ed McBain. All these novels make it plain that police work involves a great deal of time spent in an office at a police station; in the early part of the twentieth century, making endless phone calls and checking typed up lists and in the latter, gazing at computer screens. In both cases, the process of detection involves collaboration between people who may not care for each other very much. Almost every detective in fiction has a partner, an 'other' who represents certain human characteristics (in many cases, sympathy, modesty, kindness and a total absence of hubris) not possessed by the more famous detective, and this pattern is followed in police procedural novels with the important modification that often there is more than one partner. For example, in the Wallender novels, there are women detectives (who take the time to make observations about aspects of Wallender's sometimes less than scrupulous personal hygiene) and in the Martin Beck novels, there are colleagues who represent various degrees of personal ambition. As Val McDermid writes in the introduction to Sjöwall and Wahlöö's *The Man Who Went Up in Smoke*:

(Martin Beck) is part of a team, each member of which is a fully realised character. His strengths and weaknesses are balanced by those of his colleagues. He relies on them as they rely on him. This is a world where ideas are kicked around, where no individual has the monopoly on shafts of brilliant insight. Nor are the repetitive tedious tasks carried out offstage by minor minions. Both action and routine are shared between Beck and his underlings. Friendships and enmities are equally tested in the course of the ten books, and everyone is portrayed as an individual who has virtues and vices in distinct measure.[3]

What the work of Menkel and Sjöwall and Wahlöö illuminates most strikingly is, however, at least as much about the emotional life of the neo-liberal state in the late twentieth and early twenty-first centuries as about the process of detection. This question has absorbed pundits from various disciplines and political persuasions. Those on both the political right and left have argued that people in this period of history live lives of selfish abandon and pointless hedonism; the work, for example, of Christopher Lasch, Richard Sennett and Avner Offer illustrates various aspects of this position.[4] Not all these writers (and certainly not Sennett) would argue that the fault of this shift towards what is perceived as selfish (and unhappy) individualism is that of the individuals themselves. Sennett, like many others, is well aware that social pressures to achieve, consume and conform have their roots in the social and cultural fabric of capitalism. But, for whatever reason, what is evident in individual lives is unhappiness, an unhappiness unrelated, we are asked to believe by Richard Layard (author *of Happiness: Lessons from a New Science*) to our level of income.[5] The society in which Wallender and Martin Beck work is, by any measure of social wealth and prosperity, a well-off one: Sweden has long been a world wide measure of social affluence and careful and often enlightened state policies. It was also the home, students of real-life detection might note, to one of the most daring – and unsolved – political crimes of the twentieth century: the assassination in 1986 of the then Prime Minister Olaf Palme. Real-life crime detection in Sweden was clearly not as successful as in its fiction.

There are various ways in which the emotional life of fictional detectives can inform and extend our understanding of what it is like to work, as about half the population of all European countries do, for a state bureaucracy. Across Europe, in the past 30 years, there has been a considerable extension of various forms of state infrastructure: to the existing and long-standing public servants who were (and are) doctors, nurses, teachers, government officials and police officials (among others), there have been added additional white-collar and managerial forms of employment related to both assessment and audit and to various forms of policy implementation. Occasionally, these new forms of bureaucracy are the subject of attack from both left and right; they are often observed in the pages in detective fiction and always regarded with deep dislike. The people who assess what other people are doing are regarded, across Europe, with the deepest dislike. For detectives, the main complaint (apart from the considerable sums of money, which many of these state employees earn) is that they can interrupt and disrupt police work either through unasked intervention or through obstructive engagements in the process of detection. Particularly complex, in this latter category, is the way in which police work can be hampered by legal questions about procedure and by the actual relevance, if any, of police work to the general social good. Here, we arrive at one of the most contradictory aspects in Mankell and Sjöwall and Wahlöö: all these authors, and Sjöwall and Mankell particularly so, would regard themselves as politically of the left. Indeed, Sjöwall and Wahlöö have written of their work:

> We wanted to show the reader than under the official image of welfare-state Sweden there was another layer where poverty, criminality and brutality existed beneath the glossy surface. We wanted to show which

direction Sweden was heading in: toward a completely capitalistic, cold and inhuman society, where the rich got richer and the poor got poorer.[6]

Just as much as the authors make this statement about themselves, and their views, so they echo it in their fiction. Thus, in the Martin Beck novel, *The Locked Room*, the same view is put with similar passion and humour:

> The existing social system was obviously hardly viable and only with the best of will could be described as functioning at all. Even this could not be said of the police. During the last two years Stockholm had had to shelve 220,000 criminal investigations; and even of the most serious crimes – only a small fraction of the total – only a quarter were ever cleared up.
>
> This being the state of affairs, there was little that those bore ultimate responsibility could do except shake their heads and look thoughtful . . . . The only constructive suggestion put forward recently had been that people should be prevented from drinking beer. Since Sweden is a country where beer consumption is rather low anyway, it can be seen just how unrealistic was the so-called thinking of many representatives of the country's highest authorities.
>
> One thing, however, was plain. The police had largely only themselves to blame. After the 1965 nationalisation, the entire force now came under a single hat, and from the outset it had been obvious that this hat was sitting on the wrong head.
>
> For a long time now many analysts and researchers had been asking themselves what the philosophy might be that was guiding activities at National Police Headquarters. A question which, of course, went unanswered. In accordance with his doctrine that nothing must ever be allowed to leak out, the National Police Commissioner, on principle, never gave answers to anything.[7]

The passage is quoted at length since it contains, in the space of a few paragraphs, many of the comments and accusations that have been made, across the globe, about the nature of work for the state (or indeed the corporation) in the twentieth century. These complaints include over-centralization (with the accompanying loss of forms of local knowledge and individual autonomy), the absence of any democratic access to discussion about police work and a climate, in the organization as a whole, of secrecy. *The Locked Room* was first published in Sweden in 1972, and by that time there was, both within and external to detective fiction, a considerable literature about the human reality of working in the 'faceless' corporations of the multi-national, global economy. George Orwell's *1984* (published in 1949) had provided a fictional account of the possibilities of institutional power; throughout the 1950s and the 1960s, various other authors, often working within the disciplines of Sociology and Political Science, took up the various arguments about the negative impact on human beings of large-scale orga-nizations. By the time E. F. Schumacher's *Small is Beautiful* was published in 1973, a consensus was beginning to develop about the inefficiency as well as the costs to individuals of large-scale institutions.

Sjöwall and Wahlöö, writers who were both highly politicized and well read in non-fictional accounts of the social world, were clearly well aware of these debates. It is therefore no surprise to find that all their Martin Beck novels contain three consistent strands about the nature of paid work in the late twentieth century: first, that professional work (and in this case, police work in particular) is often destructive of other areas of an individual's life. Second, the definition of what work is about (and what it is for) often becomes unclear to the people doing it: both Beck and Wallender develop a great scepticism about exactly what 'crime' is. Third, and finally, and closely related to the previous question, Beck and Wallender become scep-tical not just about the actual meaning of crime but also about the justifica-tion (with exceptions such as those extremely rare serial killers) for the pursuit of criminals; a question, which then becomes a complex issue about the meaning of various forms of damage to the social fabric.

To take the first issue: the question of the difficulties that professional work imposes upon the people who do that work. Both Beck and Wallender develop (and it is something, which they share with various other British detectives) debilitating problems with their bodies. This does not surprise the reader of novels about them. Unlike those fortunate detectives Brunetti and Maigret, Wallender and Beck do not return home for regular meals (and the meals described in Donna Leon's books about Brunetti are all well worth returning home for). Wallender and Beck take their meals wherever they can, and so their diet is usually fast food, eaten as quickly as the name implies in anonymous and often depressing surroundings. Entirely predict-ably, this makes both Wallender and Beck, ill; Beck's stomach is always hurting him and Wallender develops diabetes. But, just as these men are pursuing those who have brought damage to the bodies of others, these men are effectively, if rather slowly, killing themselves. When circumstances demand that they should pursue villains, or stay awake for long hours, they both manage to do so, but the cost to themselves is visible to both readers and to the fictional people who work with them.

Just as the long-hours culture of police work (at least in Sweden) destroys the bodies of Beck and Wallender, so it destroys their social relationships. Beck, married at the beginning of the series of novels about him, is an absent father and husband. He becomes as alienated from his wife as she becomes from him; Beck, it would seem, would often prefer to be at the office or in the police car rather than at home. But, 'home' in the work of both Menkel and Sjöwall and Wahlöö has the same grim functionality as the world of work: it is a place to sleep and occasionally eat. Wallender, who lives alone, has no use for his flat except as an occasional dormitory; it is not a place in which he entertains or cooks or spends time on anything which he particularly enjoys. Beck returns to the marital home, receives the rebukes of his wife about his absence and/or his various domestic failings and then proceeds to continue to work on his small-scale models, of which the model of the ship in the bottle is a strikingly apt comment about his perception of his domestic life. When Mankell began writing his own detective novels, he commented, *à propos* the unhappy domestic lives of policemen, 'Policemen were divorced. That's all there was to it'.

It is thus that the social fabric, the intimate relations, of the lives of both Wallender and Beck collapse. Neither has any time or energy to sustain the relationships which they already have or which they wish to pursue. Eventually, Beck finds happiness with a woman who is pictured as something of a bohemian; a woman who lives outside the world of domestic respectability that his wife had been anxious to maintain. For both men, however, that conventional way of life is beset with bad faith, with demands about consumption, and fantasies generated by that same world of consumption, about what constitutes the 'good life'. The various homes, which Beck and Wallender have to enter in the course of their work, persuade them both that facades of respectability often hide great unhappiness or various forms of abuse. For example, here is Wallender, in *One Step Behind*, railing against a wealthy father who appears to have no interest in his daughter:

> . . . Wallender had had enough of the Edengren's indifference towards their daughter in spite of their son's suicide. He wondered how people could have such a total absence of affection for their children.[8]

Much of Wallender's dislike of the world of consumption seems to focus on the game of golf; his estranged wife Mona is 'living a new life with another man who played golf', and a child left alone by his parents is abandoned for a 'golf dinner'. Similarly when Beck meets Rhia, a woman who has no aspirations towards a domestic world that is organized around consumption, it is a great joy to him; it is also a great joy that the woman who becomes his partner by the conclusion of the series is an excellent cook and has a view of the social world that allows her to be both tolerant of Beck's work and yet, at the same time, share his scepticism about the value of it.

The bodies of policemen, be they male or female, attract some considerable attention by many writers of detection fiction, although it is an aspect of this fiction that this concern with the body of the detective becomes more marked as the twentieth century goes on. It is not that Miss Marple and Hercule Poirot are not 'embodied'; we are made aware that they are formed of flesh and blood and subject to the same constraints and possible ills as every other human being. But their lives are lived in ways that in themselves order the body: food arrives at regular intervals, sleep is predictable and physical danger is not part of the daily round of fictional detection. The actual discomfort of detection increases as the twentieth century goes on; both employees of the police force and private eyes are subject to the physical challenges of detection by the end of the twentieth century. Gunshots wounds, explosions, attacks with knives and other dangerous weapons all become part of the daily round of detection, a series of dangers that many detectives, because of their own frail physical state, are sometimes ill-equipped to face. In his introduction to Sjöwall and Wahlöö's *Roseanna* (a book described by Graham Greene as the best crime novel ever written), Henning Mankell observed:

> I haven't counted how many times Martin Beck feels sick in *Roseanna*, but it happens a lot. He can't eat breakfast because he doesn't feel good. Cigarettes and train rides make him ill. His personal life makes him ill. In *Roseanna* the homicide investigators emerge as ordinary human beings. There is nothing at all heroic about them. They do their job, and they get sick. I can no longer remember how I reacted forty years ago, but I think it was a revelation to see such real people as police officers in *Roseanna*.[9]

In creating Kurt Wallender, Mankell's own policeman was to be as constantly feeling as 'unwell' as Beck.

But the various detectives do go out and face the dangers of detection, at the same time as the point is often made that these middle-aged men and women are being put into the front line of a battle against criminals that does little to serve the interests of the population as a whole and a great deal to serve the interests of the rich and powerful. It is in this context that

Sjöwall and Wahlöö and Mankell, and other Scandinavian writers of detective fiction such as Jo Nesbo and Arnaldur Indridason become increasingly sceptical about the meaning of 'crime'. This moral ambiguity does not, of course, cover those cases where killers strike at random against entirely innocent people, but it does inform those occasions when Beck or Wallender (or the detectives Harry Hole and Erlander of the novels by, respectively, Nesbo and Indridason) are dubious of what it is that they are actually being asked to investigate. For example, in Nesbo's novels about crime in Norway (*The Redbreast* and *The Devil's Star*), part of what is 'criminal' and contributes to the plot of *The Redbreast*, is the way in which questionable aspects of Norway's part in the Second World War is erased from the public memory This is, to Nesbo, clearly as 'criminal' as other kinds of criminal behaviour, in that it denies or obscures what is true. This complicates the very idea of detection, since the social and political world, from which civic values about what is criminal and/or illegal are derived, has become a world of uncertainty and, and at the very worst, itself deeply dishonest. Here, in *The Devil's Star*, is Harry Hole's colleague explaining to him the function of detection in modern Norway:

> That's how we deal with the human detritus we're surrounded by. We don't clean it up, we don't throw it away; we just move it around a little. And we don't see that when the house is a stinking, rat-infested hole, it's too late. Just look at other countries where criminality has a firm foothold. Unfortunately we live in a country that is so rich at the moment that the politicians compete with each other to be the most open-handed.[10]

It is a view of Norway that finds an echo in the work of Mankell and Sjöwall and Wahlöö about Sweden. Although the person outlining to Harry Hole his view of the corruption in Norwegian society himself turns out to be deeply corrupt, he does articulate sentiments that the entirely upright Beck and Wallender share. Here, for example, are Sjöwall and Wahlöö voicing, through a defending lawyer, their own views about contemporary Sweden:

> Recently . . . large and powerful nations within the capitalist bloc been ruled by people who according to accepted legal norms are simply criminals, who from a lust for power and financial gain have led their people's into an abyss of egoism, self-indulgence and ruthlessness towards their fellow human beings . . . Someone once said that our country is a small but hungry capitalist state. This judgement is correct.[11]

Wallender and Beck face, in their daily lives, both the tedium of the work that is necessary to police the public space and yet, at the same time, have essentially no sympathy with those who profit the most by what is described as law and order. In this context, they often come close to the conclusion that what they are defending, and 'policing' is the ownership and protection of property. In the recently published and very successful novel, *The Girl with the Dragon Tattoo* by Stieg Larsson, this relationship between business, social hypocrisy and criminal behaviour is spelt out very clearly. At the same time, what is also suggested in this novel is that social 'outsiders' (in this case, the girl with the dragon tattoo) cannot be, and do not want to be, rescued by the conventional interventions of the state.[12]

These kind of connections, between 'insiders' (the rich and powerful) and 'outsiders' (the drug users, the poor and the vulnerable) are made throughout detective fiction that originates in Scandinavia. Henning Mankell and Sjöwall and Wahlöö have become the best-known Swedish authors in the English-speaking world, but, others, for example, Camilla Lackberg, have asked the same questions about the moral order of social democratic states. What all these writers realize is that the contemporary world offers individuals apparently enormous rewards, of personal happiness and wealth. Yet, to achieve these goals, individuals have to have considerable existing resources (the infamous 'cultural capital', which has been named by various sociologists as a major underlying explanation for continuing patterns of social stratification in western societies), and as ever, there is no necessary or inevitable connection between aspiration and achievement. Paid work is often tedious, demanding and badly paid, at the same time as various forms of hedonistic ideologies both articulate fantasies about, and undermine the stability and continuity of, personal relationships. Nevertheless, the majority of the population in every western society exists within these ideologies and circumstances and continues to live at peace with their neighbours and their families. But, for a tiny minority, the dissatisfactions of modern life take a more deadly direction: murderous aggression towards others. In the Henning Mankell novel, *One Step Behind*, Wallender is faced with a man (named Larstam) who kills because he hates happiness, the very quality, which social democracies with 'enlightened' welfare policies are supposed to offer their citizens. Thus, Wallender considers the murder:

> Wallender arrived at an understanding of a man who was crazy, who never fitted in anywhere, and who finally exploded in uncontrollable violence. The psychological examination corroborated this picture. Larstam had been constantly threatened and intimidated as a child and had concentrated on mastering the ability to hide and get away. He had lacked the

resources to deal with his termination from the engineering firm and had come to believe that all smiling people were evil . . . It occurred to Wallender that there was a frightening social dimension to all of this. More and more people were being judged useless and were being flung to the margins of society, where they were destined to look back enviously at the few who still had reasons to be happy.[13]

This emphasis on happiness, and how it might be attained and destroyed, is a consistent theme in the work of both Menkel and other writers of crime fiction. Inevitably, the people who have to detect serious crime come into contact with various forms of human misery: either the grief of loss of those who are loved or various forms of those human conditions and emotions such as envy, greed, jealousy and fear. The emotional world of detective fiction has always been the world of the 'dark' side of the human condition; in this context, twentieth and twenty-first century detective fiction is no different from fiction in any other epoch. Yet, what is different is what is set against this condition of misery: the pursuit of happiness that the Declaration of Independence in 1776 guaranteed.

It is unlikely that the authors of the Declaration of Independence equated happiness with indulgence and hedonism, but what they did do, and as de Tocqueville pointed out in the nineteenth century, was to unite a democratic public space with ideals of personal happiness.[13] Nothing in the Puritan heritage of the United States was then able to prevent the idea taking root that pleasure and happiness were part of the rights of every citizen: a novel and enticing idea in human history, which was then to be used to underpin various consumer paths to happiness. No writer of detective fiction writes against democratic access to goods and services, particularly the most meaningful forms of those commodities in terms of excellence in housing, education and medical care. But what they do protest about, and what all the detectives themselves clearly validate, is the equation of material rewards with happiness. Detective fiction is not a diatribe against material goods (each and every detective has certain tastes for certain material goods), but it is consistently a refusal of the central thesis of consumption in western societies that the possession of objects will automatically produce happiness. But poverty can incite hatred of others; as Wallender implicitly observes in his meditation on the captured killer Larstam, being unemployed is not just about impoverishment: it is also about exclusion and marginality. The destruction of the material basis of a person's life brings with it, Wallender and others recognize, the destruction of that person's sense of themselves. Sjöwall and Wahlöö, even more than Mankell, echo the theme of the 'social' causes of crime: *The Terrorists, The Abominable*

Man and *Murder at the Savoy* all have plots which involve various forms of forced dispossession or the misuse of wealth; the loss of the integrity of the self through prostitution (*The Terrorists*), the loss of a job (*The Abominable Man*) and material exploitation (*Murder at the Savoy*).

Given what Mankell , Sjöwall and Wahlöö have to say about the social and emotional condition of the west in the late twentieth and early twenty-first century, it is all the more remarkable that there is so little serious crime. Although to sections of the popular press across the west, crime is a rising tide, which apparently threatens to engulf us all, Western Europe is largely crime-free in the orthodox and conventional sense in which crime is gene-rally understood. That is, very few people are murdered and crimes of deliberate violence against the person are limited. Thus, we confront vari-ous paradoxes in certain recent crime-writing: first, crime-writing often presents a more negative picture of the social world than many of us might recognize, and yet, second, crime-writing is often a furious protest against the possible causes of crime. There is, therefore, both exaggeration – in the degree and presence of crime and social breakdown – and a radical politics, which condemns the material greed implicit in capitalist social relations.

This very disjunction within writing about crime allows us to consider that while writers of crime and detective fiction often offer a degree of mislead-ing accounts of the amount of crime in western societies (and certainly in the United States, the exaggeration about the number of serial and/or pathological killers), these same writers are also suggesting that many western societies need to extend their public debates about crime. The pol-itics of crime writers are far from being universally of what is described as the 'left'; indeed, many of them (both today and in the past) publicly acknowledge very different kinds of political sympathies. But the majority of European writers about crime are interested in that crucial relationship between people and crime: what it is that makes one individual, possessed of human and social characteristics that are not strikingly different from those of his or her contemporaries and peers, into a person who is pre-pared to kill. Again here, it is worth noting the differences between Europe and the United States; the latter context being one where the thesis of the 'bad' individual is more than likely to be offered as an explanation for criminal and indeed murderous behaviour. An insight into this view of the generation of a dangerous pathology is given in a novel, which is not, strictly speaking, a detective novel, but does involve the killing of innocent people. It is Lionel Shriver's *We Need to Talk about Kevin.*

The conversation about Kevin is long and difficult. The Kevin of the title is a young man born into a prosperous and educated home in New York, who nevertheless conspicuously fails to develop 'normally'. As a child, Kevin is disruptive and manipulative, patterns of behaviour, which continue into his adolescence. As Kevin's physical strength and prowess increases, so does the range and viciousness of his behaviour; in the final chapters of the novel, we see Kevin become one of the adolescent multiple killers who have shocked societies throughout the world. Rather than turning a gun on his classmates (as other real life young men have done), he attacks them with a crossbow, a gift from his parents. After the killings, Kevin's mother, understandably, attempts to establish what it is that has turned her son into a multi-murderer. In revisiting the history of Kevin's birth and childhood, his mother examines various explanations for his behaviour. Here, she recounts an interview, before the murder, with one of Kevin's teachers:

> 'Well, he wasn't too happy when his sister was born . . . We're pretty well-off – you know, we have a big house . . . We try not to spoil him, but he lacks for nothing . . . We lead the good life, don't we?'
> 'Maybe that's what he's angry about'.
> 'Why would affluence make him mad?'
> 'Maybe he's mad that this is as good as it gets. Your big house. His good school. I think it's very difficult for kids these days, in a way. The country's very prosperity has become a burden, a dead end . . .'.[14]

We Need to Talk about Kevin was published in 2003, before the so-called 'credit crunch' of 2008 began to make that easy assurance of lasting western prosperity look somewhat overconfident. Lionel Shriver is careful to avoid the suggestion that being rich and successful makes people amoral (and conversely that poor people are inevitably kind or at least less likely to be homicidal killers), but she does implicitly call into question the values of Kevin's parents. The father is, as his wife points out, wholeheartedly 'American' by which she means that he has embraced the core values and expectations of the American Dream. A Republican in his politics, Kevin's father epitomizes those ideas and values about the world, which do not recognize the limitations (or the global implications) of his values, values of which his wife, liberal and cosmopolitan, is deeply critical.

Between mother and father, there develops, on the subject of Kevin, a growing estrangement between the partners. When Kevin's mother discovers that Kevin has killed not only numbers of his classmates but also his sister and his father, we are told his now deceased father could never have understood this:

> It was possible to be a good dad, to put in the weekends and the picnics and the bedtime stories, and so to raise a decent, stalwart son. This was America. And you had done everything right. Ergo, this could not be happening.[15]

Yet, the unbelievable does happen, and as in the case of those real-life school children who have killed their contemporaries, the crimes seem to be inexplicable: the teenage killers are from prosperous homes with apparently no clear motive for their behaviour.

But this explanation, as any writer of detective fiction would recognize, is not enough. The world is, has been and always will be, populated by discontented teenagers, and yet, only a tiny proportion of them become killers. It is possible to blame the availability of guns in the United States (but again, Shriver is careful to remove this as a possible facilitator of Kevin's crime in making the parental gift the means of the crime), and it is equally possible to blame a media saturated with images of violence and physical harm to others. Computer games, it could be argued, have turned killing people into a game, in which fantasy and reality become confused. At the same time, various forms of games about killing and murder have existed for centuries; Punch and Judy shows, various forms of carnival and the board games of detection all have at their centre the construction of violence as a 'game'.

The explanation for Kevin's behaviour, which appears to have the most credence with Lionel Shriver is that his mother never had any great affection for her firstborn child. The child interrupted a happy personal life and a successful career, a career based upon providing advice about how to travel cheaply outside the confines of the United States. (A somewhat rare pastime in reality; only about 10 per cent of citizens of the United States have passports and thus experience of other cultures remains rare.) Maternal lack of affection is given a good deal of space in *We Have to Talk about Kevin*, and the bond between mother and son is only made after the murders and the incarceration of Kevin. It would, therefore, be easy to read this novel as an account of the disasters which can evolve from an absence of mother–child bonding. Against this is another possibility: Kevin, the uncontrollable child at the centre of the novel, is a metaphor for the contemporary United States, a country literally unable to 'behave'. On the one hand, this country endorses fully an agenda of entitlement and unquestioning belief in the American way of life (Kevin's father), while on the other hand, it regards the rest of the world as a playground (Kevin's mother). Even the most limited critic might be able to see the implicit problems with these views; all of which, in their different ways, are about hedonism and the making of profit.

Kevin's rather florid misbehaviour is thus perhaps easier to understand since there is no sense of a familial ethic or a way of looking at the world, which suggests either the recognition of the other (apart from being an object of curiosity) or of the emotional possibilities that exist in all human beings. As a culture, the west (particularly since the fall of the Berlin Wall in 1989 and the end of the old Soviet Union) has triumphantly naturalized capitalism as the only possible social system. But this process of naturalization is not merely social; it has also invaded the personal and private space so that the wish to be rich, to make money, to be (in the terms of the social world) successful have all become 'natural'. Yet, the 'natural' in the sense of the ways in which we can all love and hate at the same time, and experience those feelings towards the same person has disappeared in a welter of ideas about doing, as Kevin's father thought he had done, the 'right' thing. That 'right' thing is then determined by a social script, which may have little to do with the actual inclinations of the individuals concerned. The buying of pleasure is not in any sense an invention of the twenty-first century, but the scale and the expectations surely are.

It is thus not surprising that for many authors of contemporary detective fiction the version of the social world that seems to be becoming the normative ideal, has little attraction. Among Scandinavian writers, there is a discernible scepticism about the values and the achievements of these prosperous Nordic societies. Mankell, Sjöwall and Wahlöö as well as more recent authors all suggest that the prosperous, orderly societies of Scandinavian social democracy are no longer viable: the fiction of all these writers hints at a hidden (and sometimes not so hidden) social world, which threatens the surface peace and calm of these worlds. Nothing, Wallender, often remarks is mended any more; people simply thrown things away. (But then, in *The White Lioness*, Mankell is surprised to see a woman darning socks.) Just as material objects become disposable, so too do social relationships; rather than being maintained through difficulties, they are now abandoned. In their different ways, however, both Martin Beck and Kurt Wallender speak to the futility of staying in unhappy marriages; they persevere, but then do realize (although only briefly in Wallender's case) the happiness of subsequent relationships.

In this context, the search for an ethic of human existence remains paramount. From Wallender to Rebus, across cultures and continents, writers of detective fiction search less for a way of discovering the name of the murderer than for a reason to continue with their profession and for a way of making sense of their personal lives. In this sense, detective fiction, despite its occasional departures into brutality and horror, remains, at its core, fragile and vulnerable: this is a literary genre which wishes both to know and to answer considerable and important questions about human lives in an era, for many people, of unprecedented prosperity and relatively little crime.

Therefore, it is arguably a form of fiction which has a considerable relevance for the twenty-first century, not least because it suggests that simple
solutions do not answer either the mystery of 'who-done-it', but the more
complex question of why people did it, and how others might be prevented
from following the same paths. In that sense, therefore, detective fiction is
(and always has been) anti-fundamentalist in its essential tenets; there are,
of course, the exceptions in which the spectre of pathologically evil individual is raised as the answer to the mystery of the identity of a killer, but much
detective fiction avoids this reductive version of human motivation.

Central to the organizing thesis of most detective fiction (certainly the
detective fiction, which originates in Europe) is a continuation of the
Enlightenment idea that it is worthwhile to know. In the context of detective fiction, this view has the impact of differentiating the detective fiction
of, for example, Patricia Cornwell (which is concerned with pursuit rather
than explanation) from that of the tradition that has its roots in the work of
her great, earlier, compatriot Dashiell Hammett. In a passage in Hammett's
The Maltese Falcon, Sam Spade reports that he had once been employed to
locate a man who had (for no apparent reason) left his family and a stable,
ordered way of life and disappeared. Spade had done his very best to find
the man but could not. Quite by chance, a few years after the original assign-
ment, Spade comes across the man in a bar, and he tells Spade that although
he now leads a life almost identical to the one that he left, the change in his
life was nevertheless completely worthwhile. Spade is understandably puz-
zled by this choice, but what is put before the reader is both the possibility
of very fine ethical and personal distinctions: the surface (in this case, the
details of a conventional suburban existence) is not all, and to individuals
there are diverse meanings to that surface, which may often demand different kinds of actions and responses.[16]

The suburban existence, which was left by the character in *The Maltese
Falcon*, has come to signify, in the late twentieth century, much that is
oppressive about the order of western society. As we have seen, the second
half of the twentieth century saw major critiques of this way of life (*The
Feminine Mystique* being just one), but those critiques followed an earlier
literature (for example in the pages of Sinclair Lewis, George Orwell and
Georges Simenon) all of whom turned a sceptical and hostile eye on the
appearance of respectability, which the suburbs and apparently coherent
and ordered built environments came to represent. The old fairy-tale image
of the chaos and terror of the forest (the world of the Big Bad Wolf and
the terrifying gingerbread house to which Hansel and Gretel are led) was
replaced, in twentieth-century mythology by the ideal of the peaceful,

safe suburbs. The reality, as Betty Friedan and Sylvia Plath suggested in their different ways, is that the suburbs drive people, especially women, mad. Here, for example, is a passage from Plath's *The Bell Jar*, in which the heroine Esther Greenwood contemplates the life of a mother in the suburbs:

> Dodo Conway was a Catholic who had gone to Barnard and then married an architect who had gone to Columbia and was also a Catholic. They had a big, rambling house up the street from us, set behind a morbid façade of pine trees, and surrounded by scooters, tricycles, doll carriages, toy fire trucks, baseball bats, badminton nets, croquet wickets, hamster cages and cocker spaniel puppies – the whole sprawling paraphinalia of suburban childhood. Dodo interested me in spite of myself.[17]

The adjective 'morbid' in this passage returns this description of the apparently orderly to those mythical, frightening forests of fairy tales: the word suggests to the reader that perhaps we need to consider carefully exactly what is going on behind that surface impression of the 'normal'.

What is going on, as Plath points out later in the same context, is that Dodo Conway is about to be a mother of seven children. In this context, Conway, of course, brings to the pristine suburbs of New England the religion of the poor immigrants, Irish and Italian, and with this comes a powerful element of the transgressive subversion of all that the suburbs are designed to provide: an orderly, structured and normatively cohesive way of life. Dodo Conway disrupts this order, not just because her presence intimates choices (chaotic and transparently fecund) that was thought alien to the suburbs, but also because she is living out, like Sam Spade, an ethic which has little or no connection to given social rules, aspirations and expectations. (Although, of course, in another sense, Dodo Conway refuses to transgress the authority of her religion.) Middle-class people who live in affluent suburbs are simply not expected to have seven children, any more than private detectives are expected to care about cases which they cannot solve. The fictional characters Dodo Conway and Sam Spade are, however, providing a sense of those other possibilities of the social world: possibilities, which not accept absolute individual submission to the normative order.

Despite the presence in all forms of fiction of the 'outsider' figure, the social world maintains a stubborn allegiance to the view that the surface appearance of human beings and their surroundings is an accurate indication of their moral worth and purpose. Across continents and across historical time, detective fiction has refused the authority of the respectable façade: from Agatha Christie to Henning Mankell, the descriptions 'well kept' and 'neat' alert readers to the possibility that all might not be exactly what it seems. The 'quiet' person, who never disturbs his neighbours, is all too often the character whose behaviour in other contexts is less than desirable; the infamous 'loner' of psychological profiles of killers is not just a person with little taste for human society; he (although rarely, she) is also a person whose tastes lie in its elimination. Miseries and grudges held against the social world form the emotional energy, which makes possible hideous crime.

Detective fiction, as a genre, has long suggested that it is as necessary to understand a killer as to identify them. In the works of non-fiction about murderers, this impulse is similarly present, although it is complicated by two factors that are generally absent from much detective fiction. The first is that, in reality, those who commit crime, and are caught, are punished and that punishment, as many, many studies attest, seldom does anything to reform the criminal. The absence of the death penalty throughout Europe ensures that the detection of a murder does not involve yet another death; in the United States, the presence of capital punishment arguably has the effect of making fiction about murder truly ghastly, as crimes of appalling cruelty are met by punishments of equal viciousness. It is the case that the United States has a relatively high murder rate, but many of those murders are the result of various forms of feuds within communities of crime rather than those 'domestic' murders, which generally preoccupy novelists. Novelists, however, do not have to consider punishment, even if the connection between the crime and the punishment is often such that apparently, it is designed to mirror the cruelty of the murderer. It is not, therefore, that, as the writers of musical comedy, Gilbert and Sullivan put it, that 'the punishment should fit the crime' but that the crime should fit the punishment.

The second complication of 'real' murder, which is not found in fiction, is that in 'real' murder, there is considerable evidence to suggest that killers do not act with planned malevolence towards their fellow human beings – what might be described as 'rational' murder – but act largely without specifically planning a crime. If 'real' murderers attempt to establish alibis and all the other deceits necessary to avoid detection, they do so after, rather than before, the event. The literature on 'real' murderers is now extensive and high-profile crimes (for example in Britain, the Moors Murders) have led to a considerable amount of literature, much of it a salacious repetition of the details of the events. Among the many people who have written about 'real' murder, the journalist Gitta Sereny stands out; she has written on both crimes involving mass murder (aspects of the Holocaust) as well as more detailed studies of the British case of the murders committed in 1968 by the 10-year-old Mary Bell.[18]

The Mary Bell case involved the killing of two very young children; a child of 3 years and a child of 4 years by the 10-year-old Mary Bell. At the time the case inevitably involved a huge public outcry, the usual cries for revenge and general outrage and surprise that a child should be able to commit two such terrible crimes. That kind of outrage and calls for revenge were then repeated at the time of the murder, in 1993, of the toddler, James Bulger; the British newspaper the *Sun* endorsing campaigns for what was effectively lynch mob justice. Sereny, in her study of Mary Bell, does not attempt to prove Mary Bell's innocence although that is another long tradition in the study of 'real' crime and one, which has had some success in securing the release or at least the vindication of those once thought guilty. But, what she does do is to try and explain some of the circumstances of Mary's childhood and particularly, the sexual abuse, largely engineered by her mother, which it took Mary years to acknowledge. The question, which Sereny asks us to consider is, how we can recognize behaviour which is dangerous to all concerned. The answer would appear to be, and it is an answer in which Mary Bell and Gitta Sereny agree, that it is very difficult. As Mary Bell herself said, quoted in Sereny:

'There are many unhappy, very disturbed kids out there who don't end up robbing families of their children'.[19]

To which Sereny adds:

This is of course true. It is true, too, however, that we still do not understand the determining stimulus for the 'breaking point' in children who kill or commit serious crime, and which for Mary come one day before her eleventh birthday. What we do know now, what Mary's agonising recollections have shown us, is that once that breaking point is reached, the child has no way of suppressing it.[20]

The factors, which Gitta Sereny identifies as crucial in the emotional make-up of Mary Bell were the sexual abuse and the various lies, deceptions and evasions, which maintained the family. The father who was sometimes described as an uncle and the mother who made money out of prostitution all constitute what is, for many people, an ancient and familiar tale of the disordered lives of an underclass.

But that underclass, as Sereny makes clear, live in those working-class estates which replicate the suburban ideal of the middle class. Like the middle-class suburbs, the estates are distant from urban life, with degrees of separation between neighbours. This particular built environment does not, of course, 'cause' crime, but what it does do is to make it more difficult for individual disturbance and turmoil to be socially known. In every case which has involved cruelty towards children, or cruelty by children, the public cry that has resounded around Great Britain (and in other countries where similar crimes have been discovered) is that of why aberrant and potentially damaging behaviour was not known. The neighbours of the notorious British murderers Frederick and Rosemary West did not know that anything 'odd' was going on; the responsibilities of neighbours, in the case of serial killers, thus become retrospectively onerous.

In these cases of appalling cruelty, the need to 'know' always occurs after the event. But in all cases what is found wanting is the public imagination about the possible terrors underlying the ordinary, the very deceit of the public 'respectable' face about which detective fiction has consistently warned us. In the twenty-first century, many people in the west have become used to the idea that we can now live our lives in tune with our 'feelings': that curious form of naturalization, which does not question that 'feelings' might not be so entirely free from social influence as we might like to suppose. Yet, when it becomes transparently clear that an individual has given way to their 'feelings', with murderous effect, we both exaggerate our 'feelings' for revenge and refuse the possibilities of understanding. It is perhaps little wonder that the majority of contemporary fictional detectives do their very best to contain their 'feelings' for other human beings; the road to murder, they have seen too many times has been paved by an excess of feeling. 'Murder', the fictional detective Gerhard Self says in *Self's Punishment* by Bernhard Schlink, 'means never having to say you forgive'. But what Self knows is that one of the people he cannot forgive is himself: he killed the man whose crimes he could not forgive.[21]

Self's Punishment is richly instructive about possible motives for murder, since it suggests that one of the most common reasons that people kill is that they wish to end memories, to kill not just the person but the past. This analysis takes us beyond the case about the effect (important though it is) of cruelty and abuse on the human psyche; it takes us to the understanding of what we often wish to do, and what can arouse us to murderous feelings about others, is to erase our memories, to kill once and for all those recollections of both the behaviour of others to us and our behaviour to others that undermine our sense of self. It is not, therefore, the passion of the moment, which necessarily leads to murder, but the knowledge that the defining characteristic that we possess as human beings, of recall and memory, is also the characteristic that is the most potentially unnerving.

Chapter 7

'On Murder Considered as One of the Fine Arts'

The title of this final chapter is shared by Thomas de Quincey's essay of the same name, published in 1827. In the essay, de Quincey suggests to us that rather than simply condemning murder, a position that has rather little interest to it, we should turn our attention to its aesthetics, to the manner in which murder is committed. The aesthetic possibilities of murder, de Quincey writes, are numerous:

> People begin to see that something more goes to the composition of a fine murder than two blockheads to kill and be killed – a knife – a purse – and a dark lane. Design, gentlemen, grouping, light and shade, poetry, sentiment, are now deemed indispensable to attempts of this nature.[1]

Murder, seen in this way, becomes a matter of interest, of guile and cunning, of the thinking through of the place of the murder, the purpose for it and of course, the reasons for it. It is a remarkable argument, which distinguishes between banal acts of violence (for reasons of petty theft) to crimes that articulate a far more complex relationship between murdered and murderer.

For many people, any murder, for whatever reason, still contravenes the commandment of 'Thou Shalt Not Kill'. However, as de Quincey also points out, that same source of western moral authority, the Bible, is also a chronicle of murder, with some fine and distinguished murderers in its pages. Cain, de Quincey argues, is the first and in some ways the murderer who receives the most appropriate punishment: the knowledge (the fourth book of Genesis tell us) of a life that is to be spent with murder on his conscience. But, at the same time, Cain's behaviour is presented as understandable. In this context, Cain achieves the apparently unachievable: he allows us to consider that God might have had a part in the origins of the crime:

> 'And the Lord had respect unto Abel and to his offering.
> But unto Cain and to his offering he had not respect'.[2]

Making God apparently share guilt for murder is by any literary standards, remarkable.

What de Quincey's essay offers us, in the twenty-first century, is a way of thinking about detective fiction, and the 'art' of murder, as less that of a focus on an inferior genre of fiction (often coupled with adventure stories or romantic fiction in discussions of fiction) and more as a major literary form in its own right. The aesthetic, which de Quincey proposes, allows us to consider less the quality of the writing of detective fiction and more the quality of the murder itself: is the murder a simple act of aggression, greed, sexual pathology (as in much detective fiction dependent upon forensic science), or is it a form of social negotiation, a human form of the game of chess, in which real figures, rather than pieces on a board, are 'removed' from play? What is important to this form of considered murder is intelligence. Rather than the wild attack on other human beings, which is proposed in the detective fiction about serial killers or the so-called evil murderers, there lies a degree of calculation and even, in certain cases, a commitment to social improvement.

From the point of view of the person murdered, these distinctions might be somewhat irrelevant, but for those of us who survive, it does point to the perhaps comforting knowledge we can avoid being murdered if we maintain reasonably friendly relations with out neighbours and our family. If we do this, our actual chances of being murdered (as de Quincey knew and as we could realize today if we consult statistics about murder rather than media hyperbole) are very slight indeed. Here again, de Quincey recognized something which we could still usefully remember: that the creation of sensation, and especially sensationalist reporting in the media, can completely overshadow any rational account of murder and its frequency. The emergence of the 'sensation' and sensationalism was part of the western extension of print culture in the eighteenth century: a culture in which the commercial success of certain of its aspects was dependent upon its ability to create 'sensation'.[3]

Murder was (and is) a prime source of sensation, since it infringes one of the most fundamental laws of all societies: killing others is only permitted when publicly sanctioned. 'Ordinary' murder (between close relatives) is as old as human societies and has very seldom been considered as 'sensational'. But new ways of life, new social environments and new ways of killing people all gave murder, by the beginning of the nineteenth century, what might be described as a new lease of life. From the time that de Quincey was writing, two themes about murder began to appear: one was the public fear of being murdered and the other was, as these pages have suggested, a literature, and particularly a fiction, about murder. Public fears about being murdered, at least in Europe in peacetime, have born little relationship to the chances of being murdered. It is an event so rare that it inevitably attracts considerable attention, even though in the majority of cases, the murder is solved almost immediately and, predictably, a close relative, arrested.

But part of the potentially 'beautiful' murder, the murder which de Quincey sees in aesthetic terms, might also involve the murder so skilful, so astute, so supremely calculating about other human beings that the murderer is never caught. Suspicions might abound, but there is never a prosecution. In this category, both fiction and real life offer various examples. One particularly striking example in fiction is that of the woman, in a short story by Roald Dahl, who murders her husband by hitting him over the head with a joint of frozen lamb.[4] Having then telephoned the police and reported a hideous attack on her husband by intruders, the wife cooks the lamb, and we see her, at the end of the story, suggesting to the police that they might join her for dinner. A non-fictional example, which certainly echoes some of the marital discord and potential violence that underpins Dahl's story, is the case of the exploding garden shed: a tale set in real-life England in 2001. A husband (Judge Chubb) who had asked his wife for a divorce was, on that same day, killed when his garden shed apparently blew up. Although the phrase 'exploding shed' elicits a considerable response in comments on the web, and the idea of an exploding shed has been immortalized (although before the incident of the exploding shed in which the judge was killed) in the art of Cordelia Parker, suspicion remained that perhaps the shed had not blown up for entirely accidental reasons.[5] The police acted with due deference to the wife of a judge and allowed her both to bulldoze the shed and cremate her husband's body. Readers of the fiction of Agatha Christie would have recalled that the police can often be overcome with awe when faced with the English upper class but that this same class is just as likely to kill as any other.

As de Quincey realized (and as that realization was later to be translated into film and television), the 'perfect' murder reverses social expectations and assumptions about murder and enrols us on the side, less of the victim, than of the murderer. It is not so much that as the public we become enthusiastic about murder per se, but that as observers of the crime scene, and as well-informed onlookers to criminal behaviour, we are allowed to feel sympathy for (let us say) the real-life wife about to be abandoned by a husband or the wife who (literally) kills with the connubial roast dinner after a lifetime of bullying and spite. The themes of 'just reward' and 'had it coming' slip easily into out collective vocabulary, just as we know that part of the social consensus in which we live does not allow individual acts of revenge.

It is in the organization of this context, of the social wish for revenge and atonement against and by, criminals and murderers, that the western twenty-first century has increasingly reacted in diverse, and often diametrically opposed, ways. In the first place, there has long been an increasing social recognition that crime, in the most general sense, has social causes and that serious acts of aggression against others do not emerge from nowhere. Brutalization has long been identified as the surest way to create the criminal and the perpetrator of further acts of cruelty: every major English novelist from the eighteenth century onwards has recognized the connection between being hated (or despised, or half-starved or treated with various degrees of cruelty) and a desire for, often unfocussed, revenge. Institutional cruelty (of the kind described by Charlotte Bronte in *Jane Eyre* to the many accounts of brutality in male public schools) appears over and over again in fiction. The 'hangers and floggers' in politics, the media and the wider social world have always had to face opposition from those who argued, for pragmatic as well as more complex moral reasons, that meeting brutality with brutality did not produce its disappearance.

But while this debate has echoed across cultures and centuries, and played a not inconsiderable part in international politics, the constraints on the implementation of revenge for certain crimes have often been severely tested. Nowhere has this been truer than in the cases of those crimes against children which have attracted the attention of sections of the press: a social connection exists in which the poorer and the more underprivileged the readership of a newspaper is, the more likely is that newspaper to exhort its readers to quasi-vigilante acts of revenge. The British newspapers, which have become notorious for this behaviour, are the Murdoch-owned the *Sun* and the *News of the World*, both of which have directed campaigns for revenge on those who have committed (or might commit) crimes against children. The *News of the World*, from 2001 onwards, has campaigned for what has become known as 'Sarah's Law', the campaign to make available publicly information about the names and whereabouts of convicted paedophiles. The *Sun*, in 2008, has campaigned for the public shaming of those in any way involved in the agencies held responsible for the failure to prevent the death of the child known only as 'Baby P'. Despite the fact that the baby in question was killed by the violence of her mother and a male friend, the responsibility for the death has been entirely shifted to government departments responsible for child welfare.

In these campaigns, we can see at work two novel patterns concerning crime and its relation to the social world as a whole. The first is the way in which responsibility for certain acts of cruelty (and what in effect, in the case of Baby P, is certainly a number of acts, which brought about the death of a very vulnerable human being) is moved from the individuals concerned to institutions. The social norm, which appears to have been violated in the case of Baby P, is not, therefore, that the baby's parents behaved disgracefully but that state institutions failed to prevent this happening. The manifold paradox of a newspaper (or a newspaper proprietor), which has so enthusiastically embraced the idea of individual responsibility and the shortcomings of the so-called nanny state, now asserting the need for state 'nannying' is not reflected in the newspaper's editorial stance. The second novel pattern that we can observe from these campaigns is that the focus on the apparent vulnerability of children to paedophiles and those hostile to their interests is never related to the contemporary commercial sexualization and exploitation of children. Those 'innocent' children who, we are led to believe, are at risk from the multitudes of paedophiles haunting our streets, are the same children who are invited to mimic adult patterns of sexualized behaviour and dress.

Crimes against children have always attracted a particular kind of social dislike and disapproval. Given the relative powerlessness of children when faced with adults, there is little dissent from this view. But the especial fervour of the campaigns concerning children that have been mounted in the past decade is, perhaps, about something more than concern for the young and vulnerable. 'Ordinary' crime so saturates the media (indeed without crime, television media in particular might find it difficult to fill our screens) that there is a degree of tedium about its presentation. The murder of a person (or persons) is followed by pursuit by the various detectives and then all is revealed. It is so familiar, so predictable and, since the abolition of capital punishment in most of the west, so essentially lacking in drama. The death of one person is not going to be accompanied by the ritualized and institutionalized death of another; indeed, the text of some recent detective fiction suggests that there is virtually no point in apprehending killers: the political and social systems within which we live will continue to create people who murder. For many people, state 'crime', in the sense of particular policies towards other countries and/or the toleration of considerable wealth alongside considerable poverty, holds a more important place in the moral order of the contemporary world. Those kinds of policies, for many people, are the real crimes of the twenty-first century.

To restore the sense that crime, and especially murder, actually matters within the moral order of the west, demands a different kind of crime. In one sense, the novels of such writers as Patricia Cornwell have cooperated in this need, creating (and recording) new forms of bestiality in crime and allowing, as a response, considerable degrees of licensed violence. 'Shoot to kill' is the message which emerges from this literature. But although the literary creation of the ghastly, vicious and sadistic crime might satisfy some readerships, a more likely way to enter the collective fears and fantasies of the population as a whole is to create a new form of victim: the child. There is now a considerable literature about the ways in which the abolition of various forms of censorship have eroded boundaries about the portrayal of various forms of sexuality (and brutality), but the subjects and objects of these activities remain largely adult. Put a child in the place of adults and new frissons of indignation and concern are, and have demonstrably been, a result.

The cases of child abduction, cruelty towards children and so on to which the media gives us access have so far remained largely sequestered in the real world. But as taboos change and shift and disappear, violence towards children in fiction begins to be visible. Recent examples include Donna Leon's *Uniform Justice*, in which Leon's detective hero Brunetti has to investigate what appears to be a suicide at a military academy. As it turns out, the teenager who is thought to have committed suicide has been murdered, and what Brunetti uncovers in the course of the investigation is a collusion of powerful interests. But what is also interesting about this particular novel, apart from the youth of the victim, is the way in which it is agreed that the culprits should not be prosecuted; more harm would come to the boy's family through prosecution, and a consensus emerges that justice is not always done by complete obedience to the letter of the law.

It is this rethinking of the relationship of law to morality and to justice that crime fiction so ably dramatizes. Just as crime fiction has begun to deal with the possibility of child victims (adolescent victims commonly appear), so crime fiction has begun to ask questions about the usefulness of criminal prosecutions, as well as whether or not policies of incarceration can make any difference at all either to the safety of the population as a whole or to the reform of the guilty. In these debates, what crime fiction is doing is to ask questions about our relationship with the state: most radically the question asked is whether or not we need to detect, and punish, murderers. Across all continents, there is a consensus that serial killers need to be apprehended and locked up, but there is less of a consensus that institutional punishment is always necessary in the case of murder. In the west, the moral authority of the state has always been more fictional than real; the state has liked to think that it represented the views and the values of the majority of the population, but in actual fact, considerable numbers of people have always dissented from the actions of the state and made little secret of that dissent. While war, and the sense of a common enemy, has generally united much of the population, peace-time generally undermines the authority of the state. Given the domestic peace that has reigned in most European countries since 1945, the state has increasingly become regarded as the benevolent provider and arbitrator of good order and prosperity rather than as a site of moral authority.

In this context, it is possible to think of the state as most centrally concerned with the subjective life of its citizens. The state is expected to provide schools, hospitals and enough income for citizens to live in relative prosperity and with the means for consumption. Indeed, as the credit 'crunch' of 2008 has made transparently clear, a major function of the contemporary capitalist state has been to ensure that its citizens can continue to consume actively; the health of the high street and the shopping mall is the state of health which underpins the wider health of the social world. With this kind of preoccupation central to its concerns, it is not altogether surprising that the public, and the media, might ask questions about what the existing role of the state actually is, and whether or not it has actually abandoned all pretext of moral arbitration and leadership. When Bill Clinton remarked, in answer to the question about the identity of the most important political question, that 'it's the economy, stupid', he made it as clear as Marx had always suggested, that the state is the ruling committee of the bourgeoisie and primarily about the furtherance of an existing economic order. We have perhaps less sense of the class lines and allegiances of the social than was the case in the second half of the nineteenth century, but divisions of wealth are still stark throughout the west, and with those divisions of wealth remains a determination, by many, to share in that wealth.

It is the question of the protection of the interests of the rich which has remained a central organizing theme of detective fiction throughout the twentieth century. There are, of course, the many exceptions of the writers who have written about the murders caused by various forms of jealousy (although sexual jealousy is the most consistently significant), envy and fears of various kinds of social disclosure, but a central theme that has run through detective fiction, and certainly its more distinguished writers, is that of human greed. Greed, detective fiction says quite starkly and clearly, makes people kill; not just in terms of the possible loss (or gain) of money but also in terms of changes in the relationships which allow money to be made.

In this, detective fiction (again with exceptions) has been a tradition, which has never taken the social world at its face value. Those sections of the reading public, which reject the genre in ways that are often replications of Q. D. Leavis's view of 'popular' literature, and refuse engagement with writers such as Ian Rankin, who de-mythologizes one of the great cities of bourgeois culture, do so with the same energy that once refused to allow the connections between the slave trade and the wealth of Bristol merchants. Here is Q. D. Leavis (writing in 1932) finding moral decay in reading detective fiction:

> Under the head of 'mental relaxation' may be included detective stories, the enormous popularity of which (like the passion for solving cross-word puzzles) seems to show that for the reader of today a not unpleasurable way of relaxing is to exercise the ratiocinative faculties on a minor non-personal problem . . . It is relevant to note here that the author of detective novels consulted receives letters from school-boys, scientific men, clergymen, lawyers and business men generally, and adds 'I think am read more by the upper classes than the lower classes and by men more than women.' The social orders named here as forming the backbone of the detective-story public are those who in the last century would have been the guardians of the public conscience in the matter of mental self-indulgence.[6]

There is much which is interesting about this comment, not least the very idea of 'guardians of the public conscience'. But what is important about Q. D. Leavis's view is that it is not unlike those same views, which today continue to draw clear lines around various forms of fiction and the kinds of problems, which novelists explore. That minor 'non-personal problem' may well be of little interest to anyone except the relatives of the corpse but so, it might be said, are some of the problems discussed in prize-winning fiction.

A structural account of the social world is thus one, which permeates much of detective fiction. It is not, as some might like to have it, that detective (and crime) fiction is about a struggle between the good and the bad. As many writers in the genre know (and certainly as its great writers acknowledge) good and bad might be useful social binaries, but they have little place in the real world: good and bad are constructed and learned within the social context in which we live. Crime and detective writing has become ever more analytical in its account of the collusions between various sorts of badness and various sorts of apparent goodness. The social fabric is complicated both by our knowledge of the iniquities and the inequalities of that fabric and by the various failings of the state to correct and to assume authority over this social form. Hence, moral uncertainty and moral ambiguity, states in which the unthinkable and the terrible – the death of a child through murder – assumes the status of an act which re-inforces moral certainty. Attacks on children, the death of children by the neglect or cruelty of their parents, as historians would point out, is no new thing: the bond between mother and child is not always happy and loving, and commonplace resentment and lack of interest may all too easily take a suddenly callous turn. But what it allows, once publicly known, is a revival of moral certainty, an enthusiasm for morality, its terms about punishment and judgement, which has otherwise become absent.

Where attacks on children return us to, as members of a particular society, is that evocation of 'evil' as a personal trait. The press, which so enthusiastically scatters the adjective 'evil' over the heads of social workers, mothers and fathers and anyone else who has come near to a child with less than positive results is, as many people have pointed out, also the press, which has presented fantasy, and fetishistic, accounts of motherhood and pregnancy, accounts in which the baby and the child, as real and with individual needs, have little place. The delusion of the inevitable sanctity of parenthood (and motherhood in particular) is thus constructed as a given and a theme allowed to emerge, which becomes at least a part of expectations and aspirations about adults and children. No major writer of crime and detective fiction has yet produced a work which matches anything like the real-life horror of the deaths of the children killed by Mary Bell or Ian Hendry and Myra Hindley. But in this context, we might see less the refusal of writers to exploit the unbearable than the recognition by writers – who deal in the imagination rather than in fantasy – that such deaths are, just as much as the murders of adult, created.

Detective and crime fiction, whether good or bad, is a work of the imagination, an act of creation, which is both rational and creative. Media campaigns about, for example, paedophiles are fantasy: fantasies created about other people out of fantasies, which groups of individuals refuse to confront. In the case of the various media-led witch-hunts against paedophiles, the fantasy, which many in that enthusiastic, persecuting public cannot face, is the very seductive quality that children have. In his autobiography *Experience*, Martin Amis writes about the multi-murderer Frederick West and his various assaults on children, including West's own. Yet, Amis acknowledges the thoughts, which he describes as 'wayward' and which are possible when handling young children and babies: 'It feels like a sexual thought but in essence it is a violent thought'.[7] What Amis is suggesting to us, and what other authors and a long tradition of psychoanalysts have done, is that denying the physical, sensual appeal of young children is close to a form of abuse in itself. If we do not acknowledge that given quality, the quality of innocence with which all children are born, then it is all too easy to wish to project onto children an adult sexuality: the denial lays the grounds for the abuse.

Thus, the 'evil', which sections of the popular press are so anxious to condemn and, more dangerously, to seek out, is a form of the refusal and the rejection of the possibilities of the sexuality of the young. One of the (many) paradoxes of the late twentieth and early twenty-first centuries is that although we are often told that we have become more 'emotionally literate', there are considerable areas of emotional life where that claim would seem to be a little exaggerated. We have, certainly, come to recognize the importance of maintaining contact between carers and very young children. After the work of John Bowlby and Anna Freud, we would no longer see it as a good idea (as was the case in Britain in 1940) to remove very young children to unknown destinations without their most significant others, nor would we expect those same children to endure hospitalization without the presence of those same people. But while 'child centredness' has taken its place as an organizing tenet of schools and hospitals, other aspects of the culture have suggested that perhaps we have become less, rather than more, emotionally aware.

The instance where this could be demonstrated is in the case of death: the event which is crucial to much detective and crime fiction. The suspicious death of a person is to be investigated, and that forms the basis of detective fiction. Yet, at the same time, the death of a person is also a matter of loss and mourning, and it is in this sense that contemporary life has lost its sense of the impact of death on those left behind. But one of the characteristics of detective fiction is that it is a genre which continues to assert the impact of death on the survivors: from Peter Wimsey to Adam Dalgleish, famous detectives are touched by the death of those close to them, and they are marked by it. It is on this capacity of human beings to be changed and affected by the death of others that detective fiction is particularly articulate; what is recognized is that people do not 'recover' from the death of others, and that memory is a central part of the human condition.

Adam Dalgleish, his creator P. D. James makes clear, has long mourned the death of his first wife and their baby son. This tragedy is reproduced by Elizabeth George when Inspector Lynley's wife, pregnant with their first child, is killed. Both of these authors allow their heroes the capacity to be both furious and distraught with grief: a sadness, which like that of King Lear's, quite literally rages. Nor does detective fiction ignore other forms and aspects of death: there are the deaths which occur as a result of terrible accidents, and which then become the focus for revenge. There are the deaths by suicide which are the result of some form of cruelty to a particular person; there are the deaths which result from some attack on a person's integrity or values. For example, in Ruth Dudley Edwards's *Carnage in the Committee*, a father seeks revenge for the carelessness shown to his daughter, an aspirant author, by a man with considerable standing in the world of publishing:

> For all that Mary believed in her talent, she was a modest girl and she thought maybe the book wasn't good enough . . . She had an answer from Hugo Hurlingham . . . he spoke warmly about the quality and originality of her book . . . Then he took her out again and asked her to go to bed with him and she said no. After that he never answered her letters or returned her phone calls . . . She became very manic and one night she just jumped into the Thames . . .[8]

The same disappointment about the world creates the fury of a central character in Veronica Stallwood's *Oxford Exit*:

> They came in, those computer pedlars, with nothing on their minds except cost-effectiveness. Money. They swept aside the old men, the ones who loved books and cared for them, men who dedicated their lives to accuracy and scholarship, and they imposed their new regime with its modern jargon, its bastardised English and its obsession with speed and deadlines. They had no moral sense, no respect for people or tradition.[9]

In both these cases, the authors are allowing their characters to speak for what is now, as much as it was in the past, a central human predicament: how to protest and how to find a form of redemptive justice. Politics has long given voice to groups of people who have been dispossessed or the subject of grave injustice, although not always with lasting or particularly helpful results. But for individuals with a sense of grievance – the father robbed of his beloved daughter, the man appalled at the destruction of his life's work – the dominant emotional rhetoric of the twenty-first century tells us only to 'move on' or to 'seek some kind of closure'. These anodyne suggestions have become part and parcel of a political as well as a social consensus: 'moving on' has been used to justify the abandoning of, for example in British politics, a discussion of class and 'seeking closure' is used

in multiple situations where identifying a particular responsibility is thought
to have too problematic consequences.

   Against this erosion of interest in cause and effect, detective and crime
fiction propose something of a different perspective. Very little crime or
detective fiction suggests the kind of mob rule which sections of the press
come close to advocating, but what the fiction does do is to continue to
make a place in the social world for the discussion of the impact of events
on others for a consideration of the idea that perhaps 'the evil that men
does lives after them'. Modernity has always been premised on the value of
movement, progress, change and the ready abandonment of the past. Yet,
with this has disappeared a certain degree of understanding about the way
in which human beings are made and formed by the past and that sometimes it is appropriate not to forget and not to assume that latent conflicts
can be solved by 'moving on'. Those memories, which have been allowed
the greatest social space in the west in the past 50 years (for example the
huge industry surrounding the policies of Hitler's Germany towards
the Jews) have usually been the memories associated with the dominant
political agenda; the memories of those outside this agenda have been
given less public acknowledgement. Those fault lines in the social world,
which have persisted for centuries, of inequalities of class, gender and race
are given a place in detective and crime fiction, which is often absent in the
social world. Inevitably, the discussion of these fault lines can be less than
welcome, and as such, it is inevitable that 'evil' is a more easily endorsed
explanation of the behaviour of criminals and murderers than any account
which articulates a pattern in human behaviour. We do not have to make
heroes out of criminals or murderers in order to maintain our belief in the
possibilities of explaining the actions of human beings. Murder, by individuals of other individuals, is not a form of politics, even though populations
throughout the world have had to live, in the twentieth century, in states
which have maintained that civilian casualties are an inevitable, and sometimes appropriate, feature of war.

   Detective fiction in Europe (very much more than in the United States)
has a long and honourable history of opposition to capital punishment,
a form of state violence against others, which had long persisted in Europe.
Populist sentiments still express enthusiasm for this form of punishment,
and it is often associated with those kinds of crimes, generally against children, where sections of the press have done the most to excite demands
for revenge. Demands for capital punishment go hand in hand with author-
itarian views about the world and with a moral perception, which makes
clear distinctions between 'good' and 'evil'. Arguably, demands for capital

punishment (and other forms of punishment, which involve physical harm to others) are part of human fears about our own capacity for 'evil', and it is extremely difficult, for individuals in the contemporary west, to acknowledge that as much as human beings can love, so they can also hate. But as the culture in which we live teaches us, and encourages us, to love ourselves ('be good to yourself', 'you're worth it'), so it becomes more difficult to depart from our self-perception as people whose emotional range is limited to 'love', albeit often in the form of that hedonism which is most likely to involve consumption. The title of Avner Offer's *The Challenge of Affluence* continued a debate which has existed since the end of the Second World War: how can the 'rich' societies of the west find, and define, moral and ethical agendas for their citizens? That theme, of the moral vacuum of the west, is one, which detective fiction, particularly in recent work in Scandinavia, has explored. At the same time, an argument has emerged that, in the world post 9/11, 'real' detective work is now the matter of security services rather than the police: a point about this change made, with some emphasis, in Peter Robinson's *All the Colours of Darkness*. In the novel, Inspector Banks (who has made something of a study of Peter Hennessy's *The Secret State*) is warned off the further investigation of murders because it would involve the exposure of the workings of the security systems. At the conclusion of the novel, after Banks has resisted this idea, he is faced with a member of the security services telling him:

'The truth is that none of this happened', the woman went on . . . 'You can tell all the stories you want, but I guarantee you that nobody will believe a word you say. If necessary, we'll give you a legend that will land you in jail for the rest of your days.'[10]

The apparent absence of collective and individual moral agendas in the west, as well as the increased distance of the police from what sections of the political world regard as the crucial crime, and threat to the state, of terrorism is, while debateable in its existence, nevertheless an absence (real or otherwise), which has created intense moral responses. Among those responses is that of fundamentalist religion, a form of politics, which assures its believers that there is a clear morality in the world, and all that is demanded of them as human beings is obedience to it. This essentially pre-Enlightenment idea, indeed a betrayal of every form of sceptical and critical intelligence, has been seized upon by millions of people. It is part of that same coinage, which wishes to believe in 'evil', an assurance that a world (which for many people has become increasingly complex) can be understood and

even controlled. Thus, the same social pressures, which underpin fundamentalist religions and politics inform those social judgements which
encourage the assumption that 'evil' can be easily identified and attacked.
In this sense, we can understand those press campaigns for 'Sarah's Law'
and for the naming and shaming of social workers as a form of fundamentalism; the same press, which is quick to condemn what it sees as fundamentalism in non-western religions (notably, of course, Islam) demonstrates
that the ethos of fundamentalism is not primarily about religion but about
the refusal of rational thought, which allows, and gives a space for,
ambiguity.

In this context, we might perhaps do more to celebrate detective and
crime fiction, and to allow that it has a long, continuing and honourable
tradition of suggesting to us that rapid distinctions between good and bad,
between the conventional and the unconventional, are usually wrong and
based on normative expectations, which have little foundation in actual
human behaviour. From Jane Austen's heroines and Miss Marple to Kurt
Wallender, detectives (of various kinds) have challenged the view that the
conventional and the orthodox are the good and the honest. Behind those
facades, from Miss Marple's British middle class to the rich and less rich of
Wallender's Sweden, there lies both the murderous and the sinned against.
For all its many occasional simplicities of plot and language, detective and
crime fiction has one cardinal virtue which it is helpful to recognize: it
looks beyond and behind the various facades of social life; it steps away
from that comfortable view that the social world includes only good and
bad people and that social order can be maintained by the eradication of
the latter. As every criminologist knows, as we have become more prosperous, so we have become more crime-free. If we continue to buy crime and
detective detection in such considerable quantities, it is, perhaps, because a
belief in the existence of crime is central to a continuing belief in our own
capacity for moral order. As the social realities of the twenty-first century
bring many people into contact with problematic changes in gender and
ethnic identities, so writing about crime seems to offer a place of certainty
and continuity. While this remains the case for some authors writing about
crime, it is increasingly less true in many others: as authors have come to
extend and challenge definitions of crime and the criminal, so we are able
to see that crime no longer pays its social dues of allowing firm premises for
morality and the law.

Notes

Introduction

[1] Peter Guttridge, 'The Murder Rate Just Goes Up and Up', *The Observer*, 14 December 2008.

[2] *The Book of Exodus, Authorised King James version of The Bible* (London: Lutterworth Press, 1954) Exod. 21.24–25.

[3] Wendy Brown, *Regulating Aversion: Tolerance in the Age of Empire and Identity* (New Jersey: Princeton University Press, 2006).

[4] Keith Thomas, *Religion and the Decline of Magic* (London: Weidenfeld and Nicolson, 1971).

[5] Ruth Morse, 'Racination and ratiocination: post-colonial crime', *European Review*, 13 (1), 2005, 79–89.

[6] Karl Marx, *Economic and Philosophic Manuscripts of 1844* (New York: International Publishers, 1970), p. 108.

[7] Jonathan Jackson, 'Experience and expression: social and cultural significance in the fear of crime', *British Journal of Criminology*, 44 (6), 2004, 946–66.

Chapter 1

[1] At the time of writing, there were a number of prizes for the writers of crime fiction, among them the Crime Writers Association Duncan Lawrie Dagger (previously known as the Gold Dagger for Fiction) and various more specialist awards for particular sub-genres of crime fiction (e.g. the Ellis Peters award for crime-writing set in the past).

[2] Julian Symons, *Bloody Murder* (London: Penguin, 1985); Ernest Mandel, *Delightful Murder* (Minneapolis: University of Minnesota Press, 1984); T. J. Binyon, *Murder Will Out* (Oxford: Oxford University Press, 1990).

[3] Ernest Mandel, *Delightful Murder*, p. 11.

[4] M. Lee, 'The genesis of "Fear of Crime"', *Theoretical Criminology*, 5, 2001, 467–85.

[5] See, for example, Frank Furedi, *The Culture of Fear* (London: Continuum, 1997).

[6] Avner Offer, *The Challenge of Affluence* (Oxford: Oxford University Press, 2007).

[7] George Puttnam, *Bowling Alone* (New York: Simon and Schuster, 2000).

[8] Elizabeth Wilson, 'Psychoanalysis: psychic law and order?', *Feminist Review*, 8, Summer 1981, 63–78.

[9] E. J. Hobsbawm, 'The retreat of the male', *London Review of Books*, 4 August 2005, pp. 8–9.

[10] C. Day Lewis, 'Where are the war poets?', in *Word Over All* (London: Cape, 1943).

[11] Oliver James, *The Selfish Capitalist: Origins of Affluenza* (London: Random House, 2007).

[12] Richard Layard, *Happiness: Lessons from a New Science* (London: Penguin, 2006).

[13] Peter Ackroyd, *Poe: A Life Cut Short* (London: Chatto, 2007).

[14] These connections are set out by David Frisby in 'Walter Benjamin and detection', *German Politics and Society*, 32, Summer 1994, 89–106.

[15] Julian Symons, *Bloody Murder*, p. 28.

[16] Stieg Larsson, *The Girl who Played with Fire* (London: Quercus, 2009), p. 364.

Chapter 2

[1] Emile Durkheim, *Moral Education* (New York: The Free Press, 1973), p. 45.

[2] Marilyn Butler, *Jane Austen and War of Ideas* (Oxford: Oxford University Press, 1987).

[3] Jane Austen, *Mansfield Park* (London: David Campbell, 1992), p. 234.

[4] Jane Austen, *Sense and Sensibility* (London: David Campbell, 1992), p. 12.

[5] Alastair Duckworth, *The Improvement of the Estate* (Baltimore and London: Johns Hopkins University Press, 1971).

[6] Giorgio Agamben, *Marginal Notes* (Minneapolis: University of Minnesota Press, 2000), p. 86.

[7] Anne de Courcy, *Diana Mosley* (London: Chatto and Windus, 2003), p. 263.

[8] Ernest Mandel, *Delightful Murder*, p. 19.

[9] Kate Summerscale, *The Suspicions of Mr Whicher or The Murder at Road Hill House* (London: Bloomsbury, 2008).

[10] David Frisby, *Cityscapes of Modernity* (Cambridge: Polity, 2001), p. 54.

[11] David Frisby, *Cityscapes of Modernity*, p. 99.

[12] John Hayward (ed.), *John Donne* (Harmondsworth: Penguin, 1950), p. 89.

[13] Herbert Grierson (ed.), *Donne: Poetical Works* (Oxford: Oxford University Press, 1977), p. 108.

[14] Jane Austen, *Persuasion* (London: David Campbell, 1992), p. 155.

[15] Elizabeth Gaskell, *North and South* (London: Wordsworth Editions Ltd, 1995), p. 66.

[16] Jane Austen, *Persuasion*, pp. 155–6.

[17] Sarah Evans, Unpublished PhD thesis, *Becoming Somebody: Higher Education and the Aspirations of Working Class Girls*, University of Kent at Canterbury, 2008.

[18] Charles Dickens, *Bleak House* (London: Penguin, 1971), p. 53.

[19] Jenny Uglow, *Elizabeth Gaskell: A Habit of Stories* (London: Faber and Faber, 1994), p. 369.

[20] Sara Ahmed, *The Cultural Politics of Emotion* (Edinburgh: Edinburgh University Press and Routledge, 2004), p. 63.

[21] Philip Knightley, *The Second Oldest Profession: Spies and Spying in the Twentieth Century* (London: Pimlico, 2003).

22 E. J. Hobsbawm, *The Age of Capital* (London: Weidenfeld and Nicolson, 1975), p. 249.

23 E. J. Hobsbawm, *Interesting Times* (London: Abacus, 2003), p. 155.

24 See Gordon Weaver, *Conan Doyle and the Parson's Son: The George Edalji Case* (London: Pegasus, 2007) for the non-fictional account and *Arthur and George* by Julian Barnes (London: Random House, 2005) for a fictional account of the case.

25 Peter Watson, *A Terrible Beauty* (London: Weidenfeld and Nicolson, 2000), p. 5.

26 Apart from the original texts, there are excellent accounts of the relationship between modernity and the individual in Jurgen Habermas, *The Philosophical Discourse of Modernity* (Cambridge, MA: MIT Press, 1987) and Gerald Delanty, *Social Theory in a Changing World* (Cambridge: Polity, 1999).

27 Rudyard Kipling, *The Just So Stories* (London: Macmillan, 1902).

28 David Frisby, *Cityscapes of Modernity*, p. 57.

29 Gilles Deleuze, *Difference and Repetition* (London: Continuum, 2004), p. 90.

30 Walter Benjamin, 'Central Park', 'Theory of remembrance', in Howard Eiland (ed.), *Selected Writings, Vol. 4, 1938–1940*, (Cambridge, MA: Harvard University Press, 2003).

Chapter 3

1 Virginia Woolf, *Three Guineas* (London: Penguin, 1993, first published in 1938).

2 For example, there was not always the universal enthusiasm for female suffrage as is supposed. See: Julia Bush, *Women against the Vote: Female Anti-Suffragism in Britain* (Oxford: Oxford University Press, 2007).

3 Alison Light, *Mrs Woolf and the Servants* (London: Penguin, 2007).

4 Alison Light, *Forever England* (London: Routledge, 1991).

5 The *Decalogue* or *Ten Commandments of Writing Detective Fiction* by Ronald Knox are published in the Introduction to *The Best Detective Stories of 1928–29*, reprinted in H. Haycraft, *Murder for Pleasure: The Life and Times of the Detective Story* (New York: Biblio and Tannen, 1976).

6 Michael Innes (the pseudonym of John Innes Mackintosh Stewart) is among the best-known writers of the so-called don's delight detective novels. Julian Symons comments on the urbanity of Innes's novels, and Innes as a writer who 'turns the detective story into an over-civilized joke with a frivolity which makes it a literary conversation piece with detection taking place on the side'. (*Bloody Murder*, p. 115).

7 Agatha Christie, *An Autobiography* (London: Collins, 1977), p. 114.

8 T. S. Eliot, *The Waste Land* (New York: Boni and Liveright, 1922), line 223.

9 Alison Light discusses critical literature on Christie in chapter 2 of *Forever England*.

10 Jean Baudrillard, *The Gulf War Did Not Take Place* (Sydney: Power Institute Publications, 1995).

11 Agatha Christie, *The Mysterious Affair at Styles* (London: Bodley Head, 1920), p. 203.

12 Agatha Christie, *The Murder at the Vicarage* (London: Collins, 1930), p. 28.

13 Agatha Christie, *The Murder at the Vicarage*, p. 29.

14 Agatha Christie, *The Murder at the Vicarage*, p. 29.

15 K. Marx and F. Engels, *The Origin of the Family, Private Property and the State* (London: Penguin, 1985).

16 Agatha Christie, *The Body in the Library* (London: Collins, 1942), p. 15.

17 Agatha Christie, *The Body in the Library*, p. 137.

18 Agatha Christie, *4.50 from Paddington* (London: Pan Books, 1974), p. 28.

19 Ross McKibbon, *Classes and Culture: England 1918–1951* (Oxford: Oxford University Press, 1998), p. 528.

20 Agatha Christie, *4.50 from Paddington*, p. 217.

21 Evelyn Waugh, *The Letters of Evelyn Waugh* (Harmondsworth: Penguin, 1982), p. 236.

22 Dorothy Sayers, *Gaudy Night* (London: Coronet, 1990), p. 427.

23 Adrienne Rich, 'Compulsory heterosexuality and lesbian existence', in A. Snitow et al. (eds) *Desire: The Politics of Sexuality* (London: Virago, 1984), pp. 212–17.

24 Susannah Radstone, 'The sexual politics of nostalgia', in *The Sexual Politics of Time* (London: Routledge, 2007), pp. 112–59.

25 Lauren Berlant, *The Queen of America Goes to Washington City: Essays on Sex and Citizenship* (North Caroline: Duke University Press, 1997).

26 Gillian Rose, *Love's Work* (London: Chatto and Windus, 1995), p. 134.

27 Agatha Christie, *Mrs McGinty's Dead* (London: Collins, 2002), p. 103.

Chapter 4

1   Simone de Beauvoir, *The Prime of Life* (London: Penguin, 1962), p. 49.

2   Ernest Mandel, *Delightful Murder*, pp. 35–6.

3   Diane Johnson, *The Life of Dashiell Hammett* (London: Picador, 1983), p. 21.

4   Julian Symons, *Bloody Murder*, p. 126.

5   Simone de Beauvoir, *The Prime of Life*, p. 50.

6   James Burke, *Swan Peak* (London: Orion, 2008), pp. 401–2.

7   David Harvey, *The Condition of Postmodernity* (Oxford: Blackwell, 1990).

8   Diane Johnson, *The Life of Dashiell Hammett*, p. 185.

9   Ernest Mandel, *Delightful Murder*, p. 46.

10 Leonard Woolf, *Growing: An Autobiography of the Years 1904–1911* (London: Hogarth, 1961).

11 Ernest Mandel, *Delightful Murder*, p. 47.

12 Karl Marx, *Capital, Volume One* (London: Penguin,1976), p. 163.

13 Raymond Chandler, *The Lady in the Lake* (London: Heinemann, 1977), p. 393.

14 Diane Johnson, *The Life of Dashiell Hammett*, p. 126.

15 Dashiell Hammett, *Complete Novels* (New York: Alfred Knopf, 1999), p. 965.

16 Dashiell Hammett, *The Thin Man*, in *Complete Novels*, p. 802.

17 Marty Jezer, *The Dark Ages: Life in the United States 1945–1960* (Boston, MA: South End Press, 1982), p. 227.

18 This history, and the related issues, is reviewed in a number of works. See for example, Penny Summerfield, *Women Workers in the Second World War: Production and Patriarchy in Conflict* (London: Croom Helm, 1984).

19 Diane Johnson, *The Life of Dashiell Hammett*, p. 233.

20 Diane Johnson, *The Life of Dashiell Hammett*, p. 233.
21 Christine Matzke and Susanne Muhleisen (eds), *Postcolonial Postmortems: Crime Fiction from a Transcultural Perspective.*
22 Georges Simenon, *The Man Who Watched the Trains Go By* (London: Routledge, 1942), p. 136.
23 Georges Simenon, *Maigret and the Idle Burglar* (London: Hamish Hamilton, 1963), pp. 12–13.
24 Boris Akunin, the Erast Fandarin novels and Leonardo Padura, the *Havana Quartet*, featuring Inspector Mario Conde. (Akunin is published by London: Weidenfeld and Nicolson; Padura by London: Bitter Lemon Press.)
25 David Peace, *The Red Riding Quartet* (London: Faber and Faber, 2008).

Chapter 5

1 Dorothy Hughes, *The Expendable Man* (London: Persephone Books, 2006), p. 74.
2 Elizabeth Wilson, 'Bohemian Love', *Theory, Culture and Society*, 15 (3–4), 111–27.
3 Steven Box, *Power, Crime and Mystification* (London: Tavistock, 1983); *Recession, Crime and Punishment* (London: Macmillan, 1987).
4 Philip Larkin, 'Annus Mirabilis', in *Collected Poems* (London: Faber and Faber, 1988), p. 167.
5 Sara Paretsky, *Toxic Shock* (London: Penguin, 1988), p. 284.
6 Val McDermid, *The Mermaids Singing* (London: Harper Collins 1995), p. 195.
7 Michael Malone, *Time's Witness* (London: Robinson, 2002); *Uncivil Seasons* (London, Robinson, 2002); *First Lady* (London: Robinson, 2003).
8 Simone de Beauvoir, *The Second Sex* (New York: Bantam Books, 1962), p. 58.
9 Ann Douglas, *The Feminisation of American Culture* (London: Macmillan, 1988).
10 P. D. James, *The Murder Room* (London: Faber and Faber), p. 9.
11 Gayatri Spivak, 'Can the subaltern speak?' in C. Nelson and L. Grossberg (eds), *Marxism and the Interpretation of Culture* (Basingstoke: Macmillan, 1988), pp. 271–306.
12 Linda McDowell, *Capital Culture* (Oxford: Blackwell, 1997).
13 Elizabeth George, *With No One as Witness* (London: Hodder and Stoughton, 2005), p. 494.
14 Liz Stanley (ed.), *The Diaries of Hannah Cullwick: Victorian Maidservant* (London: Virago, 1985).
15 Patricia Cornwell, *Predator* (London: Little Brown, 2005), p. 65.
16 See Donna Haraway, *Simians, Cyborgs and Women: The Re-invention of Nature* (London: Free Association Press, 1991); Sarah Franklin, *Dolly Mixtures: The Re-Making of Genealogy* (Durham, NC: Duke University Press, 2007).
17 Patricia Cornwell, *Postmortem* (London: Macdonald, 1990), p. 38.
18 Patricia Cornwall, *Postmortem*, p. 38.
19 Patricia Cornwell, *Postmortem*, p. 66.
20 Patricia Cornwell, *Postmortem*, p. 67.
21 Jo Nesbo, *Devil's Star* (London: Harvill Secker, 2005), p. 150.
22 Patricia Cornwell, *Predator*, p. 215.

[23] See, for example, Donna Leon, *Friends in High Places* (London: Arrow, 2001); Barbara Nadel, *A Passion for Killing* (London: Headline, 2007).

[24] John Sutherland, 'U.S. Confidential', *New Statesman*, 13 September 2007.

[25] Donna Landry and Gerald MacLean, *Materialist Feminisms* (Oxford: Blackwell, 1993), p. 104.

[26] Jeffrey Weeks, *The World We Have Won* (London: Routledge, 2007).

[27] Tim Adams, 'The Karen Matthews Trial', *The Observer*, 7 December 2008.

[28] Gillian Rose, *Love's Work*, p. 126.

Chapter 6

[1] Slovoj Zizek, 'How to read Lacan', http://www.lacan.com (accessed on 18 April 2009).

[2] Ellis Peters (the pseudonym of Edith Pargeter) wrote 20 Brother Cadfael novels. Other writers who have set their mysteries in the distant past include Margaret Frazer, Michael Jecks and Caroline Roe. This sub-genre of crime fiction has attracted its own secondary literature, for example, Rosemary Erickson Johnsen, *Contemporary Feminist Historical Crime Fiction* (London: Palgrave Macmillan, 2009).

[3] Val McDermid, 'Introduction' to Maj Sjöwall and Per Wahlöö, *The Man Who Went Up in Smoke* (London: Harper Perennial, 2006), p. vii.

[4] Christopher Lasch, *The Culture of Narcissism* (New York: Norton, 1979); Richard Sennett, *Respect in a World of Inequality* (London: Penguin, 2003) and *The Craftsman* (London: Allen Lane, 2008).

[5] Richard Layard, *Happiness: Lessons from a New Science* (London, Penguin, 2006).

[6] Maj Sjöwall, 'Interrogation of Maj Sjöwall', in Maj Sjöwall and Per Wahlöö, *Roseanna* (London: Harper Perennial, 2006), p. 10.

[7] Maj Sjöwall and Per Wahlöö, *The Locked Room* (London: Harper Perennial, 2007), p. 55.

[8] Henning Mankell, *One Step Behind* (London: Harvill Press, 2002), p. 208.

[9] Henning Mankell, 'Introduction', to Maj Sjöwall and Per Wahlöö, *Roseanna*.

[10] Jo Nesbo, *The Devil's Star*, p. 295.

[11] Maj Sjöwall and Per Wahlöö, *The Terrorists* (London: Harper Perennial, 2007), p. 266.

[12] Stieg Larssen, *The Girl with the Dragon Tattoo* (London: Quercus Press, 2005) and *The Girl Who Played with Fire* (London; Quercus Press, 2009).

[13] Henning Mankel, *One Step Behind*, p. 438.

[14] Lionel Shriver, *We Need to Talk about Kevin* (London: Serpent's Tail, 2005), p. 333.

[15] Lionel Shriver, *We Need to Talk about Kevin*, p. 389.

[16] Diane Johnson, *The Life of Dashiell Hammett*, p. 78.

[17] Sylvia Plath, *The Bell Jar* (London: Faber and Faber, 1963), p. 122.

[18] Gitta Sereny, *Albert Speer: His Battle with Truth* (New York: Knopf, 1995); *Cries Unheard: The Story of Mary Bell* (London: Macmillan, 1998).

[19] Gitta Sereny, *Cries Unheard: The Story of Mary Bell*, p. 38.

[20] Gitta Sereny, *Cries Unheard: The Story of Mary Bell*, p. 384.

[21] Bernhard Schlink, *Self's Punishment* (London: Phoenix, 2005), p. 288.

Chapter 7

1. Thomas De Quincey's 'On murder considered as one of the fine arts' was first published in Blackwood's Magazine in 1827 and was inspired by a series of real life murders. The essay was enthusiastically received and followed by additional essays in 1839 and 1854. De Quincey's account of murder has been praised by later writers on crime, including George Orwell.

2. Gen. 4.4–5, *The Bible*.

3. Diana Souhami has described the history of one of the earliest examples of press 'sensations'; the return of Alexander Selkirk (the model for the fictional Robinson Crusoe) to Britain. See Diana Souhami, *Selkirk's Island*.

4. Ronald Dahl, 'Lamb to the slaughter', in *Collected Short Stories* (London: Penguin, 1992).

5. There are numerous web accounts of the judge killed in the mysteriously exploding shed (see, for example, www.timesonline.co.uk). For photographs and discussion of Cornelia Parker's exploding shed, see Cornelia Parker, *Catalogue*, Institute of Contemporary Art, Boston, MA, 2000.

6. Q. D. Leavis, *Fiction and the Reading Public* (London: Chatto and Windus, 1968), p. 51.

7. Martin Amis, *Experience* (London: Vintage, 2001), p. 140.

8. Ruth Dudley Edwards, *Carnage in the Committee* (London: HarperCollins, 2004), p. 236.

9. Victoria Stallwood, *Oxford Exit* (London: Macmillan, 1994), p. 111.

10. Peter Robinson, *All the Colours of Darkness* (London: Macmillan, 2008), p. 129.

Bibliography

Ackroyd, P. (2008), *Poe: A Life Cut Short*. London: Chatto & Windus.

Agamben, G. (2000), *Marginal Notes*. Minneapolis: University of Minnesota Press.

Akunin, B. (2003), *The Winter Queen*. London: Weidenfeld & Nicolson.

—(2007), *Special Assignments*. London: Weidenfeld & Nicolson.

Anderson, B. (1983), *Imagined Communities*. London: Verso.

Auden, W. H. (1980), 'The guilty vicarage', in R. Winks (ed.), *Detective Fiction: A Collection of Critical Essays*. Englewood Cliffs, NJ: Countryman.

Barzun, J. (1971), *A Catalogue of Crime*. New York: Harper & Row.

Bertens, H. and D'Haen, T. (2001), *Contemporary American Crime Fiction*. Houndmills: Palgrave.

Binyon, T. J. (1990), *'Murder Will Out': The Detective in Fiction*. Oxford: Oxford University Press.

Bleiler, E. F. (1978), *Three Detective Novels*. New York: Dover.

Buckley, J. (2006), *So He Takes the Dog*. London: Fourth Estate.

Bush, J. (2007), *Women against the Vote: Female Anti-Suffragism in Britain*. Oxford: Oxford University Press.

Calvino, H. (2003), *Hermit in Paris: Autobiographical Writings*. London: Random House.

Chandler, R. (1939), *The Big Sleep*. London: Hamish Hamilton.

—(1940), *Farwell My Lovely*. London: Hamish Hamilton.

—(1943), *The High Window*. London: Hamish Hamilton.

—(1944), *The Lady in the Lake*. London: Hamish Hamilton.

—(1953), *The Long Goodbye*. London: Hamish Hamilton.

Chandra, V. (2006), *Sacred Games*. London: Faber & Faber.

Christian, E. (2001), *The Post Colonial Detective*. London: *Palgrave*.

Christie, A. (1920), *The Mysterious Affairs at Styles*. London: Bodley Head.

—(1926), *The Murder of Roger Ackroyd*. London: Collins.

—(1930), *The Murder at the Vicarage*. London: Collins.

—(1934), *Murder on the Orient Express*. London: Collins.

—(1935), *Death in the Clouds*. London: Collins.

—(1937), *Cards on the Table*. London: Collins.

—(1937), *Dumb Witness*. London: Collins.

—(1942), *The Body in the Library*. London: Collins.

—(1950), *A Murder is Announced*. London: Collins.

—(1953), *A Pocket Full of Rye*. London: Collins.

—(1953), *After the Funeral*. London: Collins.

—(1957), *4.50 From Paddington*. London: Harper Collins.

—(1962), *The Mirror Crack'd from Side to Side*. London: Harper Collins.

—(1965), *At Bertram's Hotel*. London: William Collins.

—(1977), *An Autobiography*. London: Harper Collins.

Corley, E. (1998), *Requiem Mass*. London: Hodder Headline.

—(2000), *Fatal Legacy*. London: Hodder Headline.

—(2007), *Grave Doubts*. London: Allison & Busby.

Cornwell, P. (1990), *Post Mortem*. London: Macdonald.

—(2005), *Predator*. London: Little Brown.

—(2006), *At Risk*. London: Little Brown.

Crofts, F. W. (2001), *Antidote to Venom*. London: House of Stratus.

—(2001), *Crime at Guildford*. Thirsk: Stratus.

—(2001), *Fear Comes to Chalfont*. Thirsk: Stratus.

—(2001), *Inspector French's Greatest Case*. London: House of Stratus.

De Courcy, A. (2003), *Diana Mosley*. London: Chatto & Windus.

Dudley Edwards, R. (1995), *Ten Lords A-Leaping*. London: Harper Collins.

—(1996), *Murder in a Cathedral*. London: Harper Collins.

—(2004), *Carnage on the Committee*. London: Harper Collins.

—(2007), *Murdering Americans*. Arizona: Poisoned Pen Press.

Fleming, S. (2003), *A Fountain Filled with Blood*. London: St Martin's Press.

—(2004), *Out of the Deep I Cry*. London: St Martin's Press.

—(2005), *To Darkness and to Death*. London: St Martin's Press.

Flynn, G. (2006), *Sharp Objects*. London: Weidenfeld & Nicolson.

Fox, K. (2004), *Malicious Intent*. London: Hodder and Stoughton.

—(2006), *Without Consent*. London: Hodder and Stoughton.

Frisby, D. (1994), 'Walter Benjamin and detection', in *German Politics and Society*. (32), 89–106.

George, E. (1989), *A Great Deliverance*. London: Hodder and Stoughton.

—(1989), *Payment in Blood*. London: Hodder and Stoughton.

—(1994), *Playing for the Ashes*. London: Bantam.

—(2005), *With No-one as Witness*. London: Hodder and Stoughton.

Goddard, R. (2006), *Never Go Back*. London: Corgi.

Grafton, S. (2003), *Sin for Silence*. London: Macmillan.

Greene, G. (1950), *The Fallen Idol*. London: Heinemann.

—(1950), *The Third Man*. London: Heinemann.

Habermas, J. (1991), *The Strcutural Transformation of the Public Sphere: An Inquiry into a Category of Bourgeois Society*. Cambridge, MA: MIT Press.

Hammett, D. (1990), *The Complete Novels*. New York: The Library of America, Library Classics.

Hayder, M. (2000), *Birdman*. London: Bantam.

— (2002), *The Treatment*. London: Bantam.

Hey, V. (2002), 'Horizontal solidarities and molten capitalism: the subject, intersubjectivity, self and the other in late modernity', in *Discourse*, 23 (2), 227–42.

Himes, C. (1990), *The Primitive*. London: Allison & Busby.

Hobsbawn, E. (4/8/2005), 'The retreat of the male', in *London Review of Books*. 27(15), 8–9.

Hughes, D. (2006), *The Expendable Man*. London: Persephone.

Huxley, E. (1983), *Murder on Safari*. London: Methuen.

Jackson, J. (2006), 'Introducing fear of crime to risk research', in *Risk Analysis*, 26 (1), 253–64.

James, P. D. (1997), *A Certain Justice*. London: Faber & Faber.
—(2003), *The Murder Room*. London: Faber & Faber.
Jezer, M. (1982), *The Dark Ages: Life in the United States 1945–1960*. Boston, MA: South End Press.
Johnson, C. (1995), *Equivocal Beings: Politics, Gender and Sentimentality in the 1790s*. Chicago: University of Chicago Press.
—(1997), 'Austen cults and cultures', in E. Copeland and J. McMalter (eds), *Cambridge Companion to Jane Austen*. Cambridge: Cambridge University Press.
Johnson, D. (1984), *The Life of Dashiell Hammett*. London: Pan Books.
Klein, K. G. (1988), *The Woman Detective: Gender and Genre*. London: University of Illinois Press.
Lackberg, C. (2007), *The Ice Princess*. London: HarperCollins.
Landry, D. and MacLean, G. (1993), *Materialist Feminisms*. Oxford: Blackwell.
Larsson, S. (2005), *The Girl with the Dragon Tattoo*. London: Queraus Press.
Leavis, Q. D. (1968), *Fiction and the Reading Public*. London: Chatto & Windus.
Leon, D. (2001), *Friends in High Places*. London: Arrow.
—(2004), *Uniform Justice*. London: Arrow.
—(2005), *Doctored Evidence*. London: Arrow.
—(2008), *The Girl of His Dreams*. London: Heinemann.
Levy, R. and Srebnick, A. G. (eds) (2005), *Crime and Culture: An Historical Perspective*. Aldershot: Ashgate.
Light, A. (1991), *Forever England: Femininity, Literature and Conservatism between the Wars*. London: Routledge.
Lynch, D. (1998), *The Economy of Character: Novels, Market Culture and the Business of Inner Meaning*. Chicago: University of Chicago Press.
Magdalen, N. (1985), *Death in Autumn*. London: HarperCollins.
Maitland, B. (2000), *Silvermeadow*. London: Orion.
—(2004), *No Trace*. London: Orion.
Mandel, E. (1984), *Delightful Murder: A Social History of the Crime Story*. London: Pluto.
Mankell, H. (2002), *One Step Behind*. London: Random House.
—(2003), *The White Lioness*. London: Vintage.
Marnham, P. (1992), *The Man Who Wasn't Maigret: A Portrait of George Simenon*. London: Bloomsbury.
Marsh, N. (1934), *A Man Lay Dead*. London: HarperCollins.
—(1935), *The Nursing Home Murder*. London: HarperCollins.
—(1947), *Final Curtain*. London: HarperCollins.
Martin, A. (2007), *Murder at Deriation Junction*. London: Faber & Faber.
—(2008), *Death of a Branch Line*. London: Faber & Faber.
McBain, E. (1963), *The Pusher*. Harmondsworth: Penguin.
—(1965), *Give the Boys a Great Big Hand*. Harmondsworth: Penguin.
—(1984), *Lightning*. London: Hamish Hamilton.
—(2006), *Learning to Kill*. Orlando: Harcourt Books.
McDermid, V. (1989), *Common Murder*. London: The Women's Press Ltd.
—(1992), *Dead Beat*. London: Victor Gollancz.
—(1993), *Kick Back*. London: Victor Gollancz.
—(1993), *Union Jack*. London: The Women's Press Ltd.

—(1995), *The Mermaids Singing*. London: HarperCollins.

—(1999), *A Place of Execution*. London:HarperCollins.

—(2002), *The Last Temptation*. London: HarperCollins.

—(2006), *The Grave Tatoo*. London: HarperCollins.

Miles, R. (2003), *Jane Austen*. Devon: Tavistock.

Miller, W. (2005), 'From Old Cap Collier to Nick Carter: images of crime and criminal justice in American dime novel detective stories, 1880–1920', in R. Levy and A. Srebnick (eds), *Crime and Culture*. Aldershot: Ashgate.

Mina, D. (1998), *Garnethill*. London: Transworld.

—(2000), *Exile*. London: Transworld.

—(2001), *Resolution*. London: Bantam.

—(2003), *Sanctum*. London: Bantam.

—(2005), *The Field of Blood*. London: Bantam.

—(2006), *The Dead Hour*. London: Bantam.

—(2007), *The Last Breath*. London: Bantam.

Morgan, J. (1984), *Agatha Christie: A Biography*. London: HarperCollins.

Morrissey, B. (2003), *When Women Kill: Questions of Agency and Subjectivity*. London: Routledge.

Morse, R. (2005), 'Racination and ratiocination: post-colonial crime', in *European Review*, 13 (1), 79–89.

Neill, E. (1999), *The Politics of Jane Austen*. Basingstoke: Palgrave.

Nesbo, J., (2005), *The Devil's Star*. London: Harvill Secker.

—(2006), *The Redbreast*. London: Vintage.

Ousby, I. (1976), *Bloodhounds of Heaven: The Detective in English Fiction from Godwin to Doyle*. Cambridge, MA: Harvard University Press.

Padura, L. (2005), *Havana Red*. London: Bitterlemon Press.

—(2006), *Havana Black*. London: Bitterlemon Press.

—(2006), *Havana Blue*. London: Bitterlemon Press.

Paretsky, S. (2003), *Blacklist*. New York: G. P. Putnam.

Parker, R. (2000), *Hush Money*. London: John Murray.

—(2003) *Back Story*. London: John Murray.

Paton Walsh, J. (2007), *The Bad Quarto*. London: Hodder & Stoughton.

Peace, D. (2007), *Tokyo Year Zero*. London: Faber & Faber.

Peters, E. (1970), *The Knocker on Death's Door*. London: Macmillan.

—(1981), *Saint Peter's Fair*. London: Littlebrown.

—(1981), *The Leper of Saint Giles*. London: Littlebrown.

—(1982), *The Virgin in the Ice*. London: Littlebrown.

—(1986), *The Rose Rent*. London: Macmillan.

Porter, D. (1981), *The Pursuit of Crime: Art and Ideology in Detective Fiction*. New Haven: Yale University Press.

Priestman, M. (ed.) (2003), *The Cambridge Guide to Crime Fiction*. Cambridge: Cambridge University Press.

Queen, E. (ed.) (1944), *The Female of the Species: The Great Women Detectives and Criminals*. New York: Littlebrown.

—(1945), *101 Years Entertainment: The Great Detective Stories 1841–1941*. New York: Garden City Publishing.

Rankin, I. (2007), *Exit Music*. London: Orion.

Rees, M. (2006), *The Bethlehem Murders*. London: Atlantic Books.
Reichs, K. (2006), *Break No Bones*. London: Heinemann.
Robbie-Grillet, A. (1964), *The Erasers*. New York: New York Grove Press.
Robinson, P. (1990), *A Necessary End*. London: Viking.
—(2002), *Aftermath*. London: Pan Macmillan.
—(2008), *All the Colours of Darkness*. London: Hodder & Stoughton.
Ruggiero, V. (2003), *Crime in Literature*. London: Verso.
Sayers, D. (1963), *Busman's Honeymoon*. Harmondsworth: Penguin.
—(1990), *Gaudy Night*. London: Hodder & Stoughton.
Schlink, B. (2005), *Self's Punishment*. London: Phoenix.
Seeber, C. (2007), *Lullaby*. London: HarperCollins.
Serney, G. (1998), *Cries Unheard: The Story of Mary Bell*. London: Macmillan.
Shriver, L. (2005), *We Need to Talk about Kevin*. London: Serpent's Tail.
Simenon, G. (1942), *The Man Who Watched the Trains*. London: Routledge.
—(1960), *The Friend of Madame Maigret*. London: Hamish Hamilton.
—(1963), *Maigret & The Idle Burglar*. London: Hamish Hamilton.
—(1975), *The Man on the Boulevard*. London:Hamish Hamilton.
Sjöwall, M. and Wahlöö, P. (2002), *The Locked Room*. London:Harper Perennial.
—(2006), *The Man Who Went Up In Smoke*. London: Harper Perennial.
—(2007), *Cop Killer*. London: Harper Perennial.
—(2007), *Murder at the Savoy*. London: Harper Perennial.
—(2007), *The Abominable Man*. London:Harper Perennial.
—(2007), *The Fire Engine That Disappeared*. London: Harper Perennial.
—(2007), *The Laughing Policeman*. London: Harper Perennial.
—(2007), *The Terrorists*. London: Harper Perennial.
Slaughter, K. (2003), *Kisscut*. London: Random House.
—(2004), *A Faint Cold Fear*. London: Random House.
—(2006), *Faithless*. London:Arrow Books.
—(2008), *Skin Privilege*. London: Arrow Books.
Stallwood, V. (1992), *Deathspell*. London: Macmillan.
—(1993), *Death and the Oxford Box*. London: Macmillan.
—(1994), *Oxford Exit*. London: Macmillan.
—(1995), *Oxford Mourning*. London: Macmillan.
—(1998), *Oxford Blue*. London: Headline.
—(1999), *Oxford Shift*. London: Headline.
—(2000), *Oxford Shaddows*. London: Headline.
Stanley, L. (1992), *The Auto/Biographical I: The Theory and Practice of Feminist Auto/ Biography*. Manchester: Manchester University Press.
Summerscale, K. (2008), *The Suspicions of Mr Whicher or the Murder at Road Hill House*. London: Bloomsbury.
Sutherland, J. (13/9/2007), 'US Confidential', in *New Statesman*.
Symons, J. (1962), *Detective Story in Britain*. London: Longmans, British Council.
—(1973), *Mortal Consequences: A History from the Detective Story to the Crime Novel*. New York: Schocken.
Thomas, R. (2000), *Detective Fiction and the Rise of Forensic Science*. Cambridge: Cambridge University Press.
Tursten, H. (2003), *Detective Inspector Huss*. New York: Broadway Press.

Upson, N. (2008), *An Expert in Murder*. London: Faber & Faber.

Watson, C. (1971), *Snobbery with Violence: Crime Stories and their Detection*. London: Eyre & Spottiswoode.

Winks, R. (1988), *Detective Fiction: A Collection of Critical Essays*. Vermont: Countryman Press.

Win Spear, J. (2005), *Maisie Dobbs*. London: John Murrary.

Wise, S. (2004), *The Italian Boy: Murder and Grave Robbery in 1830s London*. London: Jonathan Cape.

Wright, E. (2004), *The Silver Face*. London: Orion.

Zizek, S. (1993), *Tarrying with the Negative*. Durham, NC: Duke University Press.

Index

Lightning Source UK Ltd.
Milton Keynes UK
UKOW041554120612

194301UK00003B/6/P